William Douglas

Soldiering in Sunshine and Storm

William Douglas

Soldiering in Sunshine and Storm

ISBN/EAN: 9783744746816

Printed in Europe, USA, Canada, Australia, Japan

Cover: Foto ©ninafisch / pixelio.de

More available books at **www.hansebooks.com**

SOLDIERING

IN

SUNSHINE AND STORM.

BY

WILLIAM DOUGLAS,
PRIVATE 10TH ROYAL HUSSARS.

EDINBURGH:
ADAM AND CHARLES BLACK.
1865.

EDINBURGH:
BALLANTYNE AND COMPANY, PRINTERS,
PAUL'S WORK.

Dedicated

MOST RESPECTFULLY

TO

MAJOR-GENERAL PARLBY

AND

COLONEL J. WILKIE

WHO COMMANDED THE REGIMENT

DURING THE MARCH AND THE CAMPAIGN,

AS A SLIGHT TRIBUTE OF THE RESPECT IN WHICH THEY WERE HELD

BY THE MEN OF THE REGIMENT,

AND BY ONE OF THE LEAST OF THEM.

PREFACE.

WHETHER a preface be actually essential as an adjunct to a book, I leave more experienced persons than myself to determine. But as custom appears to make it a common accompaniment, and as it may be expected that an author should say something about his first effort, I feel bound to speak as I respectfully make my first salute to the public. In the following pages I have endeavoured to give a true, though it may be a rather rambling description of the travels and experiences of my regiment on its march "From India to the Crimea and Home," *via* the desert, the Nile, and the Euxine, and our sojourneyings at Cairo by the way. The reminiscences of this "Soldiering in Sunshine and Storm" have been recalled, and written amid the noise and turmoil of a barrack-room, which will account for many imperfections; I therefore trust that my countrymen will kindly make allowance for defects which may be attributed to this cause, by bearing in mind that a soldier has no retreat, no home, no castle of his own, (where none dare enter if he forbid it,) like any other British workman, and so if he writes at all it must be in the midst of busy comrades, and at intervals snatched from many distracting duties.

I take this opportunity of mentioning that "Lost in the Jungle" appeared in *All the Year Round*, as likewise "Three Days at Woolmer" and a portion of the "First Anniversary of Balaklava" in the *United Service Magazine*. For permission to reprint these articles I am under obligation to the Conductors and Editors of these periodicals.

CAHIR BARRACKS, *December* 1864.

CONTENTS.

CHAPTER FIRST.

INDIA—ANTICIPATION, ... 1

CHAPTER SECOND.

FAREWELL, ... 20

CHAPTER THIRD.

LOST IN THE JUNGLE, ... 37

CHAPTER FOURTH.

THE MARCH, ... 54

CHAPTER FIFTH.

THE VOYAGE, ... 72

CHAPTER SIXTH.

EGYPT, ... 87

CHAPTER SEVENTH.

THE PYRAMIDS, ... 110

CHAPTER EIGHTH.

TO ALEXANDRIA, ... 132

CHAPTER NINTH.

VIÂ THE MEDITERRANEAN, ... 154

CHAPTER TENTH.

THE CRIMEA, ... 176

CHAPTER ELEVENTH.

CAMPAIGNING, ... 199

CHAPTER TWELFTH.

SEBASTOPOL AND THE COMMISSARIAT, . . 224

CHAPTER THIRTEENTH.

THE FIRST ANNIVERSARY OF BALAKLAVA, . . 244

CHAPTER FOURTEENTH.

TO WINTER QUARTERS AND HOME, . . . 277

CHAPTER FIFTEENTH.

THREE DAYS AT WOOLMER, ... 303

From India to the Crimea and Home.

CHAPTER FIRST.

India—Anticipation.

I THINK it is Captain Mundy who observes that "any man who will take the trouble of describing, in simple language, the scenes of which he has been a spectator, can afford an instructive and amusing narrative." With a wish to attempt something of this kind, I here give a true and simple account of what befell the 10th Hussars from the time they left their cantonments, Kirkee, Bombay Presidency, East Indies, until they arrived at the seat of war, and from thence returned to England. It is an old saying in the service, that "a soldier would even get tired of Paradise, were he stationed there longer than six months;" so in acknowledging that I was heartily tired of India, after being there, and at one station only, for upwards of eight years, I trust I shall not be considered particularly dissatisfied. For when we are with

A

the same people continually, hear the same stories over and over again, see the same objects, the same bungalows, the same horse lines over the way; where the hospital is staring at us from one flank, and the riding-school eyeing us from the other, where, on looking rearwards, are to be seen the same *patcherie*, (married quarters,) the same canteen, and the commencement of the same long road which leads to the graveyard by the river side; where morning after morning the same call (*reveillée*) awakes us, and the same *ghorrawallah* (horse-keeper) comes to carry over our *jins*, (saddles,) the same *jarrawallah* (sweeper) opens the windows and cleans out the room, the same *bobagee* (cook) brings our breakfast, which is always the same—tea, bread and butter—and asks us the same question afterwards, "*Ka khana, sahib?*" (what for dinner, sir?) receiving the never-varying reply, "Curry," for he would spoil anything else; where the same *dhobie* (washerman) comes for our clothes; the same *hodgim* (barber) daily shaves us; daily come the same drills and rollcalls; daily the sun rises about the same time, and pursues his course without even the ghost of a cloud to cast a shadow across the sameness of his path, except in the monsoons, when he disappears, and it is all cloud and no sun—when all is dark, dull, dismal, and dirty, and nothing seen nor heard but thunders and lightnings, and rain which comes pouring and splashing down in exactly the same way for weeks together—when I say, all this is continued day after day, week after week, month after month, and year after year for eight years, surely there is some excuse for "a longing after change." All the variation of this monotony lies in the seasons as they follow in their course, for we have in turn four hot, four wet, and four cold months; there is nothing to interrupt the even tenor of our way; no unexpected visitor ever drops in among us, unless it may be the cholera, which twice or thrice came to us very unexpectedly, each time decimating the regiment, and carrying off the finest and best of our men.

We certainly had books to read, but how could they be enjoyed with a hot stifling wind passing through the room, scorching all that it touched. There were likewise outdoor games, such as cricket, football, fives, longbullets, &c.; but to enjoy these properly, one would require to be bred half a salamander, or find it awkwardly warm work running about with the thermometer over 100° in the shade, a practice which, if persisted in, sometimes bore fever and ague as its fruit. And thus, what with one thing and another, we did not fancy ourselves over comfortable, (remember that by *ourselves*, I mean the rank and file,) with officers it is different, they can go in the hot months to the hills, where they enjoy a climate similar to the south of Europe, or if they get homesick, as some do, they can get two years' leave to England; and even if they take none of these privileges, what with good pay, good quarters, a good mess, a good billiard-table, and racket-court attached, and, with all these good things, horses to ride, and servants to wait on them, an officer's life in India is quite endurable. But far different to this is the life of John Private: in his bungalow there is no *punkah* to cool him, no sofa soft to lie upon, no *jilmils*

(Venetian blinds) to keep out the blazing sun, no *tatties*, (window-matting,) with natives outside throwing cold water on them, causing the heated air to become delightfully cool, no brandy in *burruff* (ice) standing temptingly to his hand, no *chuprassie, khansaman,* or *khitmutgur* to answer his call, no *purdah* (curtain) to his bed, nothing for his comfort; so that, wanting all these luxuries, or I may call them necessaries in the East, and wearied of all the sameness I have described, is it to be wondered at that we used to look forward, and wish and pray for a change, even if it were for the worse, for is not change good and necessary for both body and mind? Then there were the natives, with whom no one could ever be intimate, or could ever thoroughly understand—their ways, manners, and customs being so entirely different from ours; they wish for no improvement, they want no change, as their sires from generation to generation did, lived and died, so they wish to do, live and die likewise. *Bab ke dustoor* (it is the custom) is their reply, if anything is proposed that they think an innovation. The sameness of their country extends to themselves, and seems more fully developed in them. They still plough with a crooked piece of wood, their corn is still ground by hand between two small round stones; they still live by families of from ten to twenty in small mud hovels of the same description that has existed for centuries, the same kind of matting still serves for their bed, and the same *cummerbund* (waistcloth) for their covering; they still use cow-dung for fuel, and a carpet for their floor; their music, if such it can be termed, has undergone no change since the times of Tamerlane; in short, "as they were in the days of Noah, so are they now," and so they will continue, example and precept being alike thrown away upon them. As regards their conversion to the Christian religion, the money expended on missions in India is, in my opinion, thrown away, or nearly so, and would, I am positive, be more usefully employed, if expended in trying to convert the heathen in our own large cities. One thing, however, highly creditable to the Indian missions, is, that there is no rivalry whatever between the ministers of different sects,—Church of England, Church of Scotland, Established and Free, Baptists, Methodists, and Americans; —all work harmoniously together. And why should not this be the case all over the world, as all wish to reach the same goal, although the roads to it may vary a little? Missionaries in India have apparently discovered at last that there is but little chance of converting adults, so they have opened children's schools in all the principal villages, and in every city, where the Scriptures are daily read and explained to the native children, yet, although the attendance is numerous, the results are far from encouraging. Certainly, I have heard of whole villages in the Carnatic being converted, and, probably, people in Mysore may hear of whole villages in the Deccan turning Christian. But, for my own part, I can conscientiously assert, that during my sojourn of eight years in India, I never saw eight converts; and the only resemblance to them were those who, having committed some serious crime, had thereby lost caste. Such as these take to our religion, as a refuge for the destitute, and appropriate the name of

Christians. So perfectly is this known and understood, that the Bishop of Bombay would not take into his employ a native who would urge the fact of his being a Christian as a recommendation. The Rev. Mr Kennedy of Poonah, a really good man and true Christian, for years made it his duty to live among the natives, and by assimilating himself, as it were, to them, eating what they ate, drinking what they drank, and even making some of their customs his, endeavoured to lead them to the true faith, but even then, I regret to say, failed. He, however, still perseveres, in the hope that the seed thus sown will ultimately bring forth fruit. To his exhortations and readings from the Scriptures, they certainly would listen attentively, but only with the attention they would give to a pleasant story or fable that was intended to amuse them. The Hindoo is a mixture of cunning and simplicity, with the latter, I think, predominating. You can never make him believe nor understand anything he has not seen. Common things, that are plain and feasible to us, are utterly beyond his comprehension; and no explanation short of what the eye can see, and the ear hear, will convince or satisfy him. A Hindoo, who has not seen a steamer or a railway, can never, from any description, form an idea of a vessel being propelled without sails against wind and tide, or of a carriage being put and kept in motion without the assistance of buffaloes or horses; talk to him and try to explain about steam power and its uses, and he only comes to the conclusion that you are either a liar or a fool, or both. I remember the occasion of the first locomotive running from Bombay to Panwell, a distance of about twenty miles, the carriages were all crammed with natives who had come and taken their seats, with the firm conviction in their minds that the carriages would never start. When they actually felt them moving, and heard the engine puffing and snorting, they began to feel uneasy, a tremor ran through them, and a half belief crept into their minds that the devil had got them in hand; so being already startled, it required very little more to move them, and when the shrill shriek of the whistle was heard, it acted upon them like an electric shock,—they instantly jumped headlong out, over one another, through the doors and windows, any way out into the open air and on to solid ground, where the whole assembly dispersed to the four winds of heaven, whilst turbans and slippers, beetle-nut and chinam boxes, strewed the ground. After the panic had abated, what a spree it was to see them looking each for his own things! Some with two pairs of slippers and no turban, others with two turbans and an odd slipper, not their own, and such shouting and screaming, the air resounding with the cries, "*Mardoo-ba-a-a!*" "*Gunnoo-ba-a-a!*" "*Rowgee-ba-a-a!*"

It was a good hour before they were all satisfied, and longer still ere they could be induced to resume their places; but at last they were all again seated and quiet and fairly started, and then their amazement was at its height, for they found themselves whirled along at a speed which to them was quite as incomprehensible as it was wonderful. They reached their destination in about half an hour; but before the train could be properly stopped, out they rushed wildly; and then the cries of "*Wa-wa! ka-khoob!*" (bravo! beautiful!) which they showered upon the fire-*shigram* (engine) were tremendous, from the force and expression with which they were uttered. Their surprise was complete, and the steam-engine claimed the greater victory over their prejudices because of their former unbelief; so they jabbered and chattered as only they can jabber and chatter when all are talkers and none are listeners. They were even more at a loss in trying to understand what the telegraph wires and poles were for; and the use of these, I fear, but few of them will ever be made to understand for years to come; it was completely beyond their depth, and they puzzled and puzzled themselves over it until their heads grew giddy. They might daily be seen, standing by twenties, watching the wires for hours, in the vain expectation of seeing the messages pass along in the shape of a *cogit* or *chit*, (note;) and as they could never detect this, they came at last to the conclusion that these were only forwarded by night; nor would they believe aught else when assured to the contrary, saying that "it was altogether nonsense to suppose that a man in Poonah could communicate in a second of time with another in Bombay." One of the *muccadums* (chiefs) of horse interested himself greatly about the telegraph, but could only be made to understand it so far as this, that the wire was the means of communication; to try to explain it to him any further was only to perplex him more; so in his own way he determined secretly to fathom the mystery. He had a son, an intelligent little fellow, and he set him to work out the problem; so, one morning, giving the boy food for the day, he sent him off with directions to go into some quiet spot in the jungle, place himself underneath the telegraph wires, and watch them carefully until night, noticing all that passed up or down them. Day after day the boy was sent on this mission, and night after night he returned with the same story,—that he had seen nothing. At length, one day, while looking at the long thin line overhead, and probably tired of his useless watch, he, I suppose, fell asleep, and then he dreamt that he saw a "*tora bhuda adimi*," (very little old man,) with a gray beard and a red coat, and having a bag over his shoulder, running like lightning along the wires to Bombay. He ran home and told this to the muccadum his father, who believed it, and came the following day to me quite full of his discovery, and in great glee at having at last satisfied himself as to how the European sahibs talked to each other when a hundred miles apart!

I shall say but little about caste, that great bar to civilisation in India, only mentioning that this pride goes far beyond the Hindoos; it extends from the lowest to the most exalted European in the land. For the civil service looks down upon the military, the Queen's service upon the Company's,* and all three upon civilian tradesmen. Wherever you go this is found to be the case,—the colonel's lady taking precedence of the major's, the major's of the captain's, and the captain's of all the subalterns'; and as you descend the ladder the feeling of superiority

---

* These are supposed to be one now; but still there is between them he wide gulf of purchase and non-purchase.

over any whose income is inferior seems to increase. The next step is among the warrant rank, such as apothecaries, commissariat-conductors, and with these may be classed auctioneers, tailors, and saddlers, who fancy gentility to consist in a two-horse shigram, with black coachman to match. Next come assistant-apothecaries, sub-conductors, and such like, who, with "the pride that apes humility," scorn coaches and horses, and consider a palanquin to be the thing. There is yet another class a step lower, composed of bazaar sergeants, provost ditto, ditto on the road and tank departments, with a sprinkling of clerks belonging to the adjutant and quartermaster-general's departments. These last envy every one who appears to be better off than themselves, talk large about their family and connexions, hint obscurely that if they only chose to use their influence, how damaging it would be to those above them, are always expecting a fortune to be left to them, and always threatening to ruin the state by leaving the service,—a threat which they are far too wise ever to carry into execution. In one respect, however, all these parties seem to agree, which is in living not only up to their income, but far beyond it. Everybody appears to be of necessity in debt; and there seems to be a respectability about *that* in India which is not observable in other parts of the world. The consequence is, that a sojourn in Bombay Castle for debt is so little out of the common that no notice is taken of it beyond its appearing in general orders that *Captain Rupee* has got two months' leave to the Presidency on "urgent private affairs."

INDIA—ANTICIPATION.

Having said this much about India, I will now relate the causes of our leaving the country. I have already mentioned how heartily tired we all were of the East; and now it was with a great deal of satisfaction that we heard of hostilities having broken out between Russia and Turkey, and that England and France were inclined to join the latter, because out of this we hoped that our long-desired change might be realised. On the outbreak of the Crimean war there could be no greater anxiety shewn in any part of the world to know what was doing than that which was felt by the European community of India. The arrival of the mail from home is at all times a matter of the highest importance abroad, but this interest was shewn in a much greater degree at the period I speak of. Days before the arrival of the bi-monthly bags all the conversation was relative to the anticipated news; and as the time grew gradually nearer when the boat must come, the excitement visibly increased, and prevailed to an extent to which that at home could only bear a modified resemblance. At the middle and end of each month there was a point to which all eyes were directed. This was a lighthouse situated some few miles from Bombay, from whence the approach of the boat could be telegraphed; and the telegraph on these occasions set the whole town in a ferment. Down on the beach might be seen officials from Government offices awaiting despatches, members of the press waiting for news, merchants looking for intelligence and for lists of the latest prices, and members of both services expecting letters from home, from those who, though far away, were yet near and dear to them. All are collected, anxiously waiting; and yet, whatever their wants, hopes, or wishes might be, the first inquiry of the first person capable of answering is, "What is doing in the Crimea?" Before the anchor is dropped, the ship is surrounded on all sides by boats of every description and size, from the yacht of the port-admiral to the dingee of the bottle-wallah. The first things looked to and sent ashore are the mammoth-sized bags containing the mails, which are transferred to light carts and forwarded to the post-office with all speed, and there immediately sorted out for town and country delivery. Meanwhile the editors of the daily and weekly papers are busy with their extras, containing an epitome of the news received, which are forwarded as soon as published to the subscribers in town, and to out-stations which the electric telegraph has not yet encircled with its slight but powerful cords. There the news is seized upon by eager readers, who, as they gather tidings of what is going on in Europe, look at the small extra with kindly eyes, justly considering it a little link of that long chain which, stretching over land and sea, desert and fruitful plain, calm and stormy waters, connects them with home, though many thousand miles away.

After our troops had landed at Varna, and the Russians retired from Silistria, great things were expected from the allies; every mail was concluded to bring the news of some signal defeat of the enemy; but mail succeeded mail, and the wished-for intelligence did not arrive. At last came tidings of the sailing of the expedition to the Crimea, of the landing at Old Fort, and of the battle of the Alma. I think, nay, I am certain, that there was no class of Her Majesty's subjects who rejoiced more at this victory than the soldiers. Always on the day when a mail was due, our regimental library would be crowded, awaiting the arrival of the *Poonah Observer's* extra, and the noise and hubbub made on its coming contrasted favourably with the silence and attention paid by all when one would get on the table and "Horse Guards" or read it aloud to all assembled. Then there would probably be another meeting next day, when the newspaper being published, all the particulars were there in full, and then such discussions would sometimes ensue, relative to those high in authority, and their sayings and doings; it would have caused some of the generals to stare had they heard their actions so freely canvassed, this tribunal giving honour only when it was due, and, on the contrary, if censure was considered as deserved, it was awarded freely, and at times in a style more plain and forcible than either graceful or eloquent. But with all this, one feeling was predominant in all alike, one wish prevailed over everything else, and that was an earnest desire that it might have been our good fortune to be at home when hostilities commenced, so that we could have gone with our comrades there, to share the dangers and honours of the campaign, instead of being inactively situated as we were. And then some would hope that, being short of cavalry at home, one or two regiments might be withdrawn from India, although even the most sanguine never imagined that even if this should prove the case, it would affect us; for, taking our turn, every cavalry regiment in the three

Presidencies was before us for home service. And so time passed on, events followed each other in rapid succession, everything appeared to move but the 10th Hussars, and they were at a standstill.

I think it was somewhere about the 5th of July 1854 that an interesting cricket match was being played between two elevens of the regiment, and had just reached a very nice point of the game,—one side had been in and made a good score; the other side was now in, having but two wickets to go down, and wanting only eight runs to tie; a number of spectators were upon the ground watching the game most intently. At this moment up came our colonel at a gallop, and, riding straight between the wickets, shouted out, "Stop the play;" then, waving a despatch which he held in his hand over his head, he announced to his astonished audience that we were under orders for the Crimea! There was a pause—a pause of surprise mingled with delight,—and then a cheer burst forth, which for a moment was confined to those immediately around, and therefore comparatively low, but quickly extending to the hearers and lookers-on, was in less time than it takes me to relate, caught up by all, and cheer after cheer resounded over the parade-ground. The joyful news soon spread to the barrack-rooms, and the whole of the cantonments were quickly in an uproar; as to the cricket match, that was forgotten on the instant; the very thing which but a few minutes before was considered of the utmost importance, was now deemed not worthy of a thought; bats, balls, and wickets were sent flying; and then there was such shouting, laughing, and shaking hands among us, while in the centre of all sat our gallant and energetic little colonel on his horse, himself looking the most delighted of the happy crowd. All the talk now was, when should we start? and what we had previously been most anxious to hear, we were now afraid would really happen, which was, that the allies, by gaining a succession of victories, would terminate the war before we had time to reach them, and as it was only a letter of Readiness which had been received, the look-out now was for the Route, which should despatch us at once. As a preparatory measure, we were reviewed by His Excellency the Commander-in-chief, the late* Lord Frederick Fitzclarence, who was pleased to compliment our colonel very highly on the discipline and efficiency of his regiment, and, when expressing his regret at losing us from his command, said that he felt happy, nay, overjoyed, to think that we should have the opportunity soon of distinguishing ourselves, and, after exhorting us all to do our duty faithfully, concluded with, "Wherever you go, my good wishes and prayers for your welfare will follow." He then called upon us to give three cheers for Her Majesty—a call, to which we responded most loyally, with three times three. Whoever has spent a few years abroad will be aware that when troops have been for any length of time on one sta-

---

* Alas! little did any of us then think that he who thus addressed us, and seemed so strong and hearty, would be overtaken by the still stronger hand of death in a few short weeks. Peace be to his memory! for he was a true soldier himself, and a soldier's true friend. In him the British army lost one of its best generals, and the troops in the Bombay Presidency a commander who looked after their interests, as a father would after the welfare of his children.

tion, they acquire a practice of making themselves as comfortable as circumstances will admit of, at least so far as the furnishing and decorating of their bungalows is concerned; and when a shift comes, these articles of use and ornament, which have been accumulated at great expense and trouble, have to be disposed of for almost whatever price the dealers choose to give. Consequently, as we were not at all behind other regiments in the interior decorations of our bungalows, the route—or rather the hint to march—proved a regular windfall to the *borrees*, (native dealers.) Many will recollect Old Isaac and Shakalaná, and the harvest they reaped out of the regiment at this time. These two were in the lines, bargaining nearly as soon as the colonel had made the matter public; and there they were, day after day, carting off loads of furniture: what they made, only they themselves could tell; but, as a rule, they never gave more than about the twentieth part of its value for anything; however, few thought of the sacrifice; everything else was forgotten in the all-absorbing topic of the march. But the route did not come, it was apparently as far off as ever, and days and weeks elapsed without any other intimation arriving, which, as may easily be imagined, caused an uneasy feeling to generate among us; some (the grumblers) had all along said that "We should never go;" and, as "hope deferred maketh the heart sick," we grew very uncomfortable during this suspense. At length a letter did arrive, but it was a countermand, or at least as good as one, for it notified that the 10th Hussars should not be required that year. So all our castles in the air fell, "and like the baseless fabric of a vision, left not a rack behind," not even a plank to cling to. Most of us being now without hope henceforth despaired; and in all Her Majesty's service there was not such another grumbling, dissatisfied, disappointed, disagreeable lot as the 10th Hussars. Those who had been the most sanguine, now felt the calamity most; some declared that there had never been any order; that it was only a dream of the colonel's; and a few (the croakers) exclaimed triumphantly, "Ah, it's just what we expected all along," hugging themselves with the idea of their particular foresight and wisdom. So everything relapsed into the old way; those who had been called in off detachment, now returned; the borrees sold back the articles they had so lately purchased, in most cases being content with a profit of about four hundred per cent.; and we all sat down quietly again, with the belief that we should have to spend about eight years more in the country. But there was one in the regiment who would not give up the idea, who declared in defiance of the last order, in the face of everybody's opinion, in spite of the *Bombay Times* and the *Poonah Observer;* against the world as it were, he alone stood out and said that we *should* go : this was our colonel, and he was right. The disastrous and unfortunate charge of Balaklava brought down the scale in our favour with a thump, for simultaneously with the news of that mismanaged affair came to us the order for the 10th Hussars and 12th Lancers to proceed overland to the seat of war. There was no mistake this time; the Route had come, and we were to start as soon as the ships destined to convey us could be got

B

ready; this caused a delay of about a month, as one of them had only just been launched. The name of this vessel was the *Punjaub*, sister to the *Meanee*, and built for an East India Company's steam-frigate; she had therefore to be jury-rigged, and being without engines, there was the more room for horses.

It did not require many hours to get us ready; but as there were more horses than men, arrangements had to be made for ghorrawallahs to accompany us as far as Alexandria. Most natives have a great dislike to cross the "*Kolapani*," (black water,) and it required a great deal of coaxing, in the shape of extra pay, to persuade some of our best followers to leave home, even for a couple of months; but the certainty of a number of rupees, free rations, and their passage back on the same terms, induced them to accept the offer at last. And now, what a quantity of trips had to be made from Kirkee to Poonah, and return visits from there again. What a number of old friends to see, and to dine or sup with, for perhaps the last time; and, worst of all was the number we had to say farewell to—a long farewell to nearly all, as it has happened; for I fear that but few of us who were friends then will ever meet again on this side of the grave.

A great deal more kindly feeling springs up between Europeans abroad than at home: friends being of course few among many strangers causes a closer attachment to subsist; and there is much less of that cautious, worldly selfishness felt and shewn which we feel and see at home. People become intimate on the first introduction, without waiting for time to ripen the acquaintance into friendship.

However, from what I have observed, there is a degree of comparison even in this respect, between English, Irish, and Scotch. John Bull is an honest, hearty fellow, but he feels no particular interest in any one, unless he comes from the same village as himself. Paddy will share his bit or his sup with all, but at the same time gives the preference to one of the same religion, and from the same part of the old country he himself belongs to. Sawney is happy to see any one whose skin is of the same shade as his own; but his hand and heart are given to whoever it may be "wha comes frae north o' the Tweed," and he would consider a couple of hundred miles as nothing were he only able to travel that distance to get a shake of the hand from an old schoolfellow. I remember Alick M'Intyre, (now dead, poor fellow,) coming from Ahmednuggur to Bombay, just to be able to pass New-Year's day with a friend from Invergordon. And all this warm and kindly feeling amongst us in India is principally, if not solely, caused by the thoughts of home, and respect for those who are there. The days which they know we keep up and enjoy ourselves upon, are kept up and respected by them at home; and although thousands of miles of land and sea lie between us, we know that they are thinking of us as we are of them, and so we drink the healths of "them that's awa'" with all good feeling and good faith.

CHAPTER SECOND.

Farewell.

WE left Kirkee *en route* for the Crimea in December 1854, three days after Christmas-day, which we had kept as only Englishmen can do in foreign parts. I will speak but slightly regarding the opinion given by the published papers respecting our corps on its departure, simply stating that it was flattering in the extreme. But I cannot thus remain silent when I recall the handsome and liberal manner in which the inhabitants of Poonah came forward with a subscription for the benefit of the wives and families of our men. A committee was formed and money subscribed to a large amount; and this was done irrespective of a large sum which had been collected and forwarded to the Patriotic Fund at home. The liberality thus shewn will always be kept in grateful remembrance by the 10th Hussars. About seven o'clock A.M. on the morning of the day already mentioned, the first division composed of the right wing, was formed up in front of and at right angles to the hospital, to commence our first day's march *en route* for the Crimea, the remainder of the regiment of course being present to see us off. On the command, "Advance by threes from the right of troops," being given, three loud cheers were given for the "First Division," to which, as may be well imagined there was a hearty response; then the "Advance!" was sounded, and the band struck up "Cheer, boys, cheer!" to which tune we stoutly rode away from our old cantonments. But now that we were really leaving the old place, many and many a long look was cast behind, bidding a silent farewell to it and to all the happy hours that we had there passed; for however much we may dislike a place, it is not easy to shake off the recollections of eight or nine years; and all the pleasantest moments passed there spring up fresher than ever in our memory when parting time comes. But we marched on, the band still playing and we still cheering; and before long we reached Dapoorie Bridge, where a turn of the road shut out the old place from our view, and we felt we had looked upon it for the last time. The band then struck up another tune—"There's a good time coming;" and we, looking hopefully on into the future, bid a last farewell to all behind us, some doubtless fancying that we might meet with many a worse place before we found a better; and then the band played "Auld lang syne," and left us. We were now fairly on the road; each man, buried in his own reflections, rode carelessly along, with his thoughts on the future,—the always changing and always bright future,—building castles in the air as he rode, looking farther than the Crimea—than the war or its results,—far on to home, to arrival there, suddenly and unexpectedly, the crowding round of brothers and sisters dear, the joy of a father, the happiness of a mother, the warm welcome to be got from all. How glad and cheerful does this castle-building make us! how we think and see nothing of all that lies between us and the spot where our thoughts are!—oblivious of the dangers to be met and conquered, of the oceans and continents to be crossed, of the diseases besetting our path, of the fever, of the cholera, each more to be dreaded than the shot or steel of the enemy. Forgetful of all this, and thinking gaily of home and of the fatted calf that will be killed on the prodigal's return, we journey along, silently dreaming and picturing scenes in the future. And as we travelled onwards, every foot of ground became familiar. "It was here that I fell," says one; while another shouts, "There we lost our way." But the road, as all could see, was greatly changed for the better, and bridges spanned the water-courses that we had to wade through eight years before.

We reached Arcoodie, our first day's march, about ten A.M., and there found another sign of progress in the Accommodation Bungalow erected by the liberality of Sir Jamsetjee Jeejeebhoy, a wealthy Parsee of Bombay, who has caused these bungalows to be built at easy intervals to Panwell, for the benefit of European troops marching up and down the country. This public benefactor, who with a princely liberality has showered gifts throughout the Presidency, has in Bombay endowed a hospital. For hundreds of miles round he has caused wells to be sunk,—water is nearly as precious as bread in the East,— and has had accommodation bungalows built on all the roads that lead from station to station. The Parsees are to be found all over Western India, although, I believe, scarcely anywhere else: they are the merchants of the Bombay Presidency, and may be said to resemble the Jews in one respect, that a poor Parsee is seldom seen. They came originally from Persia. When that country was conquered by the Mohammedans in A.D. 680, they fled from it and found refuge in Guzerat, and from thence have spread all over the Presidency. They are followers of Zoroaster, worshipping fire and the sun, which they consider the essence of all good; and among their curious customs is this one, never to give any person a light, and never to extinguish a fire; even if their own houses were in flames they would not make the slightest effort to put out the fire. They are remarkably fond of flowers, and consequently of gardens; and are said to be partial to dogs, always giving a dog the first mouthful at meals. The women never shew their hair to any but their husbands and nearest relatives, wearing a white cap which closely covers it. The men are easily distinguished, as they wear a remarkably shaped cap made of shining black oil-cloth covered with gilt stars. When one of them is about to die, he or she is placed in a house that is surrounded by a high wall, and left alone without food to expire. They do not bury their dead, but place the bodies in a *Dakhma*, or "Tower of Silence." These are circular stone towers with a small iron door at the side, in form and size resembling martello towers; inside there is an iron grating over a deep pit, at the bottom of which is a reservoir connecting it with the sea or some river. The bodies are placed on this grating, where they remain until the flesh falls off the bones and is washed away by the rains; and every three or four months the priest sweeps the bones down into the reservoir, which carries them on to the river. On our first arrival I observed three towers on the hills behind Poonah, and naturally put them down as watch-towers; and I had been some time in the country before discovering that these were the Parsee burial-places, one for the men, another for the women, and the third for the children. When out on a ramble one day curiosity tempted me to visit them; but I only looked into one,—that quite satisfied me: a semi-skeleton lay on the grating, the flesh just hanging to the bones; and the remembrance of that great head, with the cheeks clinging to the jaws, the eyeless sockets, and the large bare teeth, haunted me for weeks. I required no dinner that day.

The village of Arcoodie was our first camping ground, though it could not be termed campaigning yet, as all our staff of followers accompanied us: the bobagees had gone on in advance, and our meals were got ready just as if we had been in quarters. The Accommodation Bungalow saved us the trouble of tent-pitching, and the lines being marked out, we had only to file into our places,* dismount, and picket our horses. All this took but a few minutes. Grog was then served out, and we were made as comfortable as our best friends could desire. At this place we met with a commissariat conductor and his wife, who were travelling to Sattara, and halted here during the heat of the day. In a short time the husband managed to get drunk, and fell underneath the *hackery* (covered

* See "Three Days at Woolmer," *United Service Magazine*, Sept. 1858.

cart,) where he lay helpless, while his poor wife and child lay disconsolate inside. She was pitied by us all, but none knew how to shew this to her, or to render her any assistance, for with so many men and none of her own sex, it was a rather delicate task to accost her; and she appeared to shrink from us, doubtless feeling the lonesomeness of her situation, while we could not offer her any better privacy than her own hackery afforded, and so were obliged to leave her alone, a stranger among strangers, in a country where the reverse of this is generally the case. Poor woman, she no doubt felt deeply for her husband's disgraceful condition, and towards evening she went on her lonely journey, still shrinking from the sympathy we all wished to shew.

Although we had no beds, we managed to sleep very comfortably until morning, and on the 29th we marched for Wargum, a distance of some twelve miles. Every morning we started about half-past five, and these being the cold months, the marching was delightful to us, but not so to our followers, who crept about wrapt up in *cumlies* (horse clothing,) accosting us with "*Both tanda, sahib,*" (very cold, sir,) which escaped shivering from their lips. An Indian in cold weather is the most helpless creature in the world: he can or will do nothing till the sun's rays are felt; and, looking as only a sick black can look, he crawls about with chattering teeth and shivering limbs, apparently incapable of any exertion. It is a curious thing that he always takes the greatest care of his head, which is bound up with treble the care bestowed on any other portion of his body; the next most sensitive part is apparently the stomach, round which his cummerbund is twisted; legs and arms seem to be of little consequence, so long as the head and waist are protected. We reached Wargum early, and after having breakfast, and seeing to our horses and kits, most of us set off for a stroll into the country. Those who had guns gave a very good account of the game, which was plentiful, and hares, parrots, &c., we had in abundance for supper. We saw a few peacocks, but they were too near a village for us to have a shot at them; for if the natives saw one of these killed, he would raise the country: nothing rouses the people so much as to see a buffalo, a monkey, or a peacock put to death. The Brahmin bulls have, next to the beggars, the best life going. These last always ride on horseback, and levy a very remunerative black mail on the population; the former do nothing but lounge about, and have as much loosem grass, and even sweetmeats to eat, as they choose. A Hindoo would, I believe, rather see all his relatives to the third generation, hung, drawn, and quartered, than any of the three species I have mentioned shot. I shall always remember an old soldier taking a pretty considerable rise out of me when a griffin: he said that a native would sooner see his mother hung, than see any one jump on a buffalo's back; on trying the experiment I got a pitch that I remembered for many a day afterwards.

On the 30th our destination was Carlee, a march about the same distance as that on the day previous, but a better road and finer scenery. One day's march was so like another, that a description of each is nearly needless. We had our breakfast as soon as we got in, then came the pint of porter, after that dinner, then a sleep or a stroll, and lastly, watch-setting, and to rest. At this place there are some remarkable caves, situated at about a mile and a half from the village, and approached by a steep and narrow path, winding up the side of the hill among trees, brushwood, and fragments of rock. These temples, as I should more correctly term them, are cut out of the solid rock, and the larger one is, I believe, the finest in India, and said to be over two thousand years old. A party of about a dozen of us went to visit these interesting places, and we started immediately after dinner, with the disadvantage of going when the heat was most intense. These caves or temples were rather difficult to get at, the ascent to them being one of the most never-get-there roads I ever traversed. At no part could we stand erect, and were obliged to go nearly the whole way on all fours. The best way was up the bed of a dry water-course; and at every step the loose stones, displaced by those in front, would roll down on the heads of those in the rear, causing some to wish they had never started; but still we toiled on, with the perspiration streaming out of every pore, for the sun's heat was then at its best, or, I might say, its worst, for us. Everything has an end, and so had our difficult path, the summit of which we at last reached thoroughly exhausted, dropping down at the mouth of the caves to breathe and rest. But the sight of a spring of water, cold as ice, and clear as crystal, greatly revived us; and on tasting we fancied it the most delicious that ever had passed our lips. How sweet and refreshing it was, how grateful it seemed after the toil and trouble of the ascent, when, with mouths parched with the hot wind, we were fancying that a draught of pure clear cold water was the greatest boon Providence could bestow! We were now at the entrance of the large cave, and well did the sight of this repay all the trouble we had taken. The entrance itself is enough to excite admiration, being a noble arch, a miracle of carving, on each side guarded by *Chubdars* (keepers of silence,) the figures being colossal in size. There are two apartments below and five above, where is a kind of balcony for the *nagara-khauna* (music gallery.) The temple of Chatrya is about fifty paces in length, by eighteen in width : the roof is high and vaulted, supported by pillars placed closely along the side, on which are chiselled some curious and extraordinary devices. Inside the portion to the right and left are three large figures of elephants, with mahouts and howdahs. The interior is adorned with huge figures of Siva, Vishnu, and Brahma, the Hindoo Trinity; and all the other deities of the Hindoo mythology are here delineated in shapes and positions wonderful to look at. The place is dark, being only lighted by the door, which is small and low, and by an arch above it, which is only intended to throw the light upon the Dagoba at the far end ; this is a conical umbrella-shaped stone, supposed by some to contain a hair, nail, or tooth of Bhudda. Above the Dagoba is a wooden fixture, intended probably as a sounding board, similar to what is seen in churches at home. In the centre stands the figure of an elephant. Outside is a large pillar with sixteen sides, on the top of which are four lions ; but the whole structure is now very much broken. The origin of these extraordinary excavations has been attributed to some fabulous pigmies called Pandoos, who are supposed, like the monks of old, to have worn both the surplice and the sword. The caves are said to have been the seat of learning one thousand years ago. Round to the left and in front of the rock are two smaller ones; but, after seeing the great cave, we viewed these with but little interest. And there is yet another over the large temple, to which the only access is by a kind of ladder, having an interval of four or five feet from step to step— accommodation for giants only. It was stiff work getting up the hill, but far stiffer coming down, and we all breathed freer on reaching terra firma. By the caves we had seen small cells; but they were empty, although once intended, I suppose, for the *faqueers* to finish their self-imposed penances in; but in a hole at the foot of the hill we saw one of these gentry, the most miserable object ever looked at, nothing but skin and bone; and, as if to add to his haggard appearance, he had carefully covered his body all over with wood ashes. It is, at least to us, really astonishing what pain and fatigue the Hindoo will undergo in endeavouring "to merit heaven by making earth a hell." I have seen some who had stood on one leg for years, while others engage the sympathy and extort the charity of many by holding one arm erect overhead, until in time the flesh withers and the bone sets into that position. A few I have met with who, firmly clenching one hand, have kept it closed until the nails have grown right through the palm to the other side; and it is well known that many have travelled the whole extent of land, from the Himalayas to Cape Comorin, measuring their bodies on the ground as they went. Also, there is *Charah Puja*, or hook worship, in which the devotee allows a steel hook to be passed through the muscles of his back, and in this manner is suspended from a machine like a windmill, to one of the arms of which the victim is attached: on their great feast days they can be seen thus, whirling round and round, and looking all the time as pleased as if they really enjoyed their ride. All this is done with a devotion worthy of a better cause. Khandalla was our next day's march, (the 31st,) the road to which was by far the most picturesque that we had yet travelled over, winding as it did round the foot of hills clothed with verdure to their summits, and by the sides of small lakes which reflected back their beauty, until we arrived at our camping ground, which was on a narrow ridge close by the village on the top of the Bhore Ghaut. Our tents were pitched, and the horses picketed on the right and left of the road, although there was scarcely room enough to do so, as within twenty yards of where the flank horse on the right stood, there was a clear fall of some hundred feet, whilst to the left, in contrast to this, the ground as suddenly rises, terminating in a remarkably-shaped peak of great height. This is called "Wellington's Peak," but for what reason I could not discover: the great Duke may have taken the trouble to reach the summit, or it may have been so named from its very remarkable form, or from a dozen other causes which are of little consequence: there was the Peak, and that was its name. Looking at it, however, did not satisfy some; so a few of us determined to inspect it more closely, and this could best be managed by getting to the top, a proceeding which the more cautious deemed to be among the impossibilities. We had to remain a couple of days here on account of the ships not being quite ready, and a party agreed to make the attempt that afternoon. One, however, would not wait, but started off there and then, returning after a couple of hours' absence with such a description of the perils and difficulties of the way, and the splendid view to be had from the pinnacle, that in chaff we pretended not to believe him, hinting that he had fallen asleep on the way in some *nullah*, and dreamt the remainder; but he assured us that what he described would, if we went, be found correct, and also that he had tied a handkerchief to a stick, and left it waving on the most elevated point. All this made us only the more anxious to start, being confident that what one could accomplish any other could at least try; and so, after dinner, half-a-dozen of us set off, and very soon discovered that the difficulties of the way had not been at all overdrawn. Our road was intersected by deep ravines, which we had to cross by bottoming them, and scrambling up the other side; and it was not only provoking, but really quite disheartening, when we had reached the top of one of these, sometimes to find that we were obliged to descend it again, and so relinquish the advantage but just gained with so much toil and trouble. When we had gone about half way, two of the party gave in and returned; but the remainder of us, after in vain trying to persuade them to persevere, nothing daunted, struggled on, our spirits rising with the obstacles which had to be overcome, and our task getting lighter as we saw that the higher we ascended the more lovely grew the scenery. It was in the finest part of the cold season, and before the trees and plants had lost any of their loveliness or fragrance: and the delightful perfume of innumerable flowers, the hum of insect life, and the murmur of distant waterfalls, stole softly over our senses, as we lay down from time to time to get wind. I regretted greatly my ignorance of botany when thus gazing on flowers and plants of such variety, and also that I knew so little of geology, when I was standing and passing over stones and rocks which, to the initiated, would be volumes to instruct and amuse, while of none could I give any description. What a treat this would have been for a naturalist! how he would have revelled in such a scene, lingering, resting, enjoying, and describing all around him! Even we, little as we knew, were cheered and interested by the beauty and grandeur, as on we went, scrambling and crawling, until at last we reached the summit, and here, true enough, was our comrade's flag of victory flying! Turning to look back, one of the most magnificent views ever seen burst upon our sight—rocks, rivers, gardens, lakes, hills, valleys, plains,—all lay stretched at our feet, a carpet spread by nature for miles and miles in every direction. To our right and left the different peaks of the Western Ghauts rose to our view, or, I might say, fell to it, for they all appeared beneath us; behind was the Deccan with its fertile fields, and still in view many a spot dear to our recollection; while in front, but down far, far below, was the Concan, and beyond that the sea, the glorious blue sea, that had not gladdened our eyes for years.

> "But oh, what bard could sing the onward sight,
> The piles that frown'd, the gulfs that yawn'd beneath,
> Downward a thousand fathoms from the height,
> Grim as the caverns in the land of death!
> Like mountains shatter'd in the Eternal's wrath,
> When fiends their banners 'gainst His reign unfurl'd,
> A grisly wilderness, a land of scathe,
> Rocks upon rocks in dire confusion hurl'd,
> A rent and formless mass, the ruins of a world."

From here our lines with the tents and horses, appeared to be so small that we fancied a good sized handkerchief would have covered them all. Within a few paces of the spot where we stood was a clear descent of thousands of feet; and, creeping cautiously to the edge, we glanced warily over at a scene which we grew giddy looking down on: it was awfully grand, as far as the eye could reach, only precipice towering over precipice, from the base to the summit where we were. While looking down, a strange dreadful feeling came over me, a something that whispered, "leap over;" and with the dread of being obliged to comply, I seized firm hold of the ground where I lay, and pushing myself gradually back, got away from the danger, breathing freer when I had, as it were, conquered. Did ever such a feeling come over any one else? We erected a pyramid of stones on the spot, and then prepared for the descent; and to our great surprise and pleasure a footpath was discovered, which although it took us a long way round, was very preferable to going back by the way we came up. We came down at a run, and made our way straight to the tents, when who should we find waiting there but Tom Gray, who had come all the way from Sattara to say good-bye to us. He had gone first to Kirkee, discovered that we were already on the road, and followed on till he overtook us here. His greeting always had been and now was most cordial and hearty: such a shake of the hand as he could give, and did give, as we wished each other the compliments of the season, and a " Happy New Year," (for this was New Year's eve,) was enough to warm any one's heart. Tom finished up with "This is Hogmanay, and as it will in all likelihood be some time ere we a' meet again, we will mak' a nicht o't, and see the auld year oot and the New Year in, as we do in auld Scotland." To this, of course, we were nothing loath, and after inviting two or three more to join the party, we started on a foraging expedition to the Accommodation Bungalow, to see what could be procured in the shape of materials. The reconnaissance was not successful, and we had just called a council of war, when who should turn up but young Bessingee, better known to us as "Parsee Jack," who had a supply of whatever liquors we wanted. We asked first of course, if he had any whisky, and on being answered in the affirmative, gave a cheer which was echoed back from hill and dale, until it gradually died away in some far off cavern or valley in a whispered "Good night, and joy be with you." On getting the unexpected supply, which on inspection turned out to be real "Fairntosh," the remainder was comparatively easy: first telling the bobagee to keep a constant and unlimited supply of *ghurram pani* (hot water) ready, then sending to the village for limes, sugar, and cheroots, we prepared to make all comfortable and snug for the night. When all was ready we took up our position outside the tent on a small knoll.

It was full moon, one of those cool, delightful, moonlight nights which are only to be met with, and can only be properly enjoyed, in the tropics, and the rugged and beautiful scenery around added greatly to the effect. Below us lay the road which wound in and out among wooded glens and deep ravines, into whose dark depths the silver beams of the moon could not penetrate, and at other parts shone down the faces of declivities which this planet, so glorious in India, lit up with all the clearness of day, affording a delicious contrast to our remembrance of it a few hours previous in the hot and sultry sunlight. It is at such a time that a walk can be truly enjoyed in the East, or an hour spent with real pleasure, as we were then doing, with old and true friends around, congenial spirits, with whom we could talk about old times, old comrades, and old scenes, about people and things that had passed away, people who, when revering their memory, we could discover—alas ! too late—that we scarcely valued in life as we ought to have done. But we were very happy then, telling tales, old ones many of them, singing still older songs, and by and by, as the gong told us, that in another hour eighteen hundred and fifty-four would be among the things of the past also, we crept closer together, wondering whether "the old folks at home" were thinking and talking about us as we then were about them, feeling confident all the while that they really were, and that in fancy we were round the family board, although land and sea, sea and land, lay wide between. And so, stretched out in a circle, with our heads inward, we lay on the knoll chatting pleasantly until the gong again struck—it was midnight—all of us started to our feet, and Tom Gray shouted out, "Hie, boys, it's jist chappit twal on the *gurra;* so fill yer glasses—brimmers, mind ye; but there's nae necessity to tell ye that—noo, a' stannin, comrades, 'Here's a Happy New Year to us a', and mony o' them, no forgettin' them that's awa'! Lord, wadna I hae likit to be at the Tron Kirk the nicht!" Tom was now in his glory: he gave toast after toast, drinking all our healths again and again, until at last, quite overcome, he rolled over trying to sing "Auld lang syne," and we carried him inside the tent, and made the good jolly fellow as comfortable as possible. A few of the remainder still seemed very much inclined to make a night of it, particularly Mr Patrick Blake, who, when I asked him if he meant to go to bed at all, replied, "Well, I am just like a dog at his father's funeral, I don't care whether I go or not." As the others appeared to be in the same mind, I proposed that some one should relate a story, but the proposal recoiled upon myself. On being called upon to tell a tale, as Blake was the most importunate, I rejoined that I had no objection, but as it would relate to himself, I hoped that after I had done he would give us the sequel to it. Looking interrogatively at Blake, who gave me a nod of acquiescence, I commenced.

CHAPTER THIRD.

Lost in the Jungle.

WE sailed from England in May 1846, and after a prosperous voyage of four months, landed at Bombay. Our destination was about a hundred miles up the country, to Poonah, the capital of the Deccan; but we remained at the Presidency for a few days, in the Queen's barracks, and during that time, managed to have a good look round the fort and the bazaars. This was our pastime by day; at night, we wandered over Dungaree-green, or danced at Portugee Joe's. Everything to us griffins appeared strange and wonderful, more especially the different costumes of the people, which made the scene keep ever changing. For here were to be seen not only natives, but also Chinese, with their flat faces and long tails; Parsees in their white dresses and shining oilskin hats; Beloochees from Northern India, with their long black hair and wild looks; Jews from Arabia; Caffirs from the Cape, and Bedouin Arabs;—all mingling peaceably together, to say nothing of the Ram-sami houses, their priests and fakeers, the dancing and music, and the beggars who ride on horseback.

The first day's march was to Panwell, a village about

twenty-two miles from Bombay. It was the commencement of the monsoon; so marching was far from pleasant, especially as most of us soldiers were without shoes, light clothing, beds or blankets. Some had bought white trousers on landing, but they were the exception, not the rule. However, what with the rain that poured so steadily down upon us, and the state of the road—which was at that time intersected about every quarter of a mile by a watercourse from two to four feet deep, through which we had to wade—it was of little consequence whether our trousers were good, bad, or indifferent; and boots or shoes would have been of little use, in fact an encumbrance.

As we always marched several hours before daybreak, we could see but little of the difficulties which lay in our path; and being young and strange to the country, we had no idea of the danger we incurred by travelling in such weather. We laughed and made fun of everything —at our tumbling into holes, at our bad shoes, at our being always drenched to the skin, at some of our officers because they had bought *tatoos* and rode, and at others because they hadn't and walked. We took small care of ourselves, eating and drinking whatever we fancied; and I have often thought since, that, under Providence, we owed to this very carelessness the few casualties by sickness we had upon that seven days' march; for, although we were close on eight hundred strong, fresh to the country, and above all, marching in rain and through water, lying in wet clothes on damp ground, yet we only lost two men from cholera. A deal of credit was however due to our colonel, who had always the commissariat and cooks sent on the night before, so that on our arrival in camp, a ration dram of arrack and a hot breakfast awaited us.

The next day's march was to Chowkee, a most miserable-looking place, its appearance bearing out all that we had heard of its unhealthiness; and besides this, a good many of us had reason to recollect it from another cause; for was it not here that we met with a paragon of honesty and integrity, in the shape of a Christianised native, who had taken the scriptural name of David? He could speak English well, and being a plausible fellow to boot, so managed to ingratiate himself, not only with one troop but with all the regiment, that he was in general request everywhere. Nothing was done without first consulting David; it was he who got our clothes washed, or recommended us whom to employ; and if we required anything bought, it was David that laid out the money *to advantage*, (his own, as we afterwards found.) But what raised him highest in our estimation was his manner of bullying all the other natives. Not content with calling them thieves, rogues, vagabonds, and *kola suers*, (black pigs,) he would also blackguard their ancestors as far back as the ninth generation, we simpletons never thinking that he was in league with the very people he was abusing. What an able rogue he was! and how very honest he appeared to be! Not a pice would *he* bring short in change, and would never make any charge for what he had done, leaving it always to the *gentleman's* generosity, knowing well that, from griffins as we were, he was sure to get treble the amount of what he was entitled to. Having thus gained our entire confidence, he made his *grande coupe* at Wargum. Slyly and silently he slipped from tent to tent, and from man to man, intimating confidently to each that he knew where a few—*only a few*—bottles of the best Cognac were to be procured, and that if any in this tent—they had always been friends to him—wanted a bottle or two he would fetch it, only two rupees a bottle; but they were not to tell any one else, brandy being a prohibited article. Excellent judge of human nature! he knew well "that stolen pleasures were sweet," and that the mere idea of smuggled liquors would take soldiers' fancy more than what was procured from any legitimate source. In this manner he collected about four hundred rupees, with which he made tracks to Bombay. David had all along been popular, but at no period had there been so many anxious and interested inquirers after him as on that night—his last—when he forgot to return with an equivalent in brandy for the rupees given. Everybody was stopping every-one else, to ask, "Where is David gone?" and the only answer to the question was by another being asked, "Have you seen David?" At last the truth dawned upon them, "that being strangers," he had "taken them in." We never saw him afterwards, although we often heard of him; not a regiment nor draft ever marched up the country from Bombay but David fleeced it in a similar manner; so we had at least the satisfaction of knowing that we were not the only victims of misplaced confidence.

But the incident I am about to relate happened at Khandalla, our third day's march, a place well known to all sportsmen in the Bombay Presidency. It is situated at the top of the Bhore Ghaut, one of the range of mountains which traverse Western India from north to south, and which range at this part separates the fertile Deccan from the no less fertile Concon. The sea-breeze we can feel here in all its freshness; and this, combined with the beautiful, romantic scenery, and the lofty rugged hills, causes it to be not only the most picturesque, but the most delightful encampment on our road.

It wanted still half an hour of daybreak when we reached the bottom of the ghaut, the road to the top of which is cut out of the mountain-side. It was and is a very steep, zig-zag, narrow path, and we were cautioned to keep close in to our right, as a step or two to the left would have taken us a short cut down to the bottom. For a wonder it did not rain, and we had ascended about half-way when the sun rose; slowly all above became distinctly visible, while beneath all remained still dark, and desolate. This however was not of long duration; as the sun got higher and higher the shadows below rolled gradually away and disappeared. Then was exposed to our view one of the grandest and loveliest of scenes. On all sides thousands of cascades, sparkling like crystal in the sunbeams, leaped, dashing and dancing, down the face of the ghaut. The dewdrops on the leaves glittered like diamonds. Everything looked healthy and refreshing; trees were in blossom, birds of the most beautiful plumage fluttered around, and from far in front we could hear our band playing a cheerful, heart-stirring tune. All this combined was such a relief to the dull, dreary marching of the few hours previous, that we stepped on with increased vigour, thinking mighty little of the bad road we had traversed, or the bad weather we had endured.

On arriving at our destination, it took us but a short time to pitch our tents; of course our breakfast followed, and then some of us started off for a stroll, while others lay down for a nap. At dinner time we were amused by hearing one of our sergeants, who had just returned from an exploring expedition, relate his adventures in what was considered by his audience rather a marvellous style. When he finished, a laugh went round at the account of his perils and hairbreadth escapes, which nettled him seemingly, for he threw down two rupees, offering them to any man who would descend the ravine in front, and gain the summit of a precipice that was apparently not more than half a mile from where we sat. This challenge was promptly accepted by Pat Blake and Dennis O'Callaghan, who, just as they were, without either shoes or caps, started off to attempt the feat.

It was about two in the afternoon then; and as the place seemed so near, we fully expected that they would not be gone more than a couple of hours. We looked out for their appearance on the appointed pinnacle; but three hours and more passed without our expectations being realised. We now supposed that they had failed in their attempt, or had gone farther a-field in another direction; so yet felt little or no uneasiness about them; but when another hour had elapsed and the shades of night began to close, a restless feeling crept over us all. A tiger-trap was only a few yards from our tent; so our first dread was that they had fallen a prey to some wild animal, or had tumbled into a ravine, or fallen over a precipice. While we were yet discussing these apprehensions the sun had nearly gone down; and as the twilight is but short in the tropics, we had resolved to start in search of the missing men, when O'Callaghan was descried slowly returning. Seeing that one was safe, all our sympathies were now about the other, and poor Dennis was assailed on all sides with questions as to what had become of his companion. To our astonishment and surprise, he declared that he knew no more about him than we did. "He and I parted," he said, " shortly after starting, taking different routes, having first agreed that whoever got to the point first should wait for the other." O'Callaghan had been unsuccessful in his attempt, and had consequently returned, expecting to have found Blake at home before him.

It was by this time quite dark, and the greatest apprehension was felt by all as to the probable fate of the missing man. The officers had now heard of the affair, and, under a vague idea that he might have lost himself, about one hundred of the regiment, officers and men, Lieutenant Fitzclarence leading the way, descended the gorge with lanterns. This attempt was dangerous by daylight even, therefore much more so at night, especially as none of the natives would for love or money act as guides; they certainly followed, but even that was cautiously done. And so we had to find our way as we best could, sliding, slipping, stumbling, and tumbling, until we reached the bottom, fancying all the while that every bush contained a tiger, and that every stone hid a cobra-di-capello. And when we had got thus far, what more could be done? Our lanterns but barely made the darkness visible in a spot where the sun's rays never reached. Yet what little we could do we did: bugles were sounded, pistols fired, and men shouted until they were hoarse,—all fruitlessly. After each sound or shout we waited for a reply, but none came to gladden our expectant ears—no faint halloa followed; but a stillness like death clung around, and with the feeling creeping over us that his dead body might be nigh, we spoke to each other in whispers, as if we had feared " to break the sleep that knows no waking." After remaining there nearly two hours, we were obliged to retrace our steps, with the sorrowful conviction that our poor comrade had come to an untimely end.

With a good deal of trouble we got back the way we came, and to our tents, where, as a matter of course, all the talk was about Blake. Some one now discovered that every regiment or detachment that had ever lain at this place, had lost one or more men by tigers. We were then new in the country, and all the tales we had ever heard or read of these terrible creatures came to our recollection; and such stories were related that night of their daring and determined character, that few were inclined to sleep, and one or two did not seem to relish the idea of lying next the door of the tent, dreading that a tiger would make no selection, but pounce upon the first he came to.

An affair happened about midnight which, when we discovered the cause, made our thoughts for a time run in an exactly opposite direction. A poor donkey to get shelter from the rain, which again was pouring down, had crept in between the inner and outer wall of the tent, and was smelling and sniffing underneath, trying probably to get at some bread, which lay close inside. The man behind whose head Neddy had taken shelter, on hearing the noise, sprang up suddenly, and called upon us to be silent and listen. Every one was dumb in a moment: as the saying goes, "you might have heard a pin drop." And there was, without doubt, a strong, irregular sniffing noise just outside. It only required this. All that we had heard of—all that we had been talking about, crowded at once into our thoughts. As regarded the noise, there was only one opinion of the cause; every one felt positive that it was a tiger; nothing seemed so certain, for there it was so plain and distinct, and all could hear it. It now became a question how we had best act. Should we stand where we were, wait for the monster, and boldly await his attack, or, becoming the assailants, turn out and attack him? The latter plan appeared to be the most dangerous, and as "discretion is" said to be "the better part of valour," we waited; but by waiting we acquired courage, for neither was the tent broken down, nor was the side rent asunder by the ravenous animal: there was only the sniff-sniffing still. So at last we got ashamed of ourselves; and some one remembering that all wild animals have a dread of fire, each made an impromptu torch of straw or paper: these we lit, and with a cheer, dashed boldly out,* and then discovered the cause of all our

---

* I must remind the reader that our swords, arms, and ammunition, were all in store chests, having been packed in England, and never

terror, standing and looking so meekly innocent at us, that none had the heart to turn him out of his shelter, but, giving him the bread which he had coveted, we left him to enjoy it.

We all had a hearty laugh now at our former timidity —those who had been the most nervous laughing the loudest; and so bold and brave did we then become, that I almost believe we would have attacked the real Simon Pure, had he dared to put in an appearance.

We marched the following morning to Karlee, leaving Sergeant Vallance and six men to prosecute the search after Blake by daylight; but although they spared neither time nor labour, they could get no tidings of him. The party overtook us at night, and, on hearing of their ill success, we gave up all hope. Somehow a suspicion had been gaining ground that he might have met his death either by the hand or the negligence of his comrade. "They may have quarrelled," said some, "and an unlucky blow proved fatal." So every one began to look coldly at O'Callaghan, and this he could not but observe, for if it was not openly expressed, it was strongly hinted; and thus, between the loss of his companion, and the suspicious looks of his comrades, the poor fellow was like one bereft of his senses.

We next reached Wargum, where a court of inquiry was ordered to assemble to report on the disappearance of Private Blake. Just as the proceedings of the court terminated by its returning him missing, and ordering

opened until we got to Kirkee; and as OUR teeth and talons could not compare with a tiger's, we naturally did not care about coming in contact with the jungle king.

that he should be struck off the strength of the regiment, there was a noise and uproar in the camp. All hands turned out to see what was the cause, when, to our surprise and great joy, we saw four men lifting Blake, all alive and hearty though apparently hurt, out of the mail-cart. The first to shake hands with him was O'Callaghan who, crying and laughing by turns, was accosting all the men who stood round, with "Shure, and now did I kill him?"

Blake was taken to hospital, where his right foot was discovered to be cut dreadfully, and so inflamed and swollen, that it was doubtful for some time whether it would not have to be amputated; but luckily, in time it got all right.

"Now Pat," I added, turning to the hero of my tale, "it is your turn to oblige; the liquor is good and the company agreeable, so you can have no objection." I may remark that hitherto he had always fought shy of giving an account of his adventures that night; but now fortified by grog, and the fact of our being again encamped on the same spot, had loosened his tongue, so after taking a pull at the mixture he commenced :—*

"When Dennis and I parted, I took what seemed to be the nearest road, but which in reality turned out to be the longest and most difficult. It was the most tumble-down path that ever I traversed; at one time going down the nearly perpendicular side of a water-course, and of such steep descent that one false step would have finished my wanderings; at another, scrambling up as steep an ascent, with here and there only a shrub or tree-

* I may as well remark—as some might imagine the language to be rather refined for a private soldier—that Blake had received a good education, having in fact, I believe, at one time been intended for the priesthood.

root to sustain me, and these giving way pretty often, but luckily, so far always managing, as one failed to catch hold of another; and so struggling on in this manner, I at last reached the bottom of the precipice, the summit of which was my goal.

"On casting my eyes upwards I now observed the full difficulty of the task I had undertaken, and hesitated to ascend. Above was a perpendicular rock of great height, the only apparent way to the top of which was a narrow footpath some ten or twelve inches wide, which, winding to the left up the face of the precipice, seemingly led to the summit. Underneath this ran a mountain stream, swollen by the rains to the size and velocity of a river. I could now perceive that the trial was very hazardous; but I had gone too far to return, and what I dreaded most was the jeers of my comrades at my unsuccessful attempt. The only word for me was, 'Forward!' and so I began to scramble aloft, cautiously however, and clinging close to the rock, walking on step by step, looking upwards; I dared not look down. In this manner I had got about half way when I came to an obstacle, and a serious one it proved to be. About six feet of the path had given way, staying all farther progress. I was now in a situation that might be nearly compared to that of 'Mahomet's coffin.' To return was impossible, to go forward apparently the same. I bitterly repented then having come on the expedition, or having left O'Callaghan, and would have given all the world to have been back once more in my tent. What made my situation seem more terrible was the comparative silence, and the absence of all human sympathy; for nothing could be heard but the rushing of the waters far below. If I could only but clear the gap, all might yet be well. Above my head, and within reach of my arm, the branch of a small tree hung temptingly, and I decided at last to swing myself across by that. I tried it well, too well perhaps. Then holding my breath, I made the spring: my left foot had just touched the opposite side, and in another moment I should have been safe, when snap went the twig, and down I fell, crashing through the roots and shrubs which partly covered the face of the precipice. I could not have been more than a few seconds in falling, yet in that short space of time all the principal events of my life seemed to pass before me: I also thought of my body striking the rocks, and bounding from one to the other, and that I should be dead before I reached the bottom. All this, and more, flashed with inconceivable rapidity through my brain, when my foot struck on something. I felt a sharp pain, and then found myself whirling round and round like an egg shell, among the rushing turbulent waters, which carried me onwards with great swiftness. I had just sense and strength enough to strike out for the side,—luckily I could swim well,—and reached it exhausted. I managed to crawl out, and then observed that in my right foot there was a severe cut, from which the blood flowed plentifully. I felt deeply thankful to a merciful Providence for having thus saved me from a violent death, but had only gone a few steps from the water side when I fainted. Then for a time all was a blank, though I fancied I heard sounds. They might have been the pistols or the bugles, or, more probably, the noise of the furious waters near me.

"I have no idea how long I lay in that condition. All I know is, that when I came to myself, I found that the rain had ceased, and that the sun was high in the heavens. I lay musing for a long time, feeling at first no pain; I was barely conscious of being awake, but had a pleasant kind of dream-like feeling over me; the sun was shining, the birds were singing, and the waters now quieter ran swiftly but merrily past me in their course, and to a tune which seemed in harmony with the waving boughs of the trees, and the warbling of the birds. But recollection came at last, and with that pain, as the events of the previous day rose to my memory. I looked at my foot and found that the bleeding had stopped; but the wound was very large, deep, and jagged, and that the foot was swollen to thrice its proper size. Fortunately I had got out of the stream at the side next Khandalla.

"As I lay considering what to do, I was obliged to come to the conclusion that, while I remained where I was, I should have but a poor chance of being seen by any one—my only hope—for the stream had carried me down farther into the jungle, and far from any track except the tracks of wild animals, and I could not repress a shudder when I thought of them. Knowing that my only safety lay in action, I commenced crawling in the direction of the village. My progress of course was slow, and being very weak, I was obliged to stop often to rest myself; as I was doing so, all at once I observed an animal creeping crouchingly towards me; it came nearer and nearer, and its flashing eyes were fixed on mine. My blood ran cold as the idea forced itself on me that it was a tiger, and I gave up hope then. I recollected however, having heard of men escaping from those animals by feigning death, and acting on the thought, I turned myself flat on the ground, face downward. In this way I lay for a few seconds which at that time appeared hours, but this suspense I could not bear, so, raising my head a little, and looking over my arm I carefully watched the wary advance of my antagonist. Closer and closer he came, frequently halting, and then I perceived that it was no tiger but a hyæna. This was a little relief certainly, but in my weak state, I should have been an easy prey to a wild cat. He was close to me, and his breathing was fearfully distinct. Presently, a shiver ran through my frame when I felt his nose touch my body, as he began smelling me all over. I think it was despair that kept me quiet, as I lay quite still, until he came to my head; but when I felt his cold nose touch my ear, I sprang up and gave a yell that might have been heard for a mile. At this the brute, as much frightened as I was, wheeled round, and, charging down the hill, disappeared in the jungle. When he was out of sight, I breathed freely again; but the excitement had been too much for me, and falling to the ground, I swooned away.

"I lay thus until the following morning, and I suppose it was the screeching of the parrots, and the chattering of the monkeys, who were swinging and gambolling in the trees above that caused me to awake. I could now find that I was much weaker than on the previous day, for what with the loss of blood, want of food, and exposure to the weather for two days and nights, I could scarcely move. But when I thought of my fate, '*lost in the jungle;*' when, if not found soon, I must be devoured by wild beasts, or failing that, die of hunger, I resolved to struggle on. So on I went, managing somehow or other to get along— crawling as before.

" I remember losing my belt, in the pocket of which was about two rupees; it slipped from round my waist, and I might, by simply extending my arm, have recovered it; but it did not cost me a thought; had there been five hundred times as much in it, I am certain the result would have been the same. I was fighting against weakness and hunger for my life, and all I cared for was to get forward. So I kept creeping along, slowly, certainly, and with.difficulty, but yet perseveringly, until I reached a level piece of ground, where some buffaloes were feeding. For some time, I looked anxiously about, hoping to see a human being, but could see no one. At this moment, a buffalo descried me, and he engaged my attention for the next ten minutes. Approaching within a dozen yards of me, he began lashing his tail and tossing his head. To distract his attention, I laid hold of a stone, and making a great effort, stood up and attempted to throw it at him. God help me! it fell at my feet; I was quite powerless. This seemed only to enrage the animal more, for he tore up the ground with his horns, and in all likelihood I should have been the next object for him to tear up, had not a black *chokra*, (boy,) who now saw my predicament, ran towards us, drove him off, and saved me.

" Upon discovering that I was an English soldier, he ran off to Khandalla, and in a short time returned with assistance. I was very carefully taken up and carried to the accommodation bungalow, where two European gentlemen travelling dawk down country, had just arrived. The natives had already explained to them all about me before I was brought in, and then, Indian-like, set to jabbering round about me all at once. The two Englishmen cleared the place of them, and in the spirit and with the manner of true Samaritans, washed my foot, bathed it with brandy, dressed it, got me food and drink, gave me a change of clothes, paid my fare by dawk on to where the regiment was, and, at parting, in a truly delicate and considerate manner, slipped five rupees into my hand. I shall never while I live forget their kindness; and I have regretted ever since that I did not ask those gentlemen their names. But at the time, I was too feverish and troubled to think of inquiring.

" I overtook the regiment that afternoon, and was taken to hospital, where I lay for months before I recovered."

CHAPTER FOURTH.

The March.

ON the morning of 1st January 1855, I accompanied Tom Gray a few miles on his road, and then parted with him, as it has turned out, for ever, poor fellow: he, too, has "gone the way of all flesh," and in the graveyard of Kurrachee a small headstone, erected by his comrades in the Artillery, points out his last resting-place. In the afternoon Blake and I went over the ground of his adventure eight years before. It was still a wild, lonely-looking place, but we could now hop across the stream into which he had fallen. He pointed out, far up the cliff, the spot from which he fell, and almost fancied he could pick out the rock which cut his foot. We then looked at the places where he had lain, every spot appearing to be quite familiar to him; but the greatest surprise was, that we found his belt and money lying exactly where he had dropped them: we had just been wondering whether there was any probability of our finding them, when we suddenly came on the spot; there lay all, belt, cap-pocket, and the two rupees in it! The money was discoloured and black, and the leather of the cap-pocket and belt was rotten, but there they were as they fell eight years before, and in all likelihood none but the tiger and the jackal had ever looked upon them since in that solitary place.

On the morning of the 3d, we resumed our march down the Ghauts. The road, as I have described already, is very steep. After dismounting, we advanced in files, walking and leading our horses down the path; and the road being narrow, those in front had reached the bottom long before the others in rear had started. It was a magnificent sight to see us winding down the face of the mountain that morning. The sun was shining brightly overhead, shewing us our path clearly, and for upwards of a mile beneath us the road lay like a spiral staircase covered with men and horses, who with their shining accoutrements and trappings glittering in the sun, were grand to see; and it would have been an easy feat, though not a safe one, to spring from the rear of the column to the front. At this part of the day's march I was greatly amused in watching, immediately in front of me, the descent of one of our sergeants, in the making of whom Nature had been rather sparing of material. His height was in reality about five feet three inches, but by his own standard he was a good foot over that, for like most short men he aspired to be tall, and had really gained about three inches by having tremendously high heels put to his boots. The road being very steep, I need scarcely add that the high heels threw him all on his forehand; and it would have made any one laugh as well as myself to see the desperate clutch he kept on the saddle bags to prevent himself from pitching head foremost down the ghaut. Pitying him at last, I recommended him to face about, a piece of advice that he followed, but for which, I am sorry to add, he was not in the least grateful, and in fact got quite out of temper when I afterwards related the incident and claimed credit for having saved his life. I am certain he could never have kept his hold of the valise until we reached the bottom. Our halting place on this day was Chowkee. Oh, such a miserable hole! its appearance bearing out all that we had heard of its unhealthiness.

On the 4th we reached Panwell, a village greatly in advance of Chowkee, being as clean and tidy as the other was the reverse. Since the railway had been opened thus far it had become of some importance, and was improved in every respect since we first marched up country. A considerable number of Europeans (English are always so termed there) now reside in Panwell, but their lines are as usual a long distance from those inhabited by the natives. A description of one Indian village of the better class will do for all, as they greatly resemble each other in their principal features. In the centre street of the village is the bazaar or market-place, as it may be termed, where the Borrees, or dealers in European goods, the Bunyans, or dealers in grain, and the Shroffs, or money changers, have their shop. These last make money, not only by lending it out at a high interest, but by exchanging coppers for silver: in this way, on every rupee's worth of pice they gain six pie, or three farthings. The Indian coinage consists of rupees, annas, and pie: twelve pie make an anna, and sixteen annas a rupee. There are other copper coins called pice, which are of the value of three pie, but these are not used in computation nor in accounts. The rupee ranges in value from two shillings to two shillings and threepence, varying according to the rate of exchange in London. The anna is of the value of a penny-halfpenny, the pie is worth the eighth part of a penny; and lastly come *cowries*, (shells,) sixty of which are of the value of pie. The bakers' and butchers' shops are usually at one extremity of the bazaar, the latter having their shambles in the jungle: they always go through a kind of religious ceremony before slaughtering, using the knife at all times even to buffaloes, tying them securely first and then cutting their heads off. Branching off on each side at right angles, run the different lanes where the various handicrafts reside,—viz., silversmiths, workers in iron, brass, copper, and tin; and in rear of these are to be found the dhobies, hodgims, ghorrawallahs, &c., all living clustered together. The great place is the Ram-Sami house or temple, to which they all repair several times a day, taking with them their offerings of *badgerie*, (grain,) *jaugari*, (sugar,) *ghee*, (butter,) oil, and even money; anything seems acceptable to the priests, who are no exception to the general rule. The next object of importance is the *chokee*, or police station; and next to this is the court-house; and a few doors on is the best house in the village, the *chowdra's*, (native police magistrate,) who daily holds his court, dispensing justice and giving judgment to those who fee him best. The next inhabitants of consequence in an Indian village are the pariah dogs, whose name is legion. These shew at all times an inveterate dislike to the *topee-wallahs*, (men with hats,) or Europeans; for at the mere sight of one they will turn out by twenties and follow him, barking at his heels until they see him clear of the village.

A bazaar in a village like Panwell is very picturesque at mid-day, in consequence of the many different castes, dressed in different costumes, with the occasional presence of a topee-wallah giving variety to the scene, and the native women carrying their chatties, or brass vessels for water, on their way to and from the river. This habit of carrying burdens on their heads causes them to have a particularly graceful and stately carriage, which is greatly aided by the manner in which they carry their hands, as high up as their heads, with the palms to the front, and so appear as it were, to sail along. The cause of their carrying their hands so, is the heavy silver ornaments worn on their wrists, which, if carried with a straight hanging arm, would be very tiresome to the wearer. But however handsome and graceful a native woman may look dressed in her *saree* and short silk jacket, with a chatty on her head, and silver bangles on her wrists and ankles, which jingle prettily as she walks along, the reverse of this is the case, when, wishing as some do, to appear still more engaging, she so far forgets herself as to wear a European dress. Put upon her the smartest gown, the neatest cap, shoes, and stockings, and the nicest little duck of a bonnet, and you then see the most slatternly, ill-looking, awkward creature in the world. There is nothing, without exception, that I ever saw look worse than a native woman so dressed; and most half-castes are but half a degree better, taking after their mothers in manners as well as habits.

While we were at Panwell two wealthy Bunyans, or shopkeepers, had just died; and as the bodies were to be burned that evening, we went to see the ceremony. This was to be performed by the river side, and there two large piles of wood were built, and on these, after a great deal of ceremony, the bodies were placed. The followers then commenced parading round and round the piles, dancing and screaming a wild mournful chant, while the tom-toms and other native instruments added to the clamour. At times, when the music fell to a low wail, the dancing had a kind of gracefulness in it, as they moved slowly to the tune, feet and hands keeping time; then it swelled louder, while their gestures and singing became more rapid and more piercing, the performers working themselves into a frenzy, until it reached a climax, when all suddenly ceased, and then the low wail and slow but graceful movement again commenced. As one party was fatigued another took its place, and a similar performance was gone through again. When this had been repeated several times the pile was ignited, and the wood being dry, it was soon all in a blaze; but the stench from the burning bodies made us quickly decamp. When they are consumed, the ashes are collected and thrown into the *nuddy*, (river.)

Our next and last march in India was a short one, on the 5th, to Ollwa Bunda, (landing-place,) at which point boats were waiting to take us on board our respective ships. This being only an eight miles' march, we got there early; and after dinner a portion of the troops began at once to embark, for the purpose of getting things ready on board to receive our steeds and their riders. At Ollwa we parted with our native followers,—with bobagees, dhobies, hodgims, ghorrawallahs, bheestie-wallahs, jarrawallahs, doudwallahs, and all who follow a regiment on the march in India. The poor fellows all appeared to be greatly affected as they crowded round to bid us farewell. Nearly all of them had been with us for years, and in that time an attachment had sprung up between us and them, of which neither party probably were aware until we were about to say "good-bye" for ever. Poor fellows! they were all very sad at parting; and whatever their failings may be—and who among us are faultless?—I am confident thus far, that if they are well treated, and not spoken harshly to, nor used like dogs, they will behave well in return, and shew their gratitude in numberless little ways, of which I have had many a proof. Bombay is about twenty-two miles from Ollwa by water—a great deal too far to take men and horses in sailing boats. The place is badly situated in every respect, and the temporary pier very unsuitable likewise. As the cotton boats, in which we had to embark, are all flat-bottomed and very high at the sides, a platform ought to have been constructed on an inclined plane, so that the horses might be run straight in. As it was, we were obliged to force the horses over an obstacle three feet in height, the boat's side being that much higher than the *bunda*, (landing-place.) As may well be imagined, it was no easy task to get them into the boats, at which, and at the water beyond, they were frightened; and it was not until various schemes had been tried, and all signally failed, that we hit at last upon one which answered. It was this: the horse was led up to the boat; then a rope which he had stepped over, and which was held on either side by some half-dozen men, was passed round his quarters, and with the aid of a couple of pulleys and a sailor's "Yo! heave, ho!" he was regularly hoisted over. But even when this was done, only half the work was accomplished; for it must be kept in mind that these were all stallions, that previous to this, unless when mounted in the ranks, they had never been nearer to each other than ten or twelve feet; therefore, on finding themselves suddenly so close, (not being six inches apart,) they took at once to kicking, rearing, and squealing in a manner seldom seen; and although every precaution possible had been taken as to fastening them, several managed to break both head and heel ropes, and, getting loose, plunged overboard and made for the shore, where, getting among the other horses which were being brought down, caused great confusion, and several more broke loose. All this happening more than once, much time was lost. To each boat there were half-a-dozen active men, who, as soon as a horse was shoved on board, seized him, twisted him into his place, and at once fastened him with two short heel ropes behind and two ropes to the head collar on each side in front, so that it was difficult for him to move one way or the other. A man was then placed at each horse's head after he was secured, who kept giving him hay to keep his attention employed. A party of us got away in a boat from Ollwa about eight A.M.; and as we expected to dine upon the water, took cooked provisions with us. We had a headwind, and were in consequence obliged to tack about very often, besides having the misfortune to run aground every quarter of an hour; and whenever this happened, a tremendous row and jabbering began among our boatmen, until eventually they jumped out and pushed her off. By and by we got to the sea—to where we were destined to pass a score of days; and as we looked over the expanse of waters which was to bear us on our way home, every heart swelled and every pulse beat high as we swept cheerfully along towards the *Punjaub*, which was situated on the waters a few miles ahead, off Bombay.

What a power there is in that magic word "Home!" How it causes all hearts to thrill! None but those who have been absent for years, can imagine half the enchantment that lies in that little word "home." I have seen strong men feign sickness, go into hospital, endure confinement, and swallow physic, until the pretended disease turned out a sad reality, only to get home. Others, even in that far off foreign land, I have known to desert, sans money, sans clothes, sans everything, and with the dreary prospect of walking all the way to Madras or Calcutta, not by road—for there they ran the chance of being retaken and brought back—but by unfrequented tracks, through jungles, over mountains, and across rivers, where famine, wild beasts, fever, and cholera, beset their path, depending only on the natives for a mouthful of rice and a drink of water; upon those who, were they but to touch a cooking utensil of theirs, would break it into pieces.

Yet in spite of all these dangers, would men desert, and getting clear away, never be heard of again. Whether they accomplished their object of getting home, or whether their bones are lying whitening in the jungle, never was known. This practice was not confined to our regiment; every regiment in the country had many who contrived to escape and never came back ; some, of course, failed, like Taylor of the 1st Bombay Fusiliers, who made two daring attempts—the second time not even hesitating at murder in trying to accomplish his object. His first attempt was well planned, and would have succeeded, but for an accident. His regiment was lying at Poonah, and he, with nine others, agreed to desert, beginning to lay their plans twelve months before they meant to carry them into execution. The first thing they did was to hire a bungalow in the city ; and four of them being tailors, a suit of sailor's clothes was there made for each. Taylor having been bred to the sea, understood navigation, and among other accomplishments could talk French fluently; so he was appointed captain of the party. When all things were ready, and each had saved a good sum of money, one of the party applied for month's leave to Bombay, which was granted. He, however, only proceeded as far as Panwell, where he hired a house for a week, and engaged a large boat on the pretence of making a pleasure trip the following day to the island of Elephanta; and being dressed in a suit of civilian's clothes, he had no difficulty in managing all this. The others, with Taylor, who, as I have said, had been chosen captain, had the audacity to desert in complete marching order, with muskets and side arms; Taylor having sergeant's stripes on, and his next in command corporal's stripes; and so dressed and accoutred, they marched down the road to Panwell without being questioned, because whoever they met supposed them to be on duty. They reached their destination at night, after being only two days on the road, and were met outside the village by their comrade, who guided them to the bungalow he had hired for their reception, and there they all put on their sailor's clothes. The next day they made every preparation on board their boat—laid in a month's provisions, fresh water, &c.; and when all was ready, lost no time in starting, and, getting a fair wind, were in a few days far from Bombay. They had previously agreed upon a story to relate to any vessel they might come across, and Taylor used to catechise them daily in this tale, besides teaching them a number of nautical terms and phrases, and the names of the ropes, halliards, bowlines, &c., on board a ship. In this manner they passed the time, until they reached Goa, the Portuguese settlement on the coast, and there put in. Taylor asked to see the governor, and to him made a statement that he was the captain of an American schooner, named the *Chloe*, belonging to New York, that he had sailed last from Kurrachee, with a cargo for Madras, that the night previous he had been run into by a large ship, that he had barely time to escape with his crew in the boat when the vessel sank, that he saw no more of the ship which had run him down, and so bore up for Goa, being the nearest port. The governor believed all this, and treated him and his supposed crew with great kindness, and gave them every help that lay in his power. After this assistance they sailed for Pondicherry, and relating the same tale again, were also remarkably well treated there, Taylor's knowledge of French proving of great service. A jealousy however, broke out at this place between the crew and their captain, on account of his being invited to the governor's table, while they were regaled in the kitchen; one man in particular threatening to see the governor and expose the whole affair. Taylor replied to the menace by knocking the fellow down; and, addressing the others, pointed out to them how necessary it was for both him and them that he should continue his assumed character, and that he could only do so by keeping them at a distance; and so that difficulty was at last got over. They reached Madras safely, where they told precisely the same tale, with this exception—that they were bound from Hong Kong to New York, with a cargo of tea, instead of from Kurrachee to Madras. On landing, Taylor made his report to the American consul, and was again treated better than the others, he living at a hotel, while they were put up at the Sailors' Home. It was while there that some articles of regimental necessaries were discovered on the man whom Taylor had struck; and as an account of some men having deserted from the 1st Bombays had appeared in the papers, they were detained until inquiries were made. One of their regiment was sent to identify them, and they were all brought back to Poonah, tried for desertion, and sentenced to two years' penal servitude each. On the expiration of this period Taylor rejoined his regiment, and volunteered from it to the 3d Bombays, which was just being raised. He was shortly after made corporal, and sent to the Central Training School at Poonah, established by Lord Frederick Fitzclarence, but had not been there four months when he and four others again deserted, and again he made for Panwell; and hiring a boat, proceeded to sea, accompanied by the *tindal*, or owner of the boat, who would not leave it unfortunately, as it afterwards turned out for the poor fellow. They were hotly pursued, and quickly overhauled by a steam-tug which followed them from Bombay; but the tindal was not in the boat, nor would they give any account of him. On being brought back they were all delivered over to the civil power, and tried about August 1854, for the murder of the tindal; but of this they were acquitted through some informality, and for want of evidence to prove how he had come by his end. A military tribunal, however, sentenced them to two years' imprisonment each for desertion, Taylor declaring at the time that he would never give up the idea of making his escape until he was successful, or perished in the attempt. His adventures and the cause of them would be thought extraordinary at home; but out in India they were thought nothing of. Seven years before this time, he had married a young and lovely girl, to whom it appears he was very much attached; but she proved unfaithful, and, deserting him, went to Europe with an officer of the name of S——, with whom she was still living—so he had heard. His whole desire was to be revenged; and he had sworn to allow no obstacle to stand in his path, no danger to deter him from getting to England, no difficulty to hinder him from following his wife and her paramour, until he found them; and whenever he did find them, to take a signal vengeance. I never heard of him afterwards, but doubtless if alive, he is still persevering.

To return to my story, and the element on which we were bounding along towards the good ship *Punjaub*. We arrived safely at Bombay about 5 P.M., having been eight hours in running the distance; but we were very lucky compared with some of the boats, which did not come in until two hours afterwards, and the remainder were obliged to stay on the water all night. Four vessels had been chartered to convey the right wing of the regiment; these were—the *Punjaub*, the *Earl Grey*, the *Auckland*, and the *Lord Bentinck*; the two last were steamers. I was on board the *Punjaub*, and her crew consisted of one-third Europeans, and the remainder Lascars. The getting on board of the horses was all managed in a first-rate manner, when the great difficulties under which we laboured are taken into consideration; for embarking and slinging horses were quite new to us all; and besides, the horses being crowded into small boats that were pitching about in a rough sea, rendered it dangerous as well as difficult to get these vicious creatures on board. A horse in slings mid-air is one of the most helpless-looking objects one can see, and for all the world reminded me at the time of the sign of the golden fleece, where a lamb is suspended by a girdle round the middle over the inn-door. But however docile and helpless our horses looked when being passed on board, that character was speedily lost the moment their feet touched the deck; it was then

—stand clear of their heels!—as they lashed out clean behind them half-a-dozen times; but three or four determined fellows were at their heads immediately, the slings were slipped off, and the horses passed to their places. They were stowed on all three decks in separate boxes, their heads being inwards, with small wooden troughs in front for them to feed out of. They were secured only by the head with canvas collars, to which were attached two ropes that were secured to each side of the box in such a manner that they could not smell at, far less bite each other. Beneath their feet were mats made of *kiar*, (the fibre of the cocoa-nut,) for them to stand upon, and above and in front of each stall was a pair of slings, to sling them in fine weather, not in rough, for were horses to be suspended then, the rolling and pitching of the vessel would cause them to knock against the sides and ends of their boxes, from not having the use of their feet. The greater part of the forage was packed in and round the paddle-boxes, and there being but little ballast, and the vessel carrying much top-weight, caused her to roll tremendously in a heavy sea; and when a storm arose, which I am happy to say was only once, everybody was knocking about and pitching against everything. While at Bombay, I will say a few words about it. The name is derived, I believe from two Portuguese words: *Bom*, signifying fine, and *Bahia*, signifying port or harbour; and well it deserves this name, being one of the finest, if not the best harbours in Asia. The bay has been compared to the Firth of Forth; and if one could imagine Elephanta to be Inchkeith, a resemblance might be traced;

but when one looks for the shores of Fife, and pictures the Bass and Cramond, the idea vanishes as soon as it is conjured up. Bombay is a pleasant enough sort of place in the cold months, but during the hot season it is quite another thing, for what with the hot wind that comes searching and seething into every hole and cranny, drying up all before it, and the disagreeable smells it carries along with it, together with the enervating feeling it produces, a trip to the hills, if only to get a sniff of cool air, becomes a necessity. There is certainly a machine for making ice in Bombay now, but that makes but little difference to the typhoon. It is a city of great importance, not only for its excellent harbour, but for its central position— an importance that will yearly increase as the resources of India become more fully developed. Calcutta lies too far away eastward; Madras is not at all adapted as a depôt for cotton, but Bombay must assuredly become one; first, from its proximity to Scinde and the Punjaub, the cotton-growing provinces; and secondly, from having so fine a harbour, an advantage which neither of the other Presidencies possesses, and also from its being nearer to England, especially by the overland route. It appears strange that, with all these manifest advantages, Bombay should not be the seat of Government instead of Calcutta, the one being so far superior to the other in every respect. Bombay is apparently very strongly fortified towards the sea, although many are of opinion that the remark made by the late Lord Frederick Fitzclarence, when speaking of the fortifications around Portsmouth, that he 'could see no other use for the walls than to fill up the ditches in front of them," would be equally applicable to the defences of Bombay. There is a battery on a spit of land at the entrance to the harbour, that mounts twelve guns, which on the outbreak of the Russian war was garrisoned by a troop of horse artillery from Poonah, after it was rumoured that a Russian frigate was cruising in the Indian seas; but I fancy that the Indian navy was too strong and vigilant to fear any single vessel of the enemy appearing in those seas, far less committing depredations. Bombay, as most people are aware, is an island, and not a very large one, being only about six miles in length, and from one to two miles in breadth; the harbour unites everything to be desired in a seaport; it is easy both of access and egress, possesses good anchorage, and is well adapted for docks of every description. In the native portion of the town, although nothing remarkable is to be observed, there is plenty to amuse a stranger, especially a European, who is surprised at the narrow streets, and at the buffaloes he meets at every turn, and gazes with wonder and delight at the joss houses, the faqueers, and the beggars, while he feels interested in exploring the dark, contracted alleys, which branch off at right angles to the streets at nearly every twenty yards, and in investigating the breed and colour of their numerous garrisons of dogs. But with all this there are a few drawbacks that alter the appearance of the picture; for, when on his tour of discovery, the stranger is assailed by a strong mixture of every different kind of stench under the sun, by a continual noise of people shouting in an unknown tongue, and hackeries passing on wheels that never were greased, the whole being enlivened by music so shrill and discordant as might nearly drive any sane person out of their senses, or cure the toothache in its worst form. The Hindoos allow that Europeans excel them in everything but music and making ladders: for the former you must imagine what sort of discord could be got from a broken trumpet and a kettle-drum with a crack in it; and for the latter you must imagine bare poles with notches in them about six feet apart.

CHAPTER FIFTH.

The Voyage.

IT was a great day in Bombay, when hoisting the Blue Peter to shew that we were all ready, we tripped our anchors and prepared to sail away from India. All the vessels in the harbour were in their holiday attire, with flags and ensigns streaming in the wind, while on the beach were thousands and thousands of the inhabitants assembled to see the first division of the 10th Hussars leave for the seat of war. It was about three o'clock in the afternoon of the 6th of January 1855, when we in the *Punjaub*, with the *Auckland* towing us, led the way, followed by the *Bentinck* and the *Earl Grey*, all slowly sailing from the shore. Each ship lying at anchor, as we passed her, manned the yards and cheered us in turn, to which we responded as heartily as the thoughts of the moment would allow us; while from the beach was wafted to us over the waters the strong voice of the multitude there congregated, who thus gave vent to their feelings and their desire for our welfare. As we receded from the land the distant hum came low and indistinct over the waters, and I paced the deck gazing back silently and regretfully upon the fading coast, fast disappearing from my view, and listening to the now far off and dying sounds which fell upon my ear like farewell voices, low and sweet, until all gradually sank into silence, except the ripple of the waves around the prow of the ship as she glided almost imperceptibly onwards. We were accompanied a considerable way by the commodore, Sir Stephen Lushington, in his yacht, who did not part company with us until the day began to close, when he hove to, and standing on the poop, cordially shouted "Farewell" to each vessel as she swept past him, while we in return, with manned yards, cheered the stout old sailor lustily.

Night soon drew her curtain over all and in a few hours we were far away from Bombay, steering westwards towards the Straits of Babelmandeb. Now that we were really off, there were few who could help feeling sincere regret at leaving what had been for so many years our home; and in these retrospects it is always the happiest moments which memory recalls, the hours of pleasure becoming the most vivid, while those of pain or trouble are nearly forgotten. So thinking only of the bright days that were gone, we sorrowed as we gazed at the small spark afar off, which we knew was the lighthouse off Bombay harbour. Then turning from such sad thoughts, some would easily conjure up brighter images to embellish their future. Home became uppermost in their minds, and so dreaming, they would scarcely think of the long and dangerous path they have to tread before reaching the haven of their hopes,—the perils by sea and land, the storms and shipwrecks, the fevers and cholera, the fighting and wounds. Dreaming of none of these, they see only in the foreground the sparkling visions which they called at will from the depths of their imaginations, never caring to rend the curtain and look behind, but, ignoring all darkness, would look only at the sunshine of hope.

From Bombay to Aden is 1960 miles; and steering west and by south, in ten days we reached the Straits of Babelmandeb, known also by the pleasant names of "The Gate of Misfortune," "The Straits of Shipwreck," "The Key of Death," and cast anchor at Aden on the 16th January. What a strange place is this! Though a portion of "Arabia the Happy," it is the most miserable-looking place in the world. A small peninsula cut off from the continent by a narrow neck of land, the approach to which is commanded by strange though strong fortifications; and on this tract of voltaic rock, alike destitute of tree or blade of grass, and but scantily supplied with water, a wing of a European regiment, a battery of artillery, and some sappers are obliged to drag out a sort of melancholy existence for twelve months at a stretch. Its importance as a coaling station may be said to be only an affair of yesterday. Taken possession of in 1839 by the British, first as a guarantee, and afterwards purchased by the late H. E. I. C. from the Arabs, for a sum of money paid yearly, its value has increased a hundredfold since the overland route has become the great highway for travellers to and from our Eastern dominions. The place itself has been compared to everything under the sun which has ever had a thorough roasting; and as it daily undergoes another heating process, its charred and sterile appearance increases continually; yet this unhappy-looking place is celebrated from the remotest period for its commerce, and the excellence of its harbour. On this desolate rock was accumulated the riches of the East in their transit to the natives of the West; but no effort of my imagination could people the black, barren, rocky, uninteresting ground with anything which belonged to comfort, far less to splendour. All was black, comfortless, and unfruitful; water not only scarce but bad, and the only palatable well belongs to a Parsee, who sells it as may be expected, dearly. The troops shut up here for a few months look upon it as a kind of imprisonment, far worse than a sea voyage, for no cool refreshing breeze, nor change of weather, is ever experienced; but in one respect it resembles the confinement on board ship, for the garrison is fed upon salt provisions a great portion of the time. Now I believe, Cape sheep are used, but where and how they feed them is a mystery. The Arabs apparently regretted their bargain in disposing of Aden, and several attempts have been made to retake it by stratagem. When the 1st Bombay Fusiliers were stationed at Aden in 1849, a well laid plan was made to get possession of the fort, and it very nearly succeeded. The Arabs were allowed then to come into the fort to dispose of any article they had for sale; and so by sixes at a time, nearly five hundred of them got inside and hid themselves among the many caves and hiding places in the rocks, intending to remain concealed until midnight, and then to sally out and massacre the garrison. Providentially the plot was discovered in time, and they were all turned out of the fort; and since then no more than fifty have been allowed inside at a time. The non-commissioned officer on duty at the gate keeps an account of the number who go in and come out; and whenever the prescribed number are in, no more are allowed to enter. Outside the fort Englishmen are still in danger, and no one can go five hundred yards from the walls without running the risk of having an Arab bullet through his body. So daring had they become about five years ago, that one actually made an attack upon an officer, and stabbed him at the gate of the fort, and they were only taught a lesson by a sudden movement of the garrison, who, starting one morning with three days' provisions, marched about thirty miles into the desert, took and destroyed one of their fortresses, and then returned. This they did not forget for some time, and it rendered them more cautious for a year or two; but when we were there they had begun to be as bold as they were formerly, and few of the garrison dared to go outside. We saw very few Arabs in the place: these certainly were tall, fine looking fellows; but as a contrast there were plenty of Simaulees from the African side, who could not be more distinct in every particular from the Arabs as a race, if the poles had kept them asunder, instead of only a narrow strait. Of low dwarfish stature, dirty in habits, sallow in complexion, grovelling in disposition, and with a continual outcry for *chiri-miri*, (gifts,) these Simaulees infest the water all round the ships for hours, bobbing up and down in their coloured wigs of *kiar*, like so many burned corks; the water seems their natural element, and in it they are as expert as the Maltese, in catching money when thrown to them overboard. As for their dresses, some forcibly reminded me of night shirts, by their scantiness and simplicity, but most had no dress at all. After coaling, we sailed away the same evening through the narrow channel, and in a short time our eyes were gladdened by the sight of the Red Sea. Passing the Babelmandeb peak, we were soon close to the island of Perim, which is a chip of the same block that Aden was chiselled from. The wind being still favourable, we set all sail, and, casting off the hawser with which the *Auckland* was towing us, the *Punjaub* went ahead alone, and, had we chosen, could have easily distanced her consorts. The following morning we were abreast of Mocha, which like all Eastern towns looked remarkably well from the sea, for there "distance lends enchantment to the view" really. From Aden to Suez is 1600 miles; and our course was now changed, having to steer N.W.

On the third day after leaving Aden the wind fell, and the little *Auckland* had again to take us in tow; and as she went puffing and snorting along, she looked something like a pony dragging an elephant, so great was the difference in size between the vessels. The *Punjaub* as I have already said, was a man-of-war, or frigate rather; but she had not yet received her complement of men when she was made up for our use. The crew therefore consisted principally of Lascars, who make tolerable seamen; and they are commanded by native boatswains, or *serangs*, as they are termed. It was good fun to hear the serangs shouting and giving orders when the Lascar watch was on deck. Each rope has a name by which it is known; although by the way, sailors insist that there are only two ropes on board, the others being either halliards, bowlines, whips, &c. But the native names for the different ropes are really rich, such as *burra* (large) stringie, *chotta* (small) stringie, goosie stringie, beefie stringie, onion stringie, fishie stringie. In explanation of this, it seems that the first captain who had a native crew, found it a complete impossibility to teach them the different names of the ropes, far less to get them to pull on the right ones; so being the proper man to cope with a difficulty, he attached to every rope some article of food, the name of which of course they knew; the word rope also he could not get them to repeat, so he substituted string. Then they got along surprisingly fast. He had only to shout goosie stringie, or beefie stringie, and they would all make a rush at the rope where the goose or beef hung, and pull like madmen; and in time they knew each rope by these different names, even when the article was removed from it.

We had an example one day of the difference between martial and naval laws. On board ship smoking between decks is always strictly prohibited, and very right that it should be so; for, where so much that is combustible lies about, were the laws and rules against smoking not stringently carried out, accidents might continually happen, and nothing is more dreadful than a ship on fire. Two men— a soldier and a sailor—were confined for smoking below; the soldier was punished by having his grog stopped for fourteen days, but the sailor was sentenced by the captain to receive four dozen lashes. The boatswain piped to quarters, a grating was rigged, the man strapped to it, and then the forty-eight lashes were inflicted in a far severer manner than I ever saw flogging done in the army; the sailor however, took the allowance with great nonchalance, and at the end of it put on his shirt and jacket as if nothing had happened.

Our life on board was much the same every day: we were up and stirring usually by five o'clock in the morning, principally because there was a half-pint of strong tea then served out to any one who chose to go for it; and as good tea is a grateful and refreshing drink, especially in the morning, most of us preferred getting up for it to lying an hour longer in—I was going to say bed, but our couch was made, if not on "the hard, hard ground," at least on the hard deck, where the planks were all of equal hardness; so we had no choice. At six the stable trumpet sounded, when each groomed his steed as well as he could in the narrow box he was placed in; at seven we fed them, and then went to look after our own breakfasts, which consisted of cocoa and biscuits. From that time we amused ourselves as best we could till eleven o'clock, when we went to stables again, cleaned out our horses' stalls by taking up the *kiar* (cocoa-nut fibre) matting which was underneath them, and towing it overboard for a quarter of an hour to wash it. The principal duty on board was hand-rubbing the horses' legs to keep them from swelling, which they are liable to do when standing so long; in fine weather they are slung, which eases them a good deal. At one o'clock they were fed again; then "Dismiss" sounded, and our own dinners followed, which consisted of pork and pea-soup one day, and salt beef and soup the next; but thrice a week flour, plums, and suet were served out to make puddings. Besides this we had vinegar and lime-juice issued, and a glass of grog at eight bells, (four o'clock,) stables from five to six, and then tea time came. Our evenings were usually spent in spinning yarns, singing songs, and dancing. We had a fiddler—Joe Parsons—in the troop, who being also a good singer was always in great request of an evening, when a large number would collect on the forecastle or by the cuddy door to have a dance and song. This was the usual daily routine, only broken by the appearance of some peculiar landmark which we sighted, or by a sail heaving in sight, or by the recurrence of Sunday. I often heard it remarked that the Sabbath at sea is nearly always a fine day; however bad the weather may be for six days, on the seventh it usually clears. On that day too, there is always a solemnity observable, which is more striking on shipboard than elsewhere. Everything having been cleaned and made tidy the day before, no work but what is absolutely necessary is permitted to be done on the Sabbath. From early morning all is quiet; there is a subdued tone in the voices of all, the boatswain's whistle loses much of its shrillness, the customary oaths are dispensed with, and even the ropes seem to make less noise than usual. The men are scattered about in little groups, reading or chatting quietly, dressed in their cleanest smocks, with their forage caps or billy-cocks stuck more jauntily than usual on their heads; and the sailors wear their shirts and trousers of the loudest patterns, with fancy neck-ties. In warm latitudes an awning is always placed over the main-deck,

THE VOYAGE.

which has previously been cleared of all that can be stowed away, and at four bells (ten o'clock) the men are formed into a hollow square to hear divine service. All then is still; no sound to disturb the reader but the ripple of the waves, as he distinctly reads a portion of the beautiful service of the Church of England; and as he speaks of God where God is most distinctly to be seen—in the boundless waters and the far overarching sky—all listen with apparent devoutness. A serenity is over the ship never noticed on any other day, and though there is less laughter there is not less happiness; it is if more subdued, sweeter; and as our thoughts naturally pass from religion to home, and we take out our old letters, in fancy we see loved faces far away, who on that day we know are at the little village church, making fervent responses to the supplication for mercy to be shewn to "those who go down to the sea in ships."

And so day after day passed. We met a few ships, caught several flying-fish, and shot some porpoises, ate and drank at the appointed periods, got sailorish in our ways, and pretended to be interested in the wind, which, if it puffed stronger than usual, caused us to cast our eyes critically aloft, as if we feared some of the top hamper might go by the run. While the days passed we were speeding on, on, nine knots an hour, through the Red Sea; so we sighted and passed Jeddah, and thought of the pilgrims who land there on their way to the tomb of Mohammed.

But a change in the weather came at last; and although it was for the worse, we at first rather liked it for the

F

novelty and excitement; for when the sky lowered, and heavy drops of rain began to fall long before the wind came, " Ah !" says one of the would-be weatherwise, " we shall have a squall soon." " Better that than being towed along at this rate," chimes in another. Meanwhile the dark clouds kept rising from the sea, and, towering above each other in mountain-like masses, the shapes kept ever changing as we watched them. Now they had the appearance of huge rocks and precipices, built up pile upon pile one over the other; then they altered to mountain ridges, on the summits of which towered castles; and from this mass the form of a giant seemed to rise, and with arms reaching across the sea, appeared to intend to embrace and overwhelm us. It grew darker and more dark, while the wind freshened to a gale; and the little *Auckland* in front of us was pitching and struggling amid a sea of foam, as she pulled the monstrous *Punjaub* behind her, which, with only her foresail set, threatened every minute to run over her little guide, though she to the last kept up the appearance of having us in tow. But this did not continue long; our good ship suddenly plunged ahead like a wild, unbroken courser let loose, and in a second we were right a-top of the *Auckland*. I thought we had passed over her, but fortunately she avoided us by putting her helm hard a-port—escaping by the merest hairsbreadth. The hawser, however, nearly brought her to grief. In the hurry it had not been cast off, and we were now dragging the steamer; but an axe soon settled the difficulty, and in a few minutes we were free, darting onwards through the dark waters. A light a long way astern, shewed the whereabout of our consort; but on went our vessel, like a steed uncontrolled, the waves making a clean breach over her. So much cargo being on the upper deck, and so little ballast below, she plunged, and rolled, and dipped awfully—more than I had ever seen a vessel do before; and I had doubled the Cape in the month of June—the southern winter—and there encountered many a storm. On one occasion a wave struck the ship *Brahmin* as high as the foretop-sail; but none of these gales were ever anything like this. At one moment we were on the crest of the waves and could see around us; the next moment we were in the trough of the sea, with the waves on all sides high above, and threatening to close and ingulf us; but the next instant we were again riding on the top of the waves, getting a glimpse of the sky, and then back again into the dark valley of water. There was a grandeur about the whole scene that fascinated me; and being partially sheltered by the quarter-deck, I held on enjoying the wildness around, whilst the wind shrilly whistling through the ropes and rigging, seemed a fit voice for the spirit of the storm. The horses were plunging fearfully; and some of them having got loose, broke down the wooden partitions; and then ensued such squealing and kicking amongst them as beggars all description. To stand without holding on with both hands, was nearly an impossibility; yet the trumpet sounded, "Stand to your horses,"—easier ordered than obeyed, for the vessel was lying over at an angle of 45°, and to go among vicious horses that were fighting, biting, and kicking each other, in order to secure them, was a most perilous task; but we did the best we could under the circumstances, hitting them with sticks and ropes to part them, and managing somehow to fix up the sides of the stalls in a temporary way. We were up all night long, fastening our four-footed companions, amid an uproar and war both of the elements and of the animals which might have awakened the Seven Sleepers. Yet *Private Saddler* slept through it all. Having snugly stowed himself away, he did not wake until breakfast time, when he was quite surprised to hear of all that had happened. About eight o'clock in the morning the storm abated, and we then commenced repairing the ravages it had committed. In the lower deck one of the horses, D 59, was reported dead, and as he was a regular brute both to kick and bite, and to look after, a kind of thanksgiving was uttered by all; but when about ten o'clock a fatigue party was sent down to put the carcase in slings and hoist it up on deck to be thrown overboard, lo, and behold! he was sitting quietly on his haunches nibbling some hay, and he lived for many a day afterwards to torment us all. Our voyage was now drawing to a close, and in spite of the storms, and shoals, and rocks which make the Red Sea passage so dangerous, we got safely through all. But a delay was caused by our being obliged to lie to after the storm, and wait for the *Auckland* to come up, as our orders were not to part company with her; however, she overtook us on the evening of the 30th January. We were told afterwards that the *Earl Grey* sprung a leak, and had to put back into Aden, when it was discovered that she was not seaworthy; so G troop had to be disembarked on that most wretched of all spots on the earth, and wait until a vessel came from Bombay to take them on to Suez. On the morning of the 1st of February we passed through the Straits of Shiraz, and by the island of Jubal. In the afternoon Mount Sinai was sighted, and the following morning the *Punjaub* and the *Auckland* were anchored about two miles from Suez; the anchorage being very shallow will not allow of large vessels getting any closer in shore. We immediately commenced disembarking, which was a tedious affair, there being only a kind of raft, and a couple of small boats to convey us and our chargers to the land. The raft was towed to a wooden pier, where those who were on it could get out pretty comfortably; but far different was it with those who like me landed by the small boats. We were taken to the nearest part of the beach, and when the boat's bottom touched the strand, it heeled on one side, and the cargo, ourselves and the horses, were decanted into the surf to get ashore as best we could. As might be expected, some of the horses got loose, and made much of their liberty by galloping about, shewing their joy at being once more on *terra firma* by rolling over and over in the sand. As soon as we got a number together, we moved on in succession to our camping ground, which was about a couple of miles away in the desert. Here we pitched our tents, and picketed our horses, having for picket pegs poles six feet long, and even they were of very little use in the light sandy ground, as our chargers could pull them up nearly as fast as we drove them down. We were all surprised at their restiveness, imagining that from their having had to stand for so long a time on their legs aboard ship, they would have been too tired to knock about, and would have thankfully seized upon the repose that was now offered to them; but no such feelings had they; they kept us employed the whole night, and fatiguing work we found it; for while we were engaged in tying up the one half the other half broke loose, and scampered round us, kicking and squealing in the height of their fun, and mocking us in our misery, for no one scarcely closed an eye that night. Saddler (he who slept all through the storm) attempting to get forty winks, had his head severely cut by D 39, which, in its career, galloped right over the tent in which he was sleeping, smashing the poles, and, what was far worse, placing his hoof on the poor fellow's head. On the following day the remainder of our troop disembarked; and after all was settled, some of us started to look for adventures, and to make fresh discoveries in this to us new and unknown quarter of the world.

CHAPTER SIXTH.

Egypt.

WE staid three days at Suez—a corruption, some say, of the word Oasis, while others affirm it to be a corruption of the word Sivas for Sebaste—it signifies very little which is correct. Desert-ways, we could see the telegraph houses, and naught else, except a small stone building, about a mile to the south-east of our tents. This was overhauled, and found to contain a well of very brackish water, where we had afterwards to water our horses; it was named Jacob's Well, and so became interesting to us. For our own drinking, we had plenty of delicious Nile water, so cool, so sweet, and so grateful to our parched lips after coming off shipboard; and bringing our steeds a couple of miles through the sand, in which we sank several inches at each step; and from that time we respected the Nile water nearly as much as did the Egyptians who worshipped it. This water had been brought on camels all the way from Cairo to Suez for our use, and kept there in iron tanks until we arrived; a similar supply was placed at each halting-place in the desert. Then what beautiful oranges there were for sale, and twelve for a piastre, (twopence farthing)—another luxury! and in addition to these, our rations were all that could be wished for—good mutton, good bread, and capital tea and coffee—the only drawback being that if one felt inclined to eat a little more than his rations, there was no chance of procuring it, there being no shops where extras could be purchased. There was an order for none of us to go near the town; but the very command against our going made many feel all the more anxious to have a peep at the forbidden spot. Certainly, from the slight glance we had at it as we passed through, there seemed nothing tempting to look at; and probably, but for the prohibition published in orders, none would have felt inclined to go the distance to look at it again; but the mere fact of an order against our going was an incentive to progress in that direction. So, about noon on the second day, Tom Nolan and I started to have a closer look at the town, and see what the authorities were so anxious we should not look at. Taking first the direction of Jacob's Well, we circled from there gradually round towards Suez; and as we approached it, we at once perceived that outwardly there was little to adorn the place or catch the eye. Too fastidious people might have complained of the sameness of the style in the building of the mud wall, about twenty feet high, which surrounds the town, and is loopholed on the Desert side. The entrance is a small arched gateway, inside of which now sat a Turkish sentinel, smoking quite comfortably, his matchlock resting peaceably against the wall some distance from him. "Not a bad idea that fellow has of doing sentry go," said Tom; "and what I often wonder at is, that our people have never introduced a similar seat into our sentry-boxes, seeing that *our authorities* are usually so fond of picking up anything fresh from foreigners. I'm sure it's a better way of doing duty in a warm climate, while smoking at the same time would just keep a fellow awake." I put a stop to his moralising by directing his attention to one of our officers who was coming mounted towards us at a canter from the camp, and he was now only about a couple of hundred yards behind. As it was doubtful whether he had observed us, we determined to make for the wall, as to return through the gate was now an impossibility, without being recognised: so away we went at a run. The officer passed through, and possibly would not have perceived us had it not been for the "Bono Johnny" on sentry, who drew his attention to us. He pulled up at that, looked after us, seemingly hesitating what to do. This lost him the day, for by the time he had made up his mind, we were close to the mud fortification, the top of which we easily scaled. The officer having by this time made his decision, galloped after us, when we dropped quietly down on the other side upon the sand; and as his horse could not quite leap the wall, we left him, like Lord Ullin, "lamenting," when he was obliged to retire, doubtless quite disgusted. Had we been discovered, a serious matter could have been made out of it—"disobedience of orders;" but we had no idea of being balked after having made up our minds to view the mysteries; and so, filing about, we again passed our friend in his snug berth, where he was still "blowing his bacca." Keeping to our right close to the houses, we commenced our reconnaissance; but after all, it was a hole of a place—narrow dirty streets, hovels for houses, dogs of course, and one filthy public-house kept by a Maltese with the patriarchal name of Joseph. This worthy dealt in various concoctions, which he had different names for. What he called rum I believe was a mixture of aniseed and aquafortis; and his gin was made out of spirits of tar and turpentine. Failing in ability to drink any of this stuff, we strolled down to the beach, where stood the best—I may say the only habitable —house in the place: this was the Hôtel Anglais, where everything was alike dear and bad. We then had a look at the *Punjaub*, wondering at that time what had become of the *Earl Grey*, with G troop on board, who had, in consequence of her accident, to wait for the *Feroze* to return and fetch them. We now retraced our steps, having discovered little to interest and less to amuse, with but a poor idea of Africa, wondering by the way whereabout it was that the Israelites crossed the Red Sea, and casting our eyes backwards towards Mount Sinai, thinking of "the thunders and lightnings and thick darkness upon the mount," and of "the voice of the trumpet exceeding loud, so that all the people that were in the camp trembled;" and here had sojourned those "six hundred thousand on foot that were men, beside women and children," journeying from Pi-hahiroth. As we repassed the sentinel, we found him still sitting, still smoking, and still smiling— the very picture of content; but, as Tom observed, "Why should he not be happy? seated comfortably on a cushioned seat, with his hubble-bubble by his side, and neither a stiff stock to choke him, nor tight clothing braced up and strapped down to pinch him: nothing but ease to surround him in his comfortable life—ah! why shouldn't he be happy?" And so Tom went on moralising and envying by the way. We journeyed straight ahead into the Desert for about two miles, in a contrary direction to the camp, as a precautionary measure; and when we fancied we had got far enough away, steered, as we thought, back again into the old track; but after wandering about for a considerable time, we could see nothing of our tents. I may remark that the ground was not level, but undulating; and so we just began to be a trifle afraid that we had lost our way—not very comforting, with a sea of sand on all sides; and we afraid to move in any direction, lest we should only be going further astray. At last, lying down with our ears to the ground, we listened, and then could hear the distant but welcome shrill neighs of our steeds, and immediately bearing in the direction of those sounds, we eventually reached our tents. During the time we were camped at Suez, we had frequent opportunities of seeing the mirage; and so complete was the deception, that many of the men went off to have a bathe in the beautiful fresh-looking streams overshadowed by trees, which appeared to be close at hand, and they walked on and on, the delusive image getting no nearer, but still pleasant and enticing to look at. Some who had seen them start on their useless excursion followed, and brought them to a true knowledge of what they were so anxious to get to. It was only at Suez that I noticed the mirage so plain and distinct, the air being so clear that objects could be seen for miles away in the Desert, far past the telegraph, which stands lik mileposts along the sandy way. On the day that G troop arrived from Aden, we marched our first day's journey towards Cairo; the reveille went some two hours before daybreak, and we were all ready to move off when "the gates of morning" opened. Our Arab guides led the road, I suppose by the stars that were just fading away, for there was no path into the Desert before us. At this season of the year the mornings and nights are bitterly cold in Egypt; but the sun during the day is very powerful; and this after the first morning caused us to start earlier, the reveille usually sounding about midnight, and we had consequently the better part of the march over by dawn; but our progress was slow—not out of a walk—as our horses sank at every step over their fetlocks in the soft yielding sand. The first day, February 4, I was baggage-guard, and being obliged to wait until all the camp equipage was collected, the troops had got a long way ahead before we moved off; and as the camels' pace was still slower than our horses', it was two o'clock in the afternoon before I got into the camping ground, when, tired, and hungry, and thirsty, I discovered that my rations had been eaten and my grog drunk. I found grumbling was of no use, and I was obliged to content myself for the time with a draught of Nile water, very nice and refreshing, but which unfortunately only strengthened my already too keen appetite. Accordingly, away I went on a foraging expedition, first making an attack on the quartermaster-sergeant, Boileau, but there got a repulse; all he knew or cared was, that my rations had been drawn; as regarded who had devoured them, that was no business of his. I tried other quarters, but was unsuccessful, while the more I was repulsed, the more ravenous grew my appetite; but at last I met a Samaritan at the caravansary, who, doubtless observing my wolfish look, inquired what I wanted. This I explained, when, condoling with me, and, what was far more to the purpose, taking compassion on me, he led the way inside, and placed before me a capital pie with bottled ale to wash it down. Thanking my entertainer heartily and most gratefully for the kindness, I likewise tendered payment; but he would accept of nothing, only asking if I could sell him a razor: of course I *gave* him my own, being only too happy that it was in my power to oblige him in return; whether he was master of or servant at the caravansary, I never inquired; all I know is that he deserved to be the former. On the 5th we made the second day's journey; but the days' marches were so exactly alike, that it is needless to give a description of each. From Suez to Cairo is a distance of eighty-eight miles; so the daily marches were about twenty-two miles, and, as had been the custom in India, the cooks marched the night before and got breakfast ready for our arrival. As might be expected, the march was very dull, nothing to be seen but the sand wall reaching to the heavens, that girded us round with a greater security in imagination, than stone walls or iron bars could have done. In this manner we travelled back from Pi-hahiroth to Ethan, from Ethan to Succoth, from Succoth to Ramases, and all was barren, except on the third day's march, when we passed where a large palace stands, named the Abbasayah. This was built by Abbas Pasha, completely of freestone; and such an erection in the Desert appeared entirely out of place, reminding one of a wedding party among the catacombs. On the 7th we marched for Cairo; and, as the sun rose, dispelling the night shadows, and causing the stars to wane before his presence, the Pyramids gradually came between us and the clear blue vault of heaven, drawn out plainly on the azure background. At first sight they did not create that emotion of wonder which I had anticipated. Seen from a distance of course, their immense size does not strike one, as a closer inspection does. Our quarters were near to the edge of the Desert, two handsome, newly-erected cavalry barracks having been placed at our disposal. They were built about two miles from the citadel, by the late Pasha, for his troops, and in every way they were splendid buildings—handsome gates, fine rooms, and good stabling. But here I must stop: everything requisite for cleanliness was wanting; even the horse troughs were outside, and scarcely a drop of water to be got inside, even for cooking. Egypt, like all Eastern countries, is famed for dirt, dogs, and donkeys, and other vermin, that shew there still remains a good sprinkling of the third and fourth plagues; it is, in short, as it has been described:—

> "A land of antiquities, Arabs, and asses,
> And attar, which all other odour surpasses;
> Acacias, bazaars, barley, barbers, and bats;
> Barbs, beetles, bournouses, and turbans for hats;
> Caves, caravans, caverns, the cur, and the Copt
> Who resides in a convent, close-shaven and cropt;
> Crocodiles, charcoal, cangias, cactus, and cooks,
> Whose queer craft was ne'er learn'd from cookery books;

Dahabe'ehs, dragomans, dirty dervishes,
Who delude their poor dupes as sham flies delude fishes;
Deserts, dirt, and divans, dromedaries, and drums,
Whereon, dolefully chanting, the Nubian strums;
Dates, devotees, dompalms, doves, donkeys, and dogs;
Eunuchs, eagles, fleas, flies, flax, flamingoes, and frogs;
Geese, granite, gazelles, gnats, goats, gum-trees, and goolehs,*
Which last, pray believe me, are rare water-coolers;
Hadjis, whose hallow'd journey to Mecca's great shrine
Has entitled the rogue and the saint to combine," &c.

We had to remain in Cairo for about six weeks, principally to break in a number of young horses that we were taking with us, likewise drilling a number of recruits who had joined us at Bombay from England; and we had a very pleasant time of it there. Donkey-riding formed our principal amusement, as it appeared to be also of the natives, who would at all times turn out to see a long light dragoon, with his toes touching the ground, galloping past towards the town, followed by his donkey-boy, who keeps up a continual cry to the different passengers on the right or left of the rider—a necessary precaution, when it is remembered how very narrow the streets all are, and that camels laden with wood are their most frequent passengers. As might be expected, our fellows ran a little wild in this city of the "Arabian Nights," there was so much that was strange, new, and interesting; it was all so different from anything we had lived among previously, and so preferable to India in many respects. Here we had hotels to go to, with fine cool rooms to sit down in, and the best of company to enjoy ourselves with; or we could take seats in the centre of the Eesbekiah, and

* Porous earthenware water jars.

drink sherbet under the trees, watching the passers-by, or the different groups that stood around, which, from the varying costumes of the wearers, presented a diversity of gay colours that kept continually changing. The ladies naturally engaged a great deal of our attention; we wondered, as they passed and repassed, whether they were good-looking or otherwise, trying to judge by their glances, for it was all conjecture, the long, black, narrow veils concealing every feature from view but their bright black eyes and henna-stained eyelids. One day I was seated in the square, when a little dapper chap, a European, came towards me, and, accosting me in the real Doric Scotch, and with an unmistakable Glasgow twang, began, "Gude day, sir; it's a great pleasure to us a' here, that's sae far frae hame, to hae a regiment o' our ain folk march through an oot-o'-the-way place like this." Returning the salutation, I entered into conversation with him, saying that the pleasure was not all on one side, and that, so far as we were concerned, it had been made doubly agreeable by the very handsome manner in which we had been treated by the Pasha in the first instance, and, subsequently, by all classes of our countrymen with whom we had come in contact since we arrived in Cairo. As I had surmised from the first, I found that my acquaintance was a "Glasgow chappie," of the name of Mackay, in the employment of Mr Walker, who was not only a confectioner, but a wine and spirit merchant, and general dealer, even selling revolvers. Drinking sherbet was voted slow work by my new chum, and, requesting me to follow him, he led the way to Mr

Walker's, which was only about fifty yards distant, to have, as he expressed it, "something worth drinking." It is needless to say that I accepted the invitation so freely offered; and we went across the square, up a narrow lane and through a small door, over which there was no signboard to shew who lived there, or what was disposed of inside. Through this door and up some steps, we arrived at a regular confectioner's shop, while in an adjoining apartment were kept the wines and spirits, and, in a room opposite, a stock of other articles too numerous to remember. I was here introduced by Mr Mackay to Mr and Mrs Walker; and after having some refreshments, Mackay proposed that we should go up-stairs on the roof of the house, where we could have a quiet chat, a pipe and glass. This proposition was carried into effect at once, and I speedily found myself snugly seated high above the street, underneath an awning spread out to shield us from the scorching sun. The flat roofs are regularly partitioned off, house by house, and as I saw several couches, I easily arrived at the conclusion that this served for parlour, bedroom, and all, while, at the same time, it would not be quite safe for sleep-walkers, as a look over a low parapet made me aware that a step further in that direction would take any one by a narrow, short, and deep path to the bottom. On looking across the narrow gulf between the houses, one could easily imagine how convenient a narrow plank, with a hand-rail, would be in a chamber, just to place across the chasm, and slip over to neighbour So and So's, and thus avoid the trouble of going round by the street door. And here, on the roof top, we sat, supped, smoked, and chatted, till, what with whisky and sherbet, and sherbet and whisky, we got quite jovial: Mackay sang the "Laird o' Cockpen" in a manner that I had never known equalled from the time, years before, when I heard *the* Mackay sing it, as the "Laird o' Dumbiedikes," in the theatre of Edinburgh. After this he would shew me the revolvers, and brought up a couple of those dangerous tools with powder and ball, which we loaded only to see if we could take a correct aim. For this purpose we put up a *gooleh*, (water jar,) and commenced firing at that, which, being speedily demolished, and there being a superabundance of cats hopping from wall to wall, we turned our attention to the feline specimens around us. So we kept up a regular fusilade, although with but indifferent success at the cats, all the time quite oblivious of the fact that there were other people besides ourselves on the roof; and it was only on hearing a succession of screams from the other side of the wall that we awoke to the reality that some one might have been shot. There immediately followed a fez cap with a head in it, which popped over only for a second, and then on seeing the revolvers, as suddenly popped down again. This apparition, and the screams which still continued, brought us to our senses, and, laying down the firearms, we with all speed looked over the wall and saw a sight that kept us laughing for a good half-hour. We could see the whole thing at once. An old woman had been taking a comfortable nap on an easy-chair, and while in the land of dreams, was suddenly awakened by a cat, which having been hit by one of the bullets fell on the old dame's back, and sticking its sharp claws into her shoulders, caused her to think that the Author of Evil had got her in hand; so there she was, rolling over and over with the cat still clinging to her the closer; but the moment the old lady saw us, she seemed to forget all her cat-caused calamity, and endeavoured to hide her face, shouting out, "*Dahrak ya khaivageh!*" (thy backs, O masters!) being more afraid of that being seen than aught else. The owner of the fez cap had disappeared suddenly on seeing us, and the old lady, now perceiving that we did not at once accede to her request, disappeared cat and all in the same direction. By this time, a deputation from the inhabitants of the other houses had been to Mr Walker, to request that the firing should cease, and we had consequently to migrate somewhere else, but only to Williams's Hotel at the foot of the lane, where soon my little "Glasgow callant" succumbed to the influence of sherbet and whisky, topped with a bottle of brandy. I carried him safely home at least as far as the door, against which I propped him; then, knocking, left him endeavouring to stammer out the words of his last song, "Willie brewed a Peck o' Maut," and getting a donkey, I made straight for the barracks, where I arrived just in time.

The Viceroy having expressed a wish to see the regiment manœuvre, a day was fixed, and we turned out in review order on a sandy plain between the barracks and the town. The day was one of those clear ones which are only to be met with near the desert; the sky in its deepest azure with not a breath of air stirring, while the sand on which we were formed up glistened like powdered glass in the mid-day sun. In front of us was a magnificent line of equipages and equestrians. The Pasha and his suite were mounted on splendid Arabs, whose costly harness would have made a prince's ransom, being one mass of gold, precious stones, and shells, sparkling and throwing out a thousand rays. The Pasha's body-guard came wheeling round us, some of whom would dash away singly into the desert, so far that they appeared but the smallest of specks, then dash back again at the same speed, firing their pistols and waving their lances as they went and came. The review commenced by opening the ranks, when the Pasha rode slowly along by the front and rear of each, frequently stopping and asking questions relative to the men or horses. After this we marched, trotted, and galloped past by squadrons, then, wheeling into line, advanced, and, filing to the front from the right of threes, formed, while on the move, for the sword exercise, which was gone through at the gallop. When that was finished line was reformed, and, retiring in column of troops from the right at a trot, away we went at a spanking pace to the rear for nearly a mile, when, the head of the column changing direction to the left, line was formed to the left on the new alignment. A long advance in line at a trot followed, and while on the move, the regiment changed position right back by divisions, after which, ground to the right was taken in column of troops, and then line was formed to the rear on the rear troop. On this being completed, another advance was made at the gallop, the regiment keeping in line like a wall, as it charged up at a terrific pace, toward where the Viceroy was stationed, the trumpet only sounding "Halt" when we were within ten yards of the line of spectators. This charge rather astonished most of his body-guard, if it did not frighten them. Some actually started off at a gallop, thinking they were about to be annihilated. Not much to be wondered at either, for it was rather trying for their nerves to see seven hundred sabres all at the "engage," come rushing towards them at the "attack," not sounding "halt" until within a few feet; and then, at the suddenness of the pull-up, horses rearing and bounding forward towards the frightened lookers on, as if sorry thus to be balked of their prey. The front was now changed right back, by divisions at the gallop, then the regiment retired in open column of troops from the right, reforming line to the right-about on the leading troop. This also was done at the gallop, when an advance to the front was made in echellon of squadrons from the right in succession as they formed, and then the echellon wheeled to the right, and formed line to the front. Position was again changed, right back at a gallop, and then the regiment advanced in double column from the centre and formed line to the front, with the exception of the two flank troops, which remained behind in the centre and followed as a support. The front line made another brilliant charge for a short distance, and then retired by divisions from the outward flanks of wings, when the flank troops left in rear were brought into action. As soon as space permitted, they dashed to the front from the rear of the retiring columns, and extending outwards from their inward flanks, dispersed and pursued. On the "recall" being sounded, the two troops drew suddenly and in perfect order toward their leaders, and taking their position, waited until the again advancing line came up, when they moved forward with it. An advance in parade order finished our morning's performance, which we were informed by the colonel had given the greatest satisfaction, he might say delight, to the Viceroy. Our band, too, took the Pasha's taste greatly, and he made them play tune after tune to him, making each of them a handsome present, besides giving the bandmaster a splendid Cashmere shawl. It was rumoured that Said Pasha had expressed a desire to Mr Bruce, the English Consul, to purchase the regiment out and out from our Government; and he was very much annoyed on being informed that his simple request could not be complied with.

What astonished us at first, was the money currency. An English sovereign represented twenty-three or twenty-four shillings, and each shilling seven and a half piastres,* or one hundred and fifty piastres to the pound; therefore practically a sovereign became nearly thirty-four shillings in value. Again, everything here was remarkably cheap; for instance, eggs were twopence a dozen, oranges the same; a goose could be procured for ninepence, and a turkey for a shilling; so from this tariff it may be imagined how well we all fared. Our rations ought to have cost us nothing, being all supplied gratis to us by the Pasha; but for some reason or other, we were kept under a stoppage of fivepence per diem, and

* Twopence farthing.

this money was credited to the public. The 12th Lancers followed us through Egypt, and they drew their full pay, and derived the benefit which was not allowed to us. While in the Crimea we could get no satisfaction; but after our return to England, an application was made to the Secretary of State for War, that the money thus stopped from us by mistake should be refunded, but the reply was that " the rations were a gift from the Pasha to the British Government, *not to us*, and therefore we had no claim to any of it." But why did the Lancers fare differently? By the same rule we ought to have been charged for the many comforts and articles of clothing sent out to us in the Crimea, by the people of England.

Wines were nearly as dear in Egypt as at home, and malt liquors much more expensive; yet that did not prevent us from enjoying ourselves in the first-class hotels, such as Sheperd's* and the Hôtel de l'Orient, fully determined to support the dignity of our country and the credit of our corps, as far as we could in that way. A few certainly overstepped the bounds of prudence; but they were the exception, not the rule. One day, however, there was a bit of a commotion when the overland mail arrived with its passengers. Whether it was going out or home is of little consequence; but some old martinet was of the party, and at dinner that day he heard mention made by several of having seen a drunken man in the street or square, who belonged to the 10th Hussars. Never taking the trouble to think that it might be the

* Talking of Shepherd reminds me that he paid us a visit a month afterwards, in our camp, near Karrani, in the Crimea.

same person seen by all, he jumped to the conclusion that there must have been, in broad daylight, about fifty drunken soldiers in the Eesbekiah. Of course his imagination peopled the other parts of the town with as many more, and he at once wrote off a strong letter to our colonel about the irregularity he had heard of, and stated that he would make it his duty to forward a report of the whole affair to Major-General Ferguson, then commanding the troops at Malta. Colonel Parlby happened luckily to be out that afternoon in the Eesbekiah, and himself saw the one drunken man of the regiment, whose name was Keebacks, and who thus by many-tongued rumour had swelled into fifty. This man had fallen down and knocked out some of his teeth, and he was wandering up and down inquiring of every one for his lost ivories, and because he could not find them, refused to be comforted. The colonel formed us up on parade, and when explaining, that except this man we had in no way misbehaved as yet, said that he thought it his duty to caution us against any excess, and pointed out how simply such a slight matter could be exaggerated. A mistake of a similar description occurred in the Crimea, where one or two soldiers being noticed by several hundred officers lying drunk one day in Kadokoi, each of these officers apparently related the fact in their letters to their friends. Then there was a great outcry at home about the dissipation in the army; and so loud did it become, that Sir William Codrington took notice of it, and explained the matter satisfactorily, by referring to the defaulters' sheets of the regiments at home and at the seat of war, when it was proved that drunkenness was not one-third so prevalent among soldiers in the Crimea as in England.

Being professionally equestrians, it may be imagined that we took good care never to appear as pedestrians in public, and so became excellent customers of the donkey boys, and the terror and admiration of the natives, who looked after us with astonishment as we galloped in and out of the narrow-crowded thoroughfares. They shouted after us sentences, which, had we known their import, we would never have thought of repeating; but not knowing it, we dashed on ahead halloaing their words again, and as they laughed and seemed to enjoy this, we laughed and were merry too. At first the days being short at that season of the year, it was no unusual matter in the evening for some of us to lose ourselves in this city of two hundred thousand inhabitants, where the high houses and the narrow dark lanes resembled each other so much that it was a matter of impossibility for many to find their way home. In cases of this kind, some would go to a Turkish guardroom and there lie down for the night; while others meeting with more kind and hospitable entertainers, would be taken home by them, and taken care of—of course we called these Samaritans. At times however, in the narrow dark ways the entertainer would glide so imperceptibly into the doorway in the wall, that those who followed passed on, never seeing where their guide had gone; and then followed such a hunting and trying of doors, knocking at them and disturbing the inhabitants! One of our fellows actually knocked up Mr Bruce, the English Consul, one morning about one o'clock, for the purpose of asking his aid to assist the applicant in his search after a sweetheart whom he had missed in this manner. I must state, at the same time, that the Pasha is rather particular in making his people keep good hours, and it was only during our stay that the discipline in this respect was relaxed. Whoever in Cairo is out after dark must always carry a lantern, so that he can both see and be seen, and shew by its light that his deeds are not evil.

It has been frequently said of the Egyptians that they are very jealous of their wives, and most particular about their harems; but really from what we saw and heard, I should say that they are not a bit more so than is absolutely necessary. Although the women's faces are completely covered by their long veils excepting the eyes, yet they manage to make excellent use of these organs. I never did understand properly the language of the eyes until I got to Cairo, when I could perceive that a glance from a dark eye was quite as intelligible as several sentences. When you had been thus telegraphed to, you had only to saunter carelessly after the telegrapher at a respectful distance to some sequestered spot, usually out of the town, where speech could be got at, and here very little persuasion would make the Arab or Circassian damsel drop her veil, and enter freely into conversation.

The European residents were all highly delighted at our visit, so different from the usual bi-monthly overland cargo that is unloaded here for a few hours only, and who, knowing and caring for none of them, would only visit the Pyramids and the Sphinx, and only converse with the donkey-boys, quite ignoring any English, Irish, or Scotch who might cross their path—looking upon them as foreigners or worse. Far different was it with us cosmopolites, who made ourselves at home equally with Jew or Gentile, Christian or Turk. Whenever we got into the European quarter, invitations were lavishly given to us by all we met; nor was this hospitality confined to our countrymen; every one who hailed from the other side of the Mediterranean, Greeks, Italians, and French, all vied with one another in making us welcome.

On the opposite side of the square from Shepherd's Hotel there is, or was, a snug little Italian warehouse as we should term it at home, where prime Westphalia hams and fruits of every description could be procured; wines likewise of rare vintage and fine flavour, as cards in the window informed us might be had within. Strolling in here one afternoon, a few of us received a most cordial welcome from the proprietor, a short, stout, round, jolly old fellow, whose face was the very impersonification of good-humour and kindness. I can recall him now with his shining bald pate and fat face, and while I looked at him, the idea would rise in my mind that I had seen such a countenance somewhere before. I remembered at last that years previous I had seen such another figure in a picture, "The Cellarer in a Monastery," something in the style of "Bolton Abbey in the Olden Time," with the exception that the surroundings were casks and bottles instead of venison and game. But at the moment I could not think of all this, and while I looked and wondered, I thought only of Sancho Panza, and so I christened our host as he dragged us into his sanctum sanctorum behind, where he regaled us with wine, biscuits, and cheese. One of our party happening to observe that the jovial old fellow reminded him of his father, and this being interpreted to him, he got more jolly than ever, producing some still finer wine of a fabulous age from a back bin. In this we drank his health; and at parting he forced upon us a splendid ham, which we had for breakfast the following morning. I trust that the generous old chap still lives, and is still as happy and contented as he was then. And where is Boucher, that prince of tailors and good company, that compound of all that is kind and cheerful, who, as he invited us into his shop, threw down his cutting shears and cast his measuring tape and chalk far behind him, so that he might shake hands the more freely with us. And his wife, to whom he afterwards introduced us, a nice little Frenchwoman, who, in broken English, expressed her pleasure at making our acquaintance, and what was far better, shewed by her manner that she meant it. I wonder now, and did then, what the staid steady neighbours in that quiet street thought that night of Boucher, as they heard song after song, and chorus after chorus, mingled now and then with a few cheers. Certainly they might have arrived at the conclusion that it was only a lot of mad Englishmen holding their usual orgies, and this idea would have been confirmed when we wound up at eight o'clock with a grand affair, the whole standing as they proposed the healths of our host and hostess with all the honours. While the remembrance of these happy hours is pleasant, there is also a feeling of sadness mingled with it when we think of the companions of those merry hours, then in the fulness of their prime and the strength of their manhood—and where are they now? With the exception of Boucher and his wife, (if they are still alive,) and the teller of the tale, all have made their last long journey across the dark river to the regions, we hope of light, that lie beyond. Grinley, and Lewis, and Carr lie quietly in their resting-places near Karrani, Jones died at Baidar, and Farrell only escaped the ills and perils of the Crimea to die a year or two later at Lucknow. It is a sad, sad feeling which comes over us, yet one we would not like to be deprived of, the memory of lost old friends, of those we have known and esteemed for years, but will now no more meet upon this earth. No matter how strong our conviction is, that all is for the best, that we are all journeying home, and that we have still firm and loving friends to guide and assist us on the journey, whom we care for now, as we did once for those who have gone before,—still we cannot suppress the feeling of regret which rises unbidden when we think of those departed.

CHAPTER SEVENTH.

The Pyramids.

ALL the time we were in Cairo our leisure hours were fully employed. We were engaged in our professional duties daily until one o'clock, but two or three days a week we had from that hour until evening stables, five P.M., at our own disposal, and occasionally we had a pass for the day, or got leave from evening stables, and had from dinner-time until watch-setting to ramble about. By inquiring we easily discovered what were the most interesting places, and accordingly did all the mosques and other celebrated sights here on view. The Citadel was rendered doubly interesting—not by its antiquity, although it had been built A.D. 1171—but from its founder being the "Saladin" of the "Talisman" and the "Betrothed." I was also shewn a well, of I forget how many hundred feet deep, that also bears his name to the present day—Yussuf, or Joseph. But the mosque built in the citadel by Mehemet Ali is without exception the most magnificent of all the splendid mosques in the city, a perfect diamond among rubies; it ought to be seen to be appreciated, for no description can I think give any idea of its nearly faultless splendour and chaste design. The most costly marble and expensive materials have been used in its construction; thirty-five fine columns, with their golden capitals, together with the marble walls and floor, and the superb fountain in the centre, all render it not only the most beautiful, but the most tasteful, of the hundred and odd mosques with which Cairo abounds. But all these sights, and many others, are they not fully described in the chronicles of Gardiner, Wilkinson, Rawlinson, Lipsius, and Bunsen? To our men the Mameluke's Leap, Emir Beys, was doubly interesting, both for its daring, and as it shewed what a horse well ridden could accomplish. But he, I was then informed, was not in reality the last of the Mamelukes, an old friend of Mehemet Ali's having received a hint not to attend the levee in the citadel, which proved so fatal to all but one of his brethren; I was also informed that this Bey had been obliged ever after to return and appear always in a woman's dress.

To be at Cairo without doing the Pyramids would have been like paying a visit to Niagara without seeing the Cataract, or being a month in London and never see St Paul's, or in Dublin and not walk in Sackville Street or the Phœnix Park, or at Stratford-on-Avon and not visit the house where Shakespeare was born. To have neglected either of these duties would not have shewn more of Vandalism than overlooking the Pyramids and the Sphinx; so a party of us arranged to have a day's leave, and get a nearer view of these wonders of the world. Accordingly, one fine morning,—but all mornings are fine in a country where there are neither clouds nor rain,—we were up and out of barracks before daybreak, taking with us three ghorawallahs to carry our provender for the day, which consisted of ham sandwiches and bottled porter. We then walked down to the town, and there engaged donkeys and a guide to the Pyramids of Ghizeh. Travelling leisurely a couple of miles down the river side to Old Cairo, we there came to a halt, and, dismounting, waited in a coffee-shop until the boat was ready to start, which it did quietly and without bustle about seven o'clock, taking on board donkeys, drivers, and all, for the opposite shore. After crossing the river we remounted, and, passing through a small village embowered in trees, we got upon the straight road for the Pyramids, which in the clear air never seemed to get any nearer in all these long miles. The land is cultivated close to the edge of the Desert, and within two hundred yards of this cultivation, on a rising ground, stand the Pyramids. Like other people, we were not struck with their immensity until we stood close under them; then, looking at ourselves, our donkeys, and their drivers in comparison with those mammoth erections of stone, they appeared but as grains of sand at the base of a mountain, and we felt, indeed, in all its power, our utter insignificance and their vastness. On getting near to the Pyramids, we were suddenly surrounded by about forty shrieking Arabs, all tendering their valuable—so they proved in one sense—services to escort us to the summit of the great Pyramid. Selecting a few from the many, we at once prepared for the ascent by divesting ourselves of all superfluous toggery, such as jackets, stocks, braces, &c., and leaving these in charge of our donkey-boys, and forwarding the makings of a breakfast to the top of Cheops, we put ourselves in the care of our guides and commenced the ascent. Each of us was waited upon by three Arabs—two to pull and one to push—and with this assistance we did not find the task so very difficult. Nolan and I wished to ascend without assistance; but we were made to understand that, by the Pasha's order, this is not permitted since the time when an Englishman who would go up by himself fell from the top and was killed. At a good pace we were dragged and driven up the great wide steps, until we got half-way, when we came to a part where a number of the blocks had been knocked out, and there we rested; and most of us welcomed the shady halting-place; for, what with the pace we were compelled to go at, and the height we had come, and the width of the steps we had scrambled over, a little breathing time was quite a relief. Here I may mention that our guides, as far as their dress went, were not at all fastidious; it was quite patriarchal in its simplicity, a longish shirt and a turban composing the whole, and it certainly was a useful if not an ornamental attire for going up and down that hill of stone. After a few minutes' halt, amid an incessant cry for *backsheesh* from our guides, (a demand which, for the sake of quiet, we always satisfied with a few piastres,) the ascent was continued, and in a short space of time we were on the apex, or, rather, as the extreme point has been knocked off, a little below where that had once been. There we stood on a triangle about ten yards in width, drinking a few bottles of Guinness's stout, partly in honour of the occasion, partly to quench our thirst; our pleasure being again disturbed by a second cry for backsheesh, which we again assuaged by an application of the former physic. There are only two remedies for this backsheesh disease among Arabs, and these are piastres and the bastinado. Englishmen apply the former, the Turks the latter; but which is most efficacious I cannot say. Both, like the old and new school of medicine, have their adherents, and I believe that the Turkish cure has the merit of being the speediest. Where we now stood we looked over a prospect that it had never been our lot to gaze on before. The Nile, winding for miles on either side, lay stretched out beneath us like a broad silver band; while the rich green verdure on its banks, where waved trees that in size only looked like shrubs, was a fitting binding to the bright stream, the borders of which it so surprisingly fertilises,* contrasting beautifully and strongly with the arid waste in which they are set. What recollections sprung up in our minds of the countless thousands who had looked upon these monuments of time in successive ages, and had passed away with their memories, while these stood strong as ever, apparently impenetrable to the ravages of centuries! On the selfsame spot where we stood and from which we looked down upon the valley of the Nile, the First Napoleon had also stood and gazed, and at its base had directed his soldiers' attention to these very monuments, by reminding them that "forty centuries looked down upon them and their actions." Here was cut out his name, in the well-known style of his autograph; Napoleon's, however, is only one name carved among hundreds, though there may

* Herodotus says " Egypt is the gift of the Nile."

be none other of such note. One I noticed in particular, that of the Swedish Nightingale, Jenny Lind, cut out in letters three inches long, and nearly one inch deep. When this and succeeding generations have passed away, visitors to the Pyramids will wonder who and what she was; for I fear that her fame will not be so lasting as that of Napoleon le Grand. As we stood there, the scene vividly recalled the lines of the Grampian, poet when describing the beauties to be seen from Ben Macdhui; substituting a couple of words, the description answers equally well here—

"On gray *Cheops*' upmost verge I stood,
   The loftiest cone of all that desert dun;
The seas afar were streamed o'er with blood,
   Dark forests waved, and winding waters run,
   For nature glow'd beneath the *morning* sun."

We now prepared for breakfast by unpacking the hamper of sandwiches and remaining bottled stout, and seating ourselves round *à la Turk* on the top of the great pyramid, commenced to do justice to the repast, wondering meantime what Cheops would have thought or said could he have got up and gazed at us, a lot of barbarians, (as we should doubtless have been designated by him,) knocking the necks off the black porter bottles, and hurrahing like schoolboys. If spirits do roam on the earth, and his chanced to pass that way upon the 13th of March, 1855, what a string of grievances he would have to relate to his brother pyramid, Mycernius, when next they met! But we cared little for Cheops or his chum, beyond voting them to have been regular bricks for having made themselves such slap-up extensive resting-places. Having breakfasted, we prepared for the descent, first staying to see one of our guides go down the great pyramid, up to the top of the other, and back within five minutes, which he did easily and for the low charge of four piastres. The descent although not so fatiguing, was to my fancy more dangerous than the ascent; but we all got safely down, and then made arrangements for viewing the interior, every fresh movement being met by a fresh cry for backsheesh from our guides. I had always been led to believe that the natives of India were the most difficult to satisfy in the shape of recompense; and a story is told there of an officer who made a considerable wager when travelling dawk, that he would so settle with the bearers as that they should not grumble, but be contented with what he gave them. On the completion of the journey he sent for them, and gave them a gold mohur as a gratuity, being above double their fare. They stood thunderstruck for a time, turning the piece of gold over and over in their hands as if it had been a base coin. Thinking that their consciences would not allow them to take so much more than their due, the officer inquired if they had got enough; when, to his astonishment, they whined out, "Such, Sahib, (yes, sir;) but perhaps master will give us a small sheep for supper." The Arabs of the pyramids however, I feel positive would have been content with nothing less than a whole flock, for such a grasping, avaricious crew it was never my lot to come across before or since; every quarter of an hour they raised the cry for backsheesh, and kept on repeating it until they quite gasped again.

The entrance to the great pyramid is by a small aperture about fifty feet up on the western side. Our guides, lighting candles, led the way down a sloping descent for nearly a hundred feet, and then we were lighted up a similar sloping ascent about double that distance; this was a narrow pathway by the side of the wall, at the top of which is the entrance to the small chamber in which is still to be seen the marble sarcophagus. The interior of the pyramid is wholly lined with a very hard shining granite stone, cut in blocks about twenty feet long, and six wide. After having seen all these wonders, and among them a deep well half way down in which it is said there is another chamber, we once more got back into daylight, and then had a look at the lesser pyramids and the Sphinx. This last we found nearly covered over with sand, although a road had been dug to get into the small temple in front, from which we were informed there was a communication with the interior of the body. The catacombs we only glanced at, having been made aware of the fact that one or two of these chambers had been converted by some visitors into a residence, and observing a tent, and two ladies with green veils peeping out of a catacomb, we proceeded no further in that direction. We next made another call upon the commissariat, and then mounting our donkeys, returned by the same route to the city.

Our next trip was to the petrified forest, which is situated about ten miles south from Cairo; and here was to be seen enough to bewilder and astonish any person. On all sides the trees of stone lie just as they fell, some in large clusters, others in lengthened avenues, wide apart, as where the forest had opened and become glade, and every portion of these was turned into hard flint-like stone, which would emit sparks of fire when struck together. How the change was effected, whether gradually or in one night it is for wiser heads than mine to explain; but there the great fact is: what were at one time living trees, lying in all directions as if blown down by a hurricane, or thrown down by a convulsion of the earth, and no sooner levelled, than as it were, the spirit of destruction passed over and breathed upon them, making them thus monuments for ages.

Somehow we never got tired of Cairo, at least for the period we had to stay: there was so much to be seen, so much that was new and almost incomprehensible, that each fresh sight only made us the more anxious for further curiosities. So we travelled daily east and west, south and north, all over that town so familiar by name to all readers of the "Arabian Nights," seeing no porter nor hunchback who did not remind us of one of those charming stories, and no *howwadgee* (merchant) without thinking of the Caliph Haroun Alraschid. We went through the garden, and saw the very spot where Kleber was assassinated; we wandered wonderingly through the bazaars, buying fez-caps, tobacco pouches, and anything else we could afford that was fanciful, and might be useful; and in our strolls had a few strange adventures, and heard some strange stories illustrative of Eastern manners and customs. One of the latter, as it bears upon the deceitfulness practised in those parts, I will relate.

Half-way between Cairo and the port of Boulac, once stood the palace of Mohammed Bey, the son-in-law of

Mehemet Ali, he having married the Pasha's daughter, Nazlee Hanim, and who was therefore a man of great importance and authority in the state. At the commencement of the present century the Porte, having just reason to complain of the scantiness of the revenues received from Upper Egypt, sent a firman to the Viceroy to order an inquiry to be made into the misappropriation of the revenues in that province. As Mehemet Ali, who was already contemplating how to free himself from Turkish rule, if not to supplant the reigning dynasty at Constantinople, and knew that nothing could be done without a good treasury, had himself pocketed the alleged deficit, he selected his son-in-law and another Bey to investigate the affair, concluding that one of the two would be willingly blind to the real offender, and give in a false report to the Sultan. The two investigators easily discovered that the missing moneys had all gone into the coffers of the Viceroy; but with Eastern duplicity they made out two reports, a true and a false one; the former being sent by a sure hand as they thought to Alexandria, where it would be forwarded to Stamboul; and the latter to the Pasha, for him to transmit to the Sultan. Everything was in their favour, as the true statement would arrive first. But it was "Diamond cut Diamond," "a Roland for an Oliver;" the sure hand took it safe enough, not to Alexandria though, but to Mehemet Ali, who saw at once the nice plot laid by his subordinates, rewarded the bearer, and summoned the two searchers after truth into his presence. One of these it is said died by his own hand; but the other, Nazlee's husband, returned to Cairo, and was most affectionately received by the Viceroy, who scarcely dared openly to destroy his son-in-law. But the man who had massacred the Mamelukes would not easily be balked of his vengeance, and this Mohammed Bey was well aware of, and did not allow the affectionate reception to lull him into security, knowing that his father-in-law was most to be distrusted when he appeared most kind, and therefore he feared that his days were numbered; but while setting his house in order he, like a bold man, determined to be as careful of his own life as circumspectness and wariness could make him. His wife, whatever were her many faults, was true as steel to him in this strait, and watched over her lord's life faithfully; he eating and drinking nothing but what was prepared by her own hands; and had he but continued to attend to this rule he might have lived on. But it was to be—his fate was sealed. One day his wife's nephew, Abbas Pasha, then a boy came to see him, and remained in the apartment playing round him and eating all the time. Mahommed Bey, who apparently was fond of young people, kept watching him, and among other questions asked him, "What are you eating?" "Dates," was the reply of his nephew. The doomed man asked him for one; when, from a secret pocket, the boy drew a poisoned date, which he gave to his uncle, and as soon as he saw he had eaten it, immediately but silently withdrew. A few minutes afterwards the Bey was taken with convulsions; but he knew his destroyer, and calling a faithful servant, he told him he was dying, that Abbas Pasha had poisoned him, and made Achmet swear that he would revenge his death. Achmet swore to do this, and kept his oath; but years elapsed ere the opportunity occurred: still he nourished his revenge, quietly waiting his time. On the death of Mehemet Ali, Abbas Pasha became Viceroy, when one would fancy the chance more remote than ever; but when a man has devoted his whole lifetime to a certain object, it is but rarely that he fails. Achmet was now well in years: still the one idea possessed him, and he cared not what might happen to himself or any of his family, so long as he carried out the behest of his late master. Some may think that had he been careless of his own life, and determined to effect his object, that he could easily have shot the Pasha as he drove about in public; but there was a risk in this that Achmet would not venture on, knowing that if he failed in one attempt, no other opportunity would ever be allowed him; so he matured a plan which, if it took years to complete, was at least certain to be successful. Abbas Pasha was one of, if not the very greatest monster that ever was Viceroy over Egypt. This miniature Tiberius, half tiger, half jackal, whose cruelty was only limited by his fears, committed debaucheries and unpardonable crimes, which even to mention would be sinful. Of his cruelty I will relate two instances, the last in his life I believe, which will partly shew the wretch's character. A short time before his death—for how can we call the destruction of a brute, murder?—an unfortunate Egyptian ran up to the side of his carriage to present a petition to him, seeking redress for some injustice done; and as this frightened him for a moment,—all tyrants are easily terrified, and he suspected every one who approached him,—he caused the man to be strangled to death in his presence, sitting contentedly and complacently looking on until the poor wretch was beyond suffering. The last act of his life was to cause the lips of a poor slave of his harem, who had he said told him a lie, to be sewn together; and, I am sorry to add, that the death of the executioner did not save the victim, for she died of inanition some hours afterwards. Achmet knowing this monster's propensities, sacrificed his two sons to minister to his lust. Both of these he had well tutored, making them understand that it was their duty to slay Abbas Pasha, and that if they failed in the slightest degree, or whether they made the attempt or not, they should to a certainty be put to death themselves, for he always caused those who had ministered to his pleasures to be destroyed.

At the small village of Ben-ha-el-Asal, in Lower Egypt, Mohammed Bey's murder was avenged. After a drunken debauch the Pasha retired to his sleeping tent; none were near him but Achmet's two sons, and in their company he slept his last sleep; they smothered him with a pillow, and after ripping him open, thrust in the pillow, and made their escape. But they were never sought for; and at the time I was in Cairo they were employed in some official capacity in the citadel. The medical men reported that the Viceroy had died of apoplexy, and Said Pasha reigned in his stead. Whether Nazlee Hanim was or had been an abettor of Achmet's in this design on the life of Abbas Pasha was never known. Little was thought about her after her husband's death, and even her many intrigues, which during his lifetime afforded matter for scandal in

Cairo, subsequently lost all interest: it was even mooted that this second Marguerite of Navarre had retired from the world altogether. When in Cairo I was shewn a small built-up door and window in the wall that surrounded what had been her palace; immediately opposite to this was a small coffee-shop, and at a small window in the wall some one was always stationed—a veiled woman —who, whenever she noticed a good-looking young man go in and sit down in that coffee-house, would from the window beckon him across, and if he obeyed the invitation, his fate was sealed. When he entered the little door that opened to his touch, he and all the world outside had parted company for ever. What was enacted in that "Tower of Nesle," or whether a Captain Buridan was ever enticed therein, never became known; for it is said no one ever returned to tell the tale; and as none of her own servants ever divulged what happened, it still remains a mystery whether her many lovers perished by water, steel, or poison. The scandal, however, was eventually so much talked of that Mehemet Ali ordered the door and window in the wall to be bricked up.

One day I paid a visit to the slave market, on a Thursday I think, and there saw several "lots" exposed for sale, all good looking, and all anxious to be purchased. I had seen years before, the picture of the slave market in Constantinople, and I could remember how grand and magnificent the buildings appeared, with the beautiful slaves looking from canopied doorways; I therefore expected to see something similarly grand at Cairo; but so far as regards the buildings and the appearance of the square, was doomed to be grievously disappointed. A small dirty place with a few little shops round it, in the open fronts of which stood the merchandise; the slaves all appeared very happy, and were chatting and laughing at everything and everybody who passed. Not knowing the language, I could not understand how the dealers tried to get rid of their bargains, or what words they used when puffing up the beauty of a Georgian, or praising the symmetry of a Circassian damsel, or what was said when expatiating on the clear black skin and well-moulded limbs of a Nubian. As I have already remarked, the slaves themselves seemed cheerful and comfortable enough, especially the ladies, who chatted away to, or rather at, us very gaily, passing remarks one to the other, which produced regular screams of laughter; and as that was the only thing we could join them in, we laughed heartily in chorus, and this appeared to amuse them still more. While in Cairo we had many a visit from the present Pasha, whose palace was but a short distance from our barracks; and when going round our stables one day, he took a fancy to a small white bull terrier I had brought with me from India, and which was lying down in her usual place at the top of my stall. Poor Wasp! I often wonder whether she yet lives or not; without exception she was the finest of her kind I ever saw, being the very model of an English terrier. Although only fifteen pounds weight, she would kill not only rats and bandicoots by the score, but mongooses*

---

* I thought at first that the plural of "mongoose" would be "mongeese," but learned afterwards that custom ruled it otherwise.

and wild cats by the dozen, and so swift was she that single-handed she would, and has done fifty times, run down a hare when it had got one hundred yards law. But all these qualities were as nothing compared to her faithfulness and intelligence. I verily believe that she understood every word said to her, ay, even what was going on in the barracks at the time. I remember in 1852 that the colonel was obliged to destroy a most valuable horse, in consequence of its having been bitten by a rabid dog; going mad afterwards, it had to be shot, and it need not be wondered at that Colonel Parlby gave an order to destroy all the dogs in the cantonment. There is a regular scale of rewards for the destruction of wild animals in India—at least there was in the H.E.I. Company's time—fifty rupees being given for the claws of a tiger, and five for the head of a hyæna or bison; and on such an occasion as I am speaking of, Government allows six annas, or ninepence, for every dog's head that is produced, which is paid by the regimental quartermaster. The six annas, I need scarcely add, was a great object to the natives, whose daily wage is only two annas, and who would for that amount shoot their grandmothers; consequently, in a very few days after the order was published, not a dog was left alive in the barracks of Kirkee, except Wasp. None of our men would harm a hair of her skin, and the natives knew that it was more than any of their lives were worth, to attempt to injure a dog which the English soldiers had said "should not die." Although she still remained in the room as formerly, yet she evidently was aware that it was only on sufferance, for she never now on any account went outside of the door, and the sight of a gun, with which formerly she might be enticed anywhere, would not induce her to cross the threshold. At one end of the bungalow there was a small verandah; this she selected of her own accord as a place of refuge, and whenever the sergeant-major or an officer came into the room, she would jump through the end window to her place of shelter, there remaining until the party whom it was her advantage to avoid had gone away, nor would she come in again even when called, without first satisfying herself that the coast was clear, when in she popped. But her behaviour was quite different when she heard the report of a gun; whatever part of the room she might then be in, she would at once make direct for my bed, (which was rolled up,) creep right into the centre of it, and there lie trembling. She never on these occasions thought of jumping out into the verandah, being aware that in that direction danger was to be dreaded. The "dog days" blew over in time, and little Wasp once more roamed at large, her value if possible having increased in the regimental estimation by the ordeal she had gone through so safely, and I benefited by her life having been saved before we left India. Being on detachment at Poonah, and returning one night from the station theatre with only Wasp for a companion, I was accosted and insulted by three men of the —— Foot. I may mention that I had on a light-coloured *cumlie* coat, (goat's hair,) and as I approached, they saluted me as "Hamlet's Ghost." Thinking at first that it was only pleasantry on their part, I laughed at the appellation, and attempted to pass on, but was not allowed to do so, the leader exclaiming, "Oh, it's one of the Central School ——! let us throw him in the prickly pear hedge." I had, fortunately, not allowed them to get too close, and, finding that I should have to take a hiding either quietly or fighting, I chose the latter, and, springing suddenly on the one nearest to me, by a vigorous right-hander sent him to grass. The other two at once endeavoured to close on me, and might have been successful, for I was still hampered with the coat, had not Wasp sprung upon one of them behind, and laid hold of the fleshiest part of his body with such zeal and vigour as made him yell again, and caused a complete change of tactics on his part, from the offensive to the defensive. The other, on hearing his comrade's scream, turned towards him,—an opportunity that I did not fail to embrace by giving him a slight impetus with hand and foot which sent him staggering. No sooner did Wasp see me strike him than, loosing from her first hold, she fastened on the second, and the other having by this time got to his legs, was making at me again, but he was short in his delivery, which I was not, and to grass he went once more, Wasp seizing him in turn. The two fled, leaving their comrade, who was now shouting lustily for mercy, a prisoner in Wasp's mouth. I called her off, and was partly sorry to see how she had bitten him, although I did not say so, but pointed out to him that he had got no more than his deserts, in being one of three to attack a single man; and he ran off in the middle of my exhortation, leaving me and Wasp masters of the field. The victory was wholly due to her. I should not have stood much chance, but got a severe beating, had it not been for the dog. I afterwards found out who the men were, and they expressed their regret, saying that they should never have done so had they not been half drunk. When the route came for the Crimea, I had a hundred applications for Wasp, and the men of the "drill details" at Poonah would have given me any money for her that I chose to ask; but nothing would tempt me then, and Wasp marched with the regiment at the head of my troop. The first difficulty was to get her on board of the *Punjaub*, as there is always some trouble in smuggling a dog into a man-of-war; but this was got over by putting her into a pair of saddle-bags, and I carried her and them on board slung over my left arm. She remained at nights on the orlop deck, where my horse was for three or four days, until one morning the first lieutenant, coming below, saw her running about, and, calling a midshipman, ordered him to "throw the dog overboard." Luckily I was near, and, opening the flap of my valise, in she jumped, and was lost to view, while the midshipman, though searching in every direction, could not find her. About a week after this, the first lieutenant and Wasp again came in contact, when he called out, "I thought I ordered that dog to be made away with; who owns her?" on which I stepped forward and informed him that I did. He was a good fellow after all, and could not help laughing when I shewed him the place where she had so mysteriously disappeared; and he was quite taken up with her when he himself saw her jump in, stretch out her forelegs, and resting her head on her paws, put herself into as small bulk as possible, he walked away only saying, "Keep her off the upper deck." From Suez to Cairo she did every one of the long day's marches with us, never making so much as a whimper, although from her running to and fro, she must have gone over a great deal more ground than we did; but she usually got a lift from some one towards the end of the march, being a general favourite, and but for one thing would certainly have accompanied us to the Crimea. When the time was getting near for us to proceed to Alexandria, I expected Wasp to have pups within a fortnight, and as that would happen on the march, and I remembered how she nearly died with the last litter she had, I made most anxious inquiries whether there was any possible way of having her conveyed to Alexandria by boat. No. Every one had to go by the road I was informed, so I was regularly at my wits' end. I have already mentioned how the present Pasha admired her in the stable, but was still rather surprised when a strange gentleman walked into the barrack-room, a few days afterwards, inquiring who was the owner of the white bull-terrier. Replying that I was the individual, he at once proffered me a couple of sovereigns for her, which I unhesitatingly declined. He returned the following day and offered me five; this I also declined at once. He returned again in a week's time, and raised his offer to ten sovereigns; but I would listen to none of it, for I still hoped that I might be able somehow to have her conveyed to Alexandria. The gentleman told me that I had better take his offer, for he was

I

determined to have her, and that she should not leave Cairo with me, and then gave me his direction, by which I discovered that he was the English coachman to the Viceroy apparent, and that it was for his master he wanted Wasp. I told him that I should decide one way or other in three days, and in the meantime made every exertion to get her conveyed safely by the river, but could not manage it. I then pondered over all these things, of how little hope we had had of her recovery when she had pups before, of the risk of her having them on the march, and of her having to fare badly perhaps in the Crimea, while here was a comfortable home for her to go to at once. The money I was to get for her entered very little into my calculations, and I greatly regretted the prospect of parting with her. Having called a council of war with some comrades, I laid the case down, and asked their advice on the subject, when the conclusion was come to that she must be sold, one sagely remarking that if she were not sold for ten sovereigns, somebody would steal her and dispose of her for five. So on the evening of the third day, Blake and I walked down to the palace with Wasp, and on making inquiry for Mr ——, were at once admitted. Going in and out through long passages that had no windows, but were lighted by lamps placed at short intervals, we were ushered at last into a splendidly-furnished dining-room, where we were joined in a few minutes by the present Pasha's coachman in his dressing-gown. He gave us a most cordial welcome; and producing some excellent sherry, invited us to sit round and help him to discuss it. The business we had come about was quickly done. He drew ten sovereigns carelessly from a bag which apparently contained as many hundreds, tossed them down on the table, and the transfer was effected. Poor Wasp had become the property of another! I can still recall her pitiful look on our leaving. She evidently knew what had happened, and never attempted to follow us; but gave a low piteous cry as we caressed her at parting. But that was not the last I saw of her, for on the following day, when we were at stables, she ran in, looked in my face, gave a sharp quick bark, ran out and up stairs into the room, where she immediately crawled under my blanket and hid herself. Her new master was soon after her, when he informed me that she had jumped from a wall twenty feet high, which he was taking her round the top of that morning for exercise, and scampered off at once to the barracks. The wonder was, considering the state she was in, that she did not seriously injure herself. I now offered him back his money and a sovereign besides, to cry off the bargain; but he said that twenty sovereigns would not repurchase her, and carried her off—poor Wasp! The coachman behaved remarkably well to us during the few days we had to stay, taking us down to shew us over the Pasha's splendid garden at Shoubra, which is certainly a great credit to the head gardener, Mr Train, a Scotchman. Our days in the city of the caliphs came at last to an end, and on the 25th of March we had orders to march the following day, to make room for the 12th Lancers, who, on their way from Bangalore in Madras, were now only one day's march behind us in the desert.

CHAPTER VIII.

To Alexandria.

ALL arrangements having been made for our march, which was to be down the left bank of the Nile, and Cairo being on the right bank, a bridge of boats had to be constructed for us to cross from Boulac to the Isle of Rhoda, and from thence another bridge to the opposite shore. We marched away about ten in the morning, and passed through the most fashionable portion of the city. Shepherd's Hotel was gaily decorated with flags as on a gala day, and every window in the Eesbekiah was filled with spectators. A crowd of Copts and Turks lined the pathway, while behind all surged the mob of Cairo, rough and unruly as all mobs are. There were Arabs with their camels and burnouses, the chatting chaffing donkey boys, fair-haired Jews, villainous-looking Greeks, cunning Maltese, and sleek Armenians, the money-changers and usurers of Egypt, while craning above all, rose the curved necks and long faces of a number of dromedaries. There was also a number of unseen spectators, who made us aware of their presence by knocking against the wire-gauze windows, which so jealously hid the beauty of their occupants from our sight; but we could only sigh as we thought of their charms, and ride on lamenting.

On reaching the bridge of boats at Boulac, a guard of Turkish infantry was formed up to receive us, and also a number of Turks and Egyptians, blazing with scarlet and covered with gold embroidery, wonderful to see. And there were bands of music. Such bands too! If noise constituted harmony, nothing, I am certain, could have equalled them; but, like the native melodies of India, to any other ears it was the worst description of misery to be obliged to sit and listen. On each side of the bridge, and stationed about five yards apart, was a row of soldiers, for what I could not imagine. It could not be to keep back the crowd, for the river was behind them, and certainly not for the purpose of keeping us on the bridge. At any rate, there they were. Nubians, real men of colour, with faces as black and shining as a pair of polished boots—quite a superior article to the Ethiopian serenaders of our concert halls. They had large, heavy pipe-clayed belts, and a mongrel sort of European uniform, in which they looked very uncomfortable, and which we could perceive at a glance would be quickly discarded with a feeling of real relief, when they got home off parade. And to the sound of this dreadful music, and between the line of glittering firelocks held out in front of these strange Ethiopian faces, with their gleaming, almond-shaped eyes and protruding lips, we passed by files across to Rhoda, and from the island to the other bank. Here we had some amusement when watering our horses in the Nile, from seeing several rolling in the stream, rider and all, each in turn rising dripping from his watery bed, but evidently with quite different feelings as regards the effects of the bath, the steeds being quite refreshed, and shaking themselves with evident pleasure, while the riders, in their wet togs and boots full of water, looked awfully damp and miserable.

Our first day's camping ground was by the village of Ghizeh, which we did not reach till about three o'clock in the afternoon, and immediately got our horses in the lines picketed, the tents pitched, and all comfortably at dinner in half-an-hour's time. The encampment was beautifully situated, our tents being among a grove of palm and date trees, while the gigantic black masses of the Pyramids filled the background in the distance. When work was over, we lay down outside, watching the blazing sunset, the full, dark, flowing river to our front, and the dim expanse of level ground on either side; and so we rested until dark, when the moon, in her first quarter, rising with appropriate crescent, shed her pale light on the groups of European soldiers, the white tents shewing clear among the trees, with the horses in rear, and behind all moving about restlessly, the towering shapes of camels and dromedaries, that kept ever shifting, now falling into one mass, now breaking up into groups that were fitfully lighted by the glare of camp fires. And so, smoking, or singing, or talking, the different parties passed the time away, until wearily they dropped to sleep, being lulled thereto by the ripple of the water as it forced its way through the bulrushes which fringed the banks.

The following day was a halt, and on the next our

destination was the "Barrage." What that was, whether village, town, desert, or fortified place, none of us knew, and no one could or would tell us. The tents were struck and packed, and the regiment formed up for the march by 3 A.M., and bitterly cold we found it. The sharp air and the dense fog chilled us all as we sat waiting for the order to move off; but the trumpet soon rang out the "Advance;" and moving by files along the high narrow pathway by the side of the Nile, we pursued our march. The guides with their paper lanterns were in front, and next to them the band, which kept playing away in the mist, followed by the remainder of the regiment; who, with a species of blind devotion, followed each man after the other, having all the time a sort of idea that if the file in front marched into the Nile, all the rest to a dead certainty would follow in after him. Nothing could be seen of the road in front, nor on the right hand or left, nor above or below; nothing but the fog all around us, and a thin shadowy outline of the man and horse in front; but it was all right; we left it to our steeds and they made no mistake, but kept on along the narrow road without even a stumble. In an hour or two the sun began to warm us with his rays and to dispel the mist, which, as it gradually gathered up and rolled on one side, disclosed to us interesting Egyptian villages with their gardens of *mishmish* (apricot) trees, and fields of grain, and beans in every degree of cultivation; for in a land of perpetual summer you see all at once "seed-time and harvest, and flowery spring;" there is no winter to change the bright green leaves of flowers and plants to dull withered brown; and we remarked fields side by side—one with fresh blades of green, the other with ripe ears of gold. But amid all the cultivation not an inhabitant was to be seen. The march of a regiment, especially of cavalry in Egypt, is as devastating in its consequences as a flight of locusts, and is therefore avoided by all on its route as if it were a pestilence; for Egyptian soldiers seize everything from the poor villagers without purchasing: food for themselves and fodder for their horses, are taken without the slightest compunction as a matter of right, and no one dares to complain, for the Pasha is lord of all in the land. This was the cause of the villages being uninhabited, and the fields destitute of their husbandmen; no living thing was to be seen except the dogs, which barked at us from a distance, and the vultures that soared over head. The *felaheen*, (peasantry,) not knowing the difference between us and their own military, fled from their homes at our approach, carrying with them their flocks and herds; and had it not been for the supplies daily ordered by the Pasha, and which, I suppose, the Sheiks were obliged to find, we should have been starved. But if evil news flies fast, good tidings is but little behind; and about the third day the villagers found out that we were neither robbers nor Egyptian soldiers, but paid and paid well for whatever we required; and then, not only eggs and milk were brought into our camp, but plenty of ducks, geese, and turkeys; and the days of plenty were now quite as troublesome to us as the days of famine had been, for the *fellahs* (peasants) would have us to buy whether we wanted or not.

About 9 A.M. we reached the Barrage, which turned out

to be neither a town, a village, nor a mud fortification, but a magnificent iron suspension bridge, which here spanned the Nile, and on either side splendid stone towers forty feet high, built in a castellated style with miniature embrasures, bastions, and ravelins. It was here the railway would cross we were informed, and this was corroborated by the long embankments we saw forming here and on the other side. The next day's march was to Gatta, and we started for that place about the same time, and had to march along a precisely similar road, and were accompanied by a similar dense fog, as on the morning before. As in India, and on the march across the desert, the troop's cooks and linesmen * always preceded the regiment the night before, so that a hot breakfast always awaited us. Gatta resembled any other Egyptian village, being composed of numerous flat-roofed mud huts, with a scarcity of windows and chimneys, which would appal any sanitary commissioner who believed in light and ventilation. The huts are thatched very lightly with branches of palm, and have each a small courtyard surrounded by a mud wall, which is the haunt of the harem, donkeys, and all. The pigeon-houses however, gave quite a substantial air to the whole place, and although built of mud, are whitewashed all over, and have the corners decorated with ochre; while all around hundreds of blue pigeons are cooing about all day. The pigeon-houses always occupy the centre of the mound on which all the villages in Egypt are built, to prevent their being overflowed at the periodical inundations of the river. The graceful tapering palm-trees with

* A corporal and private of each troop accompanied the quarter-master to take up the lines for the tents and horses.

their feathery branches, greatly add to the beauty of the villages, and act as a shade; while the groves of dark sont trees on the plain afford a pleasant retreat to the wearied fellah as he toils in the fields, or tends the sacke'eah * or shadoof by the river side. Our next day's journey was to Salameh, where there was nothing to interest or amuse, and on the following day we marched to Micklek, where we had a halt day, April 1, which may fitly come under the same description.

On the 2d, our route was to Kaffir Boullin, and we had just got our horses picketed and the camels unloaded, when we were startled by hearing a tremendous shouting in the rear, and on looking in that direction perceived that it was caused by the camel-drivers, who were here relieved from their forced service, and turned us over to a fresh party

---

* The sacke'eah and shadoof are machines used to irrigate the land; the first being worked by oxen, is composed of a number of buckets attached to an endless rope, all wound upon a drum, similar to the dredging machines used for raising mud in most harbours. As one lot of buckets is descending, the other lot is ascending full of water, and these in turn discharge their contents into a trough partly open at one end, from which a small stream is kept perpetually flowing through the parched fields. The shadoof is of a much similar construction, of one fellah power. This is simply a bucket, to the handle of which is attached a pole; this is fastened at right angles to the end of a second pole, balanced like a see-saw on a cross beam, supported between upright posts. The extreme end of the see-saw is weighted by a lump of clay, equal in weight to the bucketful of water. The machine is placed on the river bank, in which the fellah has dug a trench, to admit the stream to a little pool under his feet, in which he can dip the bucket, which is then lowered by its long handle, and easily raised by the aid of the countervailing clay weight. The advantage that the fellah has is, that he has only to pull down a weight from over his head, which his own weight assists him to do, while the clay weight in fact lifts the water for him.

who had just arrived. I could now account for the style of free living practised by the camel-drivers all along the line of march, whom I had daily observed as they neared their destination, to dismount from their camels and make forcible raids into the bean fields that skirted the road on either side, and in defiance of the prayers, threats, and entreaties of the fellahs, carry off armful after armful of fodder. Sitting disconsolately by their camels were the fresh lot, who had been brought from a distance to convey our baggage to Alexandria, and their sheik appeared to be the most unhappy of all. It certainly is peculiarly hard upon them thus to be obliged, without fee or reward, to leave their crops, and go miles away from their families at the command of the Pasha.

The next day's march was to Gubarri; and we here left the Nile to our right, taking the straight road to Alexandria. This was a long day's march, and we felt proportionately fatigued when we got in. Here we were encamped close by the side of a canal, one of those main arteries from the Nile that feeds and irrigates the land; it was very difficult however to water our horses in the canal here, owing to the steepness of the banks; and several men slipped in and caught a similar ducking to what they had on the first day's march. The following was a halt day, which was gratifying so far as it allowed of our having a slice of sport here, that we might not have been able to get had it been otherwise. An Arab chief having heard of our arrival, rode into the camp on the following morning, and gave a challenge to ride any of our officers a race for a thousand piastres. The stake was not valuable; but for the credit of the corps, our officers were

anxious that he should be beaten, and all were eager to
accept his challenge. Of course it would not answer to let
a dozen run at the single man ; so the Colonel allowed
Captain T—— to do so. The chief's horse was a
beautiful little gray Arabian, with every mark of blood,
quite a model of what a horse ought to be. The match
was necessarily an off-hand affair, the chief having all the
advantage on his side; doubtless his horse was in good
condition, and he was a lighter man by a couple of stone
than Captain T——. About noon most of the regiment
was assembled on the high steep banks of the canal to
witness the contest, and after a few necessary preliminaries,
the riders were brought to the post ready for the start.
The chief with his turban and flowing white dress reminded one forcibly of a Saracen, and he was as nervously
impatient as his restive snorting steed; while the Englishman in a neat silk racing jacket and buckskins contrasted
favourably in our opinion with the son of the desert, and
was cool, calm, and collected, and his horse apparently as
quiet and as much at ease as himself. When both were
ready the signal was given by firing a pistol, and a beautiful start was effected; the chief springing his horse instantly to the top of his speed, dashed away ahead like
the wind, evidently of the opinion that the race was virtually over and he was the winner. And to a novice this
would have appeared to be the case, for Captain T——,
with his hands low down and his horse well together, was
nearly two hundred yards behind when half the distance
was run, and apparently it was as the facetious Jerry
Noon once expressed it, "All Woolwich Arsenal to a

sentry box." But the chief did not know that he had the best rider of the Bombay Presidency, if not in India, behind. We could see the gap gradually and surely closing at every stride. When within between one and two hundred yards from the goal, Captain T—— was at his girths; a few more strides and he was leading; and the chief was eventually beaten by a dozen yards. The beaten horse was completely blown, and could not have galloped another quarter of a mile, while ours was fit to run the distance over again; this superiority being entirely owing to Captain T——'s judgment in riding. The chief seemed to feel his defeat sorely, not for the money, but the thought that his horse, his pride, that had hitherto distanced every other that he had contested with, was now beaten so easily by a Giaour, was gall and wormwood to his sensitive temperament. We all felt sorry for him when he rode away looking so different from what he had done a quarter of an hour before; then so proud and confident, now so desponding and dejected, he evidently never thought that the fault was his own, and that had the riders been changed, the result would have been different.

The next day's march was to Dahamanhour, the largest and most populous, and I may say the only, place worthy of the name of "town," between Cairo and Alexandria. We had heard a good account of it all the way, and so naturally expected to have a pleasant time of it here. After attending to our horses and getting all done, we strolled through the place and found that it was only a village on a largish scale. There were the same kind of shops, kept by the same kind of people, in the same description of streets, dirt and dogs, donkeys and doves, and all else that composes a dreary Egyptian town, except the fair sex: these had all been whisked away in the night, and now not one female form was to be seen. It happened to strike us that this had been the case all along our way, and on inquiring what had become of all the dear creatures, we were informed that the Pasha had always had them shifted a day's march behind us; for instance, the morning we marched into Dahamanhour, the women had all been transported back to Gubarri about midnight: very thoughtful of the Pasha, and I suppose kindly meant; but it was a kindness that none of us appreciated. I heard then that the Egyptians are very jealous of their wives, and as I observed before, they have every reason to be so; certainly there is a *little* encouragement for the wives, as the Mohammedan law, relative to a wife's infidelity, requires a much greater amount of proof than is necessary to carry conviction in our divorce courts; the camel-driver of Mecca having declared it indispensable that there should be four credible eye-witnesses to prove any act of adultery. This decree was issued in consequence of very strong and circumstantial evidence against his favourite wife Ayesha, who apparently was no better than she ought to have been. The Prophet would not believe the three witnesses, and settled the affair by putting another article in the Koran to meet the case: this laid down that four witnesses were requisite. So the ladies are said to have it nearly all their own way, doing just as they like, in spite of eunuchs and closely-guarded harems, and thankful that the Prophet was so hard of belief.

At Dahamanhour I had the pleasure of meeting with some Scotch engineers, who were employed on the railway that was at that time in construction; and as one of them was not only from Edinburgh, but of a period contemporaneous with myself, I spent a most comfortable evening with him, talking about Auld Reekie, our schoolboy days, and the "bickers" (stone battles) between the South Side and Carnegie Street, to which part the engineer had belonged, and could recall with me many a hard-fought battle, in which we had both been engaged, on opposite sides in the Meadows. In the land of the Pharaohs we sat and chatted of our boyish feuds, how we nicknamed them "Keelies," and they in return termed us "Puppies;" also about Tom U——, our leader, better known among us in those days as "Long Tom Coffin," when he, at the head of the boys of Buccleuch Place, George Square, Park Place, &c., met the opposite faction of the South Side and Carnegie Street. How we met at Hope-Park End, and while the battle was at its height, with plenty of ammunition, (caps full of stones,) and the blood up, and the enemy pressing us hard, our leader despatched a strong detachment under his lieutenant, Norman M'——, to take the foe in reverse; and he, with some fifty picked *men*, making a detour by Buccleuch Place Mews, and round by the Archers' Hall, burst suddenly upon the enemy's rear with a shout and shower of stones, which proved irresistible. The battle was over—the enemy broken, fled from the field in all directions, and were pursued towards Bruntsfield Links. We talked, too, of the snow-ball riot of the students in 1839, which we, as schoolboys at the time, had taken an interest in ; of the rioters marching over the Bridges by sections of threes, with short thick sticks under their arms, and Blenerhasset at their head ; of their gallant defence at the College steps, against all the power of Captain Stewart and his police ; of the military (was it not the 93d ?) being called out, and the Riot Act read by the Provost; of the noble stand which the students made, until the bayonet points were within a foot of their breasts; the subsequent flight and capture of the ringleaders in detail ; their appearance at the Police Court; their trial afterwards, their "noble defender," Patrick Robertson, and their acquittal. Branching from that, we spoke of Dicky Weston's Library, and the account of the whole which appeared in the pamphlet, entitled "Magna Charta." Of these, and many other "bickers" and escapades, we sat and chatted and passed the hours joyously, until the gray tints dimming the eastern sky warned us that it was time for retiring.

How happy do such unexpected rencontres in a foreign land make one! Recalling our schoolboy days, we, as it were, bound back again over the wide abyss of time, and are again young, joyous, happy, and free. And how glad I was whenever I came across an Edinburgian in India ; but of the many I only recognised two, and one of these did not remember me. The first was among a batch of recruits going towards Ahmednugger. The following being a halt day, I inquired, as was customary in like cases, if there were any Scotchmen with them, for the purpose of inviting them up to dinner with us. There were three, two from the Calton of Glasgow, and one from "mine own romantic town," and him, as soon as I saw him, I recognised to be the son of old Henshaw, who years before had been the George's Square gardener, and who, like Peerie Weerie, by his short temper, afforded excellent fun for us boys. Many must still remember him. The other I met in a similar manner, but he recognised me at once, calling me by name as I passed his tent, and rushed out and shook me by the hand for a minute, before I recalled the features of my old schoolmate, Tom Duncan. We had fought many times as boys, never through ill-will, but only for love, just to see who was the best, the result varying alternately, to the best of my recollection. Poor Tom now lies at Sukkur, a victim to the cholera, which there destroyed a third of his regiment. When he first came to B——'s school, he had just arrived from Glasgow, and his talk, quaint and strange to our ears, made amusement for the others. I reminded him what a shout of laughter there was on his first entering the playground, when, standing on the grass plot in the centre, he so simply asked, "Daur we pou the gowans?" and also of the trick we played upon him, when we sent him into Maclauchlan's, the hair-dresser's shop, to inquire for "Fuddy," and the yell he gave when the good-natured old fellow laid hold of him, and drawing a thick stick from a bundle, made him believe that his last hour had come. How many of that school are now alive? Very few I fear; but numbers there must be who can go back a quarter of a century and recall to memory old Maclauchlan, the hair-dresser of Nicolson Street, his elegant shop, under the sign of the Civet Cat—his neat

K

and tasteful attire—his powdered head, and his pardonable vanity, conspicuous in the gold watch, the large gold-linked guard, the diamond rings and shirt studs, which he wore not at all *unbecomingly, and his cross snarling liver-and-white-coloured dog. And many more will remember his back parlour, or shop rather, where used to congregate daily at noon, numbers of students from the College, who liked no fun better than listening to the choice scandal and witty talk of old Mac, who had the reputation in those days of being able to tell a tale as well, if not better, than any man in the city. With us schoolboys he had gained the euphonious name of Fuddy, a nickname which he could not bear to hear, and we, of course, took an especial delight in dropping in, at least once a day, and blandly inquiring " if Fuddy was at home ?" or wishing him " Good morning," by the misnomer he detested. For my part, I for weeks never omitted calling on my way to school at Mr B——'s in George Street, going round by Nicolson Street, and over the North and South Bridges, instead of going by the nearer road, across George IV.'s Bridge, and the Mound. As it was considered that there was some risk attending this demonstration of respect, it was usual to reconnoitre the approaches first, and ascertain whether or not he was safe behind his counter; if so, the advances could be securely made, as the enemy was too strongly entrenched behind his high glass-case-covered

* For years, when a boy, I never could properly tell the difference between him and the late Major Alexander of Boydston; but I should not have liked to say so to the gallant Major, though he was not a proud man, for I have heard him boast of having washed his own shirt when in the Peninsula, and then lain in a haystack till it was dry.

counter, to be able to sally after us. At that time we all firmly believed that he was the possessor of several Polar bears, and that were he to catch any of us, we should be thrown in to make a morning or evening repast to those animals. This fear caused us to be most wary, and not to attempt to attack unless there was time to retreat safely afterwards; but "the pitcher that goes often to the well, gets cracked at last," and so I found it practically. One morning as was my custom, I paid my respects to Maclauchlan, and as was usual afterwards, on his making a rush at me ran off, with the full intention of placing the South Bridge between us before I halted; but before I had got fifty yards away, a crowd, collected round a man who had fallen in a fit, overcame my sense of self-preservation, and I pulled up to see what it was all about, and afterwards forgot all about Fuddy and his cane, and his bears, and proceeded leisurely to school. But Mac had watched me from his shop-door, and seeing me halt had called his maid-servant, pointed me out, telling her to follow me and bring back word where I went to. All unconscious, I walked on to school, where about an hour afterwards Mr B—— was called out, and I remained trying hard to construe some difficult passage in Cornelius Nepos,* when I heard my name called, and was informed that my presence was required in the parlour. A vision of some friend calling to see me, and perhaps a holiday and a half-crown tip, rose at once uppermost in my mind;

* Irreverently termed by us in those days "Curley Neeps"—a book, the very mention of which to the present day, gives me a tingling sensation in the fingers.

but all was suddenly dispelled when, on entering the room, there stood bodily before me, the now thrice-to-be-dreaded Maclauchlan, with his gold-headed cane and other paraphernalia, who, with a snap and a growl exclaimed, "That's the scoundrel!" Mr B—— evidently did not know him; but on his informing him of the whole affair, I was ordered at once to beg Mac's pardon. This I would not do. A false shame prevented me. I feared what the other boys might say if they knew I had begged a barber's pardon, for so we scoffers termed him. I consequently got a flogging, but so long as I received the condolence of my fellows, and got applauded for my pluck, I little cared. Tradition stated that the name of "Fuddy" was acquired by Maclauchlan in his younger days, and when a still greater buck than at the period I speak of, and when fashionable hair-dressers in a manner led the *ton* in a certain class of society, having distinguished himself in a way which I will attempt to relate. At that time as I have heard, Robertson of the High Street, a contemporary of his, used to ride hired blood horses, and see the hounds throw off regularly, and Maclauchlan as may be imagined, was not a whit behind him. So, as the tale goes, it was while exercising on his steed one fine morning, that he met a young and handsome lady, and, with the assurance that he was famed for, managed to introduce himself, and further made himself so agreeable, that, when at parting he expressed a wish to be allowed to call the following day, the permission was granted. Maclauchlan, I may remark, carried a card case, with only his name on the cards, for when out of it, he invariably dropped the shop, and on the following day, when he called at Queen Street, took out what he thought was his own card, and sent it in. By one of those accidents which are supposed to make or mar a man, the servant-girl when brushing his clothes the day before, had found in his pocket a card of Lord F——'s, then attending the University, and a customer of his. The girl thinking it was her master's card, carefully put it in his card-case, and so he unknowingly gave it as his own. The remainder can be easily surmised; a most cordial reception from the young lady and her mamma followed, and an invitation to a party the next evening. This further and unlooked-for condescension was justly appreciated by the worthy perruquier, and punctual to the appointed time, in full fig, he drove up in a noddy to the house. A loud rap-tap at the door by the jarvie, who then let down the steps with a bang, and as the doors opened, Maclauchlan, with a hop-step-and-a-jump, sprang out from one into the other. He was known and expected, for before he had time to take breath, the name of Lord F——, was passed up by the footman at the door, thrown at another up stairs, caught by him, and cast to the next as Lord Fardue, and this last, being a little deaf, gave it in to the room as "Lord Fuddy," to the horror of the young lady, and her maternal relative. Utterly unconscious of his new title and dignity, but perfectly conscious of his own importance, and of the awe and respect shewn him, he glided gracefully and majestically up stairs, and passed through the wide open doors of the drawing-room, where, awaiting to receive him, all wreathed in smiles, were his host and hostess, and standing timidly behind them, the dear delightful creature he had met. The feeling was enchanting, and bowing low, and smiling to all around, he advanced. At that moment he was far above things perruquial; curling tongs, combs, and scissors, had vanished, and were buried in oblivion, like Hannibal at Cannæ, Cæsar at Pharsalia, Napoleon at Austerlitz, at one gigantic bound he had placed himself far above his former ken. As Waterloo was to Wellington, this night would have been to Maclauchlan the making of him, but for an exclamation from one in the throng who knew him professionally, which dashed down the whole superstructure to its base; this was, "Hang me if it isn't Maclauchlan the hairdresser," and the unfortunate Mac was buried in the fall of his pyramid. I will draw a veil over the remainder of that evening. The barber returned again to his tonsorial duties a sadder and a wiser man, and perhaps when he thought of what was, and what might have been, still a vainer man. The story, as may be expected, got wind, and the following day various exaggerated accounts were flying about, the last of these being, that on the night in question, a carriage and four with postilions, were in waiting just round the corner, to convey an expectant couple to Gretna Green. Whether this was, or was not the case, was never known, as Mac kept his own counsel; but the name that the last footman gave into the drawing-room stuck to him to his dying day—Fuddy.

From Dahamanhour, where we had another halt, we marched to Kaffir Dewan, a place of little consequence, and on the following day, the 7th of April, we marched into Alexandria. This was our longest day's march, and we were accordingly proportionately fatigued as we got nigh to the city. But this wore off in a great measure when we had passed through the suburbs, and got into the better part of the town, when our eyes were greatly refreshed by the substantiality and almost elegance of the buildings and streets; and the number of windmills about the city was really wonderful to see. Extending for miles along the summit of the small hills, they could be observed with their huge arms in motion, but no two moving seemingly in one direction or at one time, which gave them an appearance as if they were all running with their heads up towards the town. Groves of date-trees lined the road on each side, while we passed never-ending strings of camels, laden with every description of burden, and through and among these, in and out, appearing and disappearing, were donkeys of every kind, equipped anyhow and ridden by every description of riders, Franks and Turks, howadgees (merchants) and sailors, cadiis and cooks, moolahs and dragomans, while all the time their donkey boys kept up a continual cry, warning the foot passengers to look out, by shouting such words as these—*Shimalek!* (to thy left,) *Yemeinah!* (to thy right,) *Riglack!* (thy foot,) *Wish shak!* (thy face,) and to an Osmanli, *Sacken!* (take care,) &c.

The barracks so far as cleanliness, comfort, or accommodation were concerned, were not to be compared to those at Cairo. In the first place there was no stabling for our horses, which we had to picket in the barrack-yard as best we could; and, in the next place our quarters, the mere sight of them was enough,—dark, dirty, dismal holes, without windows, and round which a kind of guard bed was placed. On this there certainly were some blankets, but these were already occupied by fleas, as the saying is, "as large as jackasses." We left them to enjoy the luxury, preferring to lie in the open air with our horses. After stables, I managed to get outside to have a glimpse of the town, and made for the principal square. I had considered the Esbeekiah in Cairo a fine place; but for splendour it is not at all to be compared to this. The houses are so much more magnificent; and a beautiful marble obelisk stands in the centre, under which gushes up a sparkling fountain of pure cold water, the mere sight of which refreshed one, as a sea breeze does a weary traveller. In this square reside the different Consuls, whose houses could be easily told by the flagstaffs on the roofs, from each of which floats the flag of their respective nations. What struck me most with amazement in Alexandria was the huge carriages—regular family affairs—capable of holding a score or more comfortably. Just fancy an octagon summer-house, or a Chinese pagoda on wheels, and that not only elaborately carved, but painted, and gilt all over! Fancy still further, some wretched horses drawing it, whose harness, composed of many brass ornaments and a little leather, is connected together by ropes and bits of string, and you will have a fair idea of a fashionable carriage in Alexandria. I looked at Pompey's Pillar, when on my way to visit a place of far more importance to a soldier and a Scotchman; this is a field a short distance to the left of the pillar, where the brave old Sir Ralph Abercrombie fell. I have as much as possible refrained from entering too particularly into details descriptive of the Overland Route, believing that thousands upon thousands are now as familiar with this tract of land as they are with the railway from London to Dover or Southampton, either by personal experience, or from reading the many books which have from time to time appeared concerning the Desert, the Pyramids, and the Nile.

CHAPTER NINTH.

Viâ the Mediterranean.

A SHIP is far from being a pleasant place while the process of embarkation is going on, and more especially when, as with us, a number of horses have to be got on board. In addition to the usual creaking of blocks and tackle, there was a perpetual squealing and kicking going on among our steeds, mingling with which could be heard a steady chorus of, " Walk away with it, lads ! " " Lower handsomely ! " " Steady ! " " Ease away ! " while the chafing of ropes, and the solo performances of the boatswain on his shrill whistle, altogether made a noise and commotion easier imagined than described. However from the steamer being alongside of the pier, the horses were got on board with much less trouble than at Bombay; all we had to do was to take hold of the reins, and, running up the gangway, the horse followed ; and in this manner all the horses of the first squadron (D and H troops) were speedily on board the *Etna*. This vessel, one of the Cunard line of steamers, was nearly new ; she was ready to start for Sebastopol by three o'clock in the afternoon, and with the Blue Peter flying, we ran out of the harbour, steaming past the mole that defends its entrance, and then steering northward towards the Grecian Archipelago, passing in turn its many islands, and those we have lately ceded to Greece. Bearing still in the same direction we reached the Hellespont, when we steered eastward, sailing slowly past classic ground where Troy is said to have stood, marked now only by a number of sandhills and a few hovels. Passing this and many Turkish forts we arrived at Gallipoli, where English, French, and Turkish men-of-war were lying securely at anchor; and on shore a town of tents shewed where the allied soldiers were encamped. It was night when we left Gallipoli—the many lights on shore making it resemble a Chinese "feast of lanterns." Up steam and away; some on watch, the others to sleep, and to wake up in the morning and find themselves entering in the bright sunshine the sea of Marmora, while the continuous thud thud of the screw-propeller causes a jar throughout the vessel. Still we sped on, the distance hourly decreasing; and on the following morning were in the Bosporus, through which we glided, looking carelessly at the low batteries which are placed at such short distances apart on either side of us, the muzzles of their guns being on a level with the surface of the water. On—past all these, and as the waters spread gradually open, we glided quietly past the Golden Horn, and the splendid city of the sultans burst upon our view. The magnificent amphitheatre before our eyes, the glittering mosques, the white houses with their trelliced windows, the sycamore and palm trees, the gardens down to the water's edge, while, passing over the azure bosom of the Bosporus, hundreds of caiques leaped along like things of light and beauty,—all render it the most beautiful city in the world to look at, more like a splendid scene in a Christmas pantomime than anything in reality. We here dropped anchor to await orders, and in the meantime we looked on the many places of interest that surrounded us. There was the Turkish cemetery, extending for five miles along the Asiatic shore, which, while a resting-place for the dead, is also a burrow for hundreds of living dogs by which it was infested. Casting our eyes more to the right, they alight on a plain square brick building, which is the Scutari Hospital; but nearer still to us is a much larger pile, several stories higher, many feet longer, with towers at each corner; this is the Scutari barracks, capable, it is said, of holding ten thousand men; yet when, as was necessary, it was turned into a hospital, there was not even room for the thousands of wounded and sick sent from the Crimea. Away to our left front was Pera, the European quarter, where we directed our eyes, but nothing interesting could be distinguished. We passed our gaze gradually round until it was fastened on a large and beautiful mosque, St Sophia. We were informed by an old *salt*, who also pointed out the sultan's palace and his harem, and likewise directed our attention to a small iron gate on the water, which he told us never opens in the daylight, but that in the dead of night, sacks with victims inside, weighted with heavy stones or iron, have been conveyed through it in small boats out into the centre of the deep blue water on which we were so peacefully floating, and there cast in and sunk with a deep gurgling sound; and as he told us this, we looked out over the water and saw the gilded caiques gliding innocently over the Bosporus in all directions, looking as gay and beautiful as if such cruel deeds, and such hideous vices as jealousy, hatred, and revenge were unknown. Our orders came down in the afternoon; so, up with the anchor for the last time, we steamed away from the lovely spot, passing the creek which leads up the "sweet waters," close in shore,—so close that we could look into the little wooden houses that were reflected in the blue element beneath them. Fortifications and batteries, batteries and fortifications, nothing else on either side of the narrow deep channel could be seen,—all so demurely covered by long waving grass mounds, that from a distance they would never have been taken to conceal guns and magazines. Numerous forts also on the heights, with the crescent waving from their summits—an emblem we acknowledged by dipping our flag to each as we passed. So it was on, on; and as we entered the borders of the dark Euxine, it seemed quite appropriate that the sun should be setting behind us, causing all in front to look black and dismal, recalling the description given in the Odyssey of the aborigines of this (the Chersonese) far-off region in Horace's day, "as those dwelling beyond the ocean stream, immersed in darkness and unblest by the rays of Helios," (the sun,) while we had but to look backwards to see a beautiful sunset, covering the banks and heights of the Bosporus with glorious tints, which, as the sun sank lower and lower in the west, gradually softened into gray—a scene which the following lines so well describe, that I have again ventured to quote from the same poem already twice resorted to:—

> "First died upon the peaks the golden hue,
>   And o'er them spread a beauteous purple screen,
> Then rose a shade of pale cerulean blue,
>   Softening the hills and hazy vales between.
> Deeper and deeper grew the magic scene,
>   As darker shades of the night heaven came on;
> No star along the firmament was seen,
>   But solemn majesty prevail'd alone."

Steering still in the same course towards the Chersonese, we sighted at seven o'clock on the morning of the 15th of April, the long, bold range of cliff on the shores of that peninsula, after a fine passage of some forty hours from the Bosporus, and all eyes were intently watching those cliffs and wondering, as we kept sailing on towards the huge wall of bluff rock that rises perpendicularly from out of the sea. A white building to our left perched in the crevice of the rock, was pointed out to me as the Monastery of St George, not much of a place to look at from the sea, but it well repays a visit made to it from inland, being a charming oasis among the wilds of the Sebastopol plateau. As we approached nearer, we could plainly perceive the mountains of Baidar to our right, covered with rich verdure from their summit to their base, where wooded dells wind, and the olive and vine clothe mountain slopes of remarkable beauty, intersected by streams whose waters sparkling in the sunbeams gushed down tumultuously, whilst from out of the dark foliage of the horse-chestnuts which overshadowed them, white chateaux gleamed forth, giving relief to the sombre shade that the Pharos pass threw across the sunny landscape. At last we could see the old Genoese castle on the summit of the rock, and the long running wall of defence down its side to the mouth of the little Balaklava creek becomes quite apparent, and we knew that we were now close to the very spot where the ill-fated *Prince* and her companions were dashed to pieces in the gale of the 14th of November 1854. The *Etna* heaved to and signalled, and presently out came a small tug steamer with orders for us to proceed inside; and steaming slowly we made for a small fissure in the rock, which, as we approached, gradually opened, disclosing in large painted letters the words " *Cossack Point.*" Making direct for that, and turning round, we found ourselves in the now famous harbour of Balaklava, and were speedily warped round into our places. That night we remained on board, but I think very few slept soundly, being so anxious to get on shore. I kept wondering how far off Sebastopol was from where we were, and if from the top of the hill that towered over us the fortress could be seen, while I heard the boom from the distant guns and was anxious to be closer. It was only curiosity that I wished to indulge. I had no bloodthirsty inclination to gratify as regards the enemy; but never having seen a town regularly approached and pounded to pieces by batteries of guns, I wanted to have ocular demonstration of how it was done. In the morning we were all astir early and commenced disembarking, but early as we were, there was a little active middle-aged man already in waiting, who, as the business proceeded, seemed to be here, there, and everywhere all over the ship, and always at the right place in the right time, who would lay on to a rope and pull as a sailor, or drag a stubborn horse on shore as a soldier, who, by his energy and determination, infused a spirit of activity and work into all around him; by his dress you might consider him a nobody, yet by his actions he proved that he was in himself a small host, one who considered work as play, and hard work evidently a pleasure, unlike many of the officials * I afterwards saw in the same place, who were not only an annoyance and a hindrance themselves, but the cause of annoyance and hindrance in others. On inquiring afterwards who was this hard-working indefatigable man, to my great surprise I was told, Port-Admiral Boxer, and yet in a few months, I may say weeks afterwards, when he was in his grave, prematurely there through nothing but hard work and over anxiety, it was attempted to take the blame of wretched mismanagement and inattention to duties from off the shoulders of the living, and pile it on those of the dead Admiral.

There being a right as well as a wrong way of embarking and disembarking horses, and as the former is decidedly the better plan, I may as well describe the way which I have invariably seen carried out in my own regiment, and which I have never seen equalled by any other. On arriving alongside of the vessel on which they are going to embark, the men should be formed up in single rank, which, as the usual column of march is in files or sections of threes, there is no difficulty in doing, they should then be ordered to dismount, the left files reining back to do so, to

* Captain Gordon of the Quartermaster-General's Department was one of the few noble exceptions.

unsaddle and pack up for embarkation. Meanwhile, the officer should go on board and see that all was ready and clear there to pass on the horses; he should also select some handy convenient place where the saddles, &c., could be stowed away and got at easily. While he was doing this the men would be unsaddling, the first thing to be taken off the horse being the corn-sack, which would be unlapped and opened; then comes the sheepskin, which should be first doubled lengthways and then folded into three, and placed flat at the bottom of the sack. After this the valise, mess tin,* and wallets would be taken off, the two latter and the nosebag placed above the sheepskin, and when the saddle was taken off, it should be laid open on the ground, panels upwards. In the centre the bit, bridoon, breastplate, &c., would be placed carefully, and on the top of these the valise, the whole being rolled tightly round and strapped together with the surcingle, and placed inside the cornsack with the points of the panels upwards, and the numbdha being placed on the top of all. In times of peace it is as well to pack the belts and arms also in the cornsack, the sword and carbine fitting easily down the side, and the belts, &c., going on the top of the numbdha; the mouth of the sack would be then tied up, and all ready to carry on board. Then commencing with the horses, they would be passed on board in succession from the left, and taken below and then on deck, the furthest off stalls being filled first. When the horses were all put in their places, then the packed cornsacks should be carried on board, and stowed

* For a voyage exceeding a couple of days these would be kept out.

away in precisely the same order as the horses. When disembarking the saddles, &c., the sacks would first be taken out, and placed at intervals from the right in two rows, in precisely the same manner as they had been taken up, and so every man would be exactly in the same place as he was when he dismounted, and when his horse was brought out he would only have to open the sack and take out the belts and arms, (if they were packed,) then out with the numbdha which he would place upon the horse's back, then the saddle, then undoing the surcingle take out the valise, bit, and bridoon, placing them on the ground, carefully adjust the breastplate, crupper cloak, and baggage-straps, and taking the saddle up place it on the horse's back, and proceed with the saddling and fastening on of baggage, which would all go on inversely to the way it was taken off. Then the men would put on their accoutrements and stand to their horses, and when all were ready the order would be given, "Prepare to mount" —"Mount"—and all would be at once in their places without confusion.

In short voyages, and especially where troops have to disembark within the circuit of the enemy's vigilance, or where they are liable to be engaged at once, everything would be kept on the saddles, ready to place on the horses' backs, and these should be carefully piled one on the top of the other in exact rotation,* as the horses were put on board, so that in disembarking, the horses in

---

* On the upper deck, by the main hatch, would be the best situation for the saddles, covered with a tarpaulin to keep them dry, and fastened with a couple of ropes across; they would in that way take no injury.

succession could be brought out of the stalls, saddled if necessary on board, which a couple of men could do in a minute and a half, and taken on shore.

As we got on shore and saddled, we marched away to camp in small parties, meeting on our road strings of mules with Maltese drivers going to the harbour for stores, mounted orderlies and officers travelling in all directions, and then we came to the wooden town of Kadokoi, with its rows of wooden shops, where anything that a soldier required—from a needle to a tent or a sentry box—could be procured. On the right were gangs of navvies working away at the railway to the front; many of them, however, I fancied, not labouring with the same zeal I had seen them display at home. A very fanciful and expensive toy to Government was that "Army Works Corps" in the Crimea; the men were paid seven and sixpence per diem, had double rations, a double allowance of grog, and from what I observed, a double allowance of rest to any other corps or class in or near Balaklava. There was certainly every inducement to them to take it easy; being allowed splendid tents, first-rate iron bedsteads, and good beds to lie on. Any morning that they felt disinclined to work, they had only to send their compliments to the doctor, and say they "were indisposed," and at once they were placed upon the sick list. Having no idea of military discipline, either themselves or their officers, nothing like restraint was ever employed; while of one thing they were perfectly aware, which was, that work or play, Government had always to pay and find them their rations, and that if things did not suit, they had only to strike and they would be sent home. Thus it was that the navvie work on the railway was principally done by Tartars and Maltese, and the military roads to the front were made by the infantry. I am only relating facts without any exaggeration, which all who used their eyesight, and were ever about the Army Works Corps can testify. I have observed about one half on the sick list, among a small detachment of them which was encamped on an eminence just above the French wateringplace. I have, while on guard at that watering-place, been an eye-witness to the comfortable time these sick men had of it. All they did was to drink, smoke, and play at cards, or stroll down with their hands in their pockets and chat to the guard, and all were of opinion that John Bull was the best master they ever had.

Our regiment was camped on an eminence near to the village of Karrani, where a few Greek damsels still resided, and where a Greek church still stood. The nearest lines to Kadokoi were occupied by a troop of R.H.A., and the Greys, Royals, 11th, 17th, 4th Light, 4th Heavy, 5th Dragoon Guards, &c., followed in succession. A steep hill separated us from the remainder of the cavalry, for our horses being all stallions, it was necessary to keep them and the others as far apart as possible; but the hill was of little use, and whenever any of our animals got loose of a night, which some were almost sure to do, the straight path down the hill was invariably taken by them, and then would ensue such an uproar and confusion below, as caused that particular portion of the camp to wish that the 10th Hussars had remained in India. In such cases a messenger was always despatched up the hill to us, for some men to be sent down to take the brutes back. No other dragoons would go near them when loose; nor need this be wondered at, when it was well known that one day when we and the 12th Lancers were watering at the same place together, they being on one side, and we on the other, one of our horses leaped over the trough in spite of all his rider could do to prevent him, and seizing hold of a man of the 12th, dragged him from his horse and worried his hand off like a dog. And when we were returning from Baidar afterwards, a sergeant and his man halted on the way, the former giving his horse to the latter to hold, and he immediately charged Pte. Peacre openmouthed; he, to save himself, thrust out his right hand, but D 3 (the horse's number) laid hold of his thumb, pulled him down, and although a big bit was in its mouth, gnawed the thumb off completely. But their heels were equally dangerous, or more so, than their teeth; many of our men had their legs broken, several were severely injured, and Carpenter of H Troop did not live a couple of hours after he was kicked, his chest having been driven completely in. But with all their bad habits and vices I, and I am certain all Indian soldiers, would always prefer them to the English troopers, they are so much more handy, faster, surer footed, and capable of undergoing double the fatigue that the cavalry horses at home can endure. All cavalry horses are named and numbered, the initial of the names being taken from the troop's letter, and the number being progressive. My horse was Donald, D 71. I have with me still a souvenir of him, for when he was turned over to the Turkish Government at Scutari on our leaving for England, I cut off a bit of his mane although I did not need it to keep him in my memory, for on parting with him I felt as much as if losing a comrade whom I had known for years. The poor fellow seemed to know that he was leaving home when the Osmanlis took him in charge, and they appeared to be not at all proud of the job. I expect they had heard terrible accounts of our chargers, for there were two men to take over each horse; and the most laughable thing of all was, to see a couple of musicians, two kettle-drums in each stable, tum-tumming away to keep the horses quiet; which, I should say, had quite a contrary effect, as the noise was enough to drive a herd of donkeys mad. But to return to Donald—of the purest breed of Herat, colour nearly black, a small head like a deer, surmounted by a pair of small tapering ears, which nearly met when cocked, long flowing mane and tail, eyes dark, sparkling, and full as cups, he was altogether a perfect picture—his action was unequalled, and in fact he had not a bad point about him. Yet he had one bad habit—he kicked, but only when you were on his back, he had a temper which in other respects was like a lamb; you could groom him or take him anywhere you liked, and he never bit or kicked man or horse in his life. The cause of his kicking at all was ill-treatment, and so was not his fault, as I will explain. On his joining the regiment in India, a man of the name of O'Malieu took him up, and fearing that he would be taken away from him by some non-commissioned officer, he put a curry comb under his tail. Now a horse, when anything hurts it, has not the sense to free itself; for instance, if a horse is pricked by a bayonet, it will immediately force itself further on the point instead of drawing backwards; and so in this case, finding the sharp teeth of the curry comb painful, he gripped it all the firmer, kicking furiously all the while; and he never forgot this lesson; from that day he always kicked, and it was a most difficult matter to get the crupper on him ever after. There was one most remarkable fact connected with Donald, which was, that no horse, however vicious, would either bite or kick him. In Ismid he stood between two of the worst horses in the troop, D 19 and D 67, and daily either one or the other would break his head ropes, or slip his collar and get loose, yet neither of them ever touched D 71. I have known 19 jump over his back to get at 67, and 67 go round behind him to get at another horse; but whatever horse was loose Donald escaped scatheless. Sure-footed as a cat, fast in his paces, able to leap any hedge or ditch he was put at, and good-tempered and affectionate with it all. I trust that I will be excused for talking so much of him. Although eight years have passed since I lost him, I still think regretfully of him, and sincerely trust that he met with a kind master.

To return: this rambling habit of our steeds in Balaklava caused us a great deal of trouble, and one of them set us all at defiance. Whoever has been at Balaklava will remember at the head of the valley, where the cavalry division was encamped, a high and steep rock, called the French Hill, round the base of which the road wound. To the best of my recollection it was Vinoy's Division that was camped on its crest. Well, one morning one of our horses was found absent from his picket, and word was brought up to us that he was causing a vast deal of diversion among the lines of the 4th Light Dragoons. Half a dozen of us were despatched after him, and when he saw us he made straight for the road I have mentioned. Dividing our party, three went one way and three the other; and closing round we drove him straight on towards the rock. Now we have him—thought we; but as we got closer to him he began to scramble up the face of the rock, while we stood thunderstruck at the bottom! On he went ahead, while we, ashamed to be beaten by a horse in a match of climbing, followed on. Only once he hesitated, and that was when he had got about half way up, when he stopped and looked down; but, whatever his thoughts might have been, the sight of us following seemed only to confirm him in his determination, for on he pushed ahead as before, and reaching the summit safely galloped over among some French horses, when we managed to secure him. Had I not seen him do this, I should never have believed it possible that any animal but a goat would have gone up where he did, without ever stumbling. Had he stumbled he would have fallen to the bottom and been dashed to pieces, but as I have already stated, our horses were as sure-footed and nimble as cats.

On the following day, the 17th, Head-Quarters, with the second and third squadrons, arrived in the *Himalaya*, and the fourth squadron the next day in the *Trent*. We still kept the *rowties* (Indian tents) that we had brought with us, which however if more roomy, were not so handy as the bell tent for a campaign, though they answered well enough for a standing camp, such as ours was. The horses were picketed as near as possible in front of the tent, where were the men to whom they belonged, and the saddles, with valises, &c., fastened, all ready to put on the horses' backs, were laid outside ready to the hand. Our boots and spurs and lace jackets were on, our pelisses under our heads for pillows, our belts and arms conveniently placed, so that if a sudden call came, even in the middle of the night, every man could have turned out in a few minutes and without confusion. Although but six months had elapsed since the battle of Balaklava, yet the appearance at this time of that field, would have led any one at first sight to imagine that as many weeks, I might even say as many days, had not passed since the combat. Skeletons of horses still lay all round as they fell in their harness; not far in front of these was the body of one of our dragoons, the 1st Royals, I think, and in advance of that the remains of a Russian. Both of these must have been overlooked when the dead were buried. The Russian vedette, a Cossack, at this time was posted on Canrobert's Hill, close to our lines; in fact, overlooking the harbour, while our own solitary vedette was posted on an eminence to the left of the valley, commanding a view of the plain behind the enemy's outpost. This state of affairs will not be surprising, when it is known that our force of cavalry, at the time that we landed, did not exceed from twenty to thirty file. This was all that the Balaklava charge, and the severe winter, had left of our heavy and light brigades, all that remained of ten regiments, viz., 1st Royal Dragoons, 2d or Scots' Greys, 4th Royal Irish, 5th and 6th Dragoon Guards, 8th and 11th Hussars, 4th and 13th Light Dragoons, and 17th Lancers. Men were not so scarce as horses; for instance, the 11th Hussars had only seven horses in the regiment, and as three of these were sick, only four could be mounted, and the cavalry division, as it was very inappropriately termed, cut rather a motley figure on parade, red jackets and blue, heavy and light hussars and lancers, and even then they formed but a weak squadron. Consequently, when the 10th Hussars came, numbering over seven hundred sabres, we did not get there before we were absolutely wanted, and fortunately we were only the advance of several thousands who were following after us. First arrived the 12th Lancers, then the Carabineers and the 1st Dragoon Guards, whilst strong drafts of men and horses were coming in daily to strengthen the skeleton regiments, and all of these by the end of June composed a cavalry force more considerable than had been mustered at Waterloo. We had each two blankets; one that was served out to us in the Crimea, and the other, that was worth its weight in gold, which was given to us by the Pasha of Egypt; this was made of camel's hair, and was nearly waterproof, needing a great deal of rain to penetrate through it, and being several yards long and double, it was very useful, in make exactly like a Scotch plaid, but not so heavy, which was another good quality. With these two blankets and our sheepskins we made a most comfortable bed,— quite luxurious we thought it, after coming off outlying picket on a wet and cold morning. As for the rations, they really were not so bad, for if salt beef and biscuits are always to be had, there is very little fear of starvation. We only went one day without provisions, and that was through a mistake. This happened when we were along with Omar Pasha's force at Baidar, and I believe that a few sheep, which belonged to the Turks, disappeared that afternoon, and were cooked in some manner or other by some of our foragers, so that we did not all starve. Into one tent a couple of ducks came in about dark, and in a minute they were decapitated, plucked, and in a cloth, ready for boiling, while our officer's servant was making vain inquiries regarding them. When cooked, they were called *pudding*, and as such, went down remarkably well, I believe. The preserved vegetables that we got were very acceptable indeed, and we very soon found out the best manner of cooking the salt beef and pork. I can assure any one, that when the meat is first boiled for a couple of hours in the piece, then taken out and the water thrown away, then cut up small, adding some pounded biscuit, and preserved vegetables, if they can be got, and a little seasoning of pepper, then covered with water, while it all stews together for two hours more, a mess will be furnished fit for a prince. We had always coffee or cocoa for breakfast, and tea for the evening meal. Bread was served out about twice a week, rather coarse and sometimes mouldy, but it was a great deal better than none. To buy bread was dear—about sixpence a pound—often dearer, and other things in proportion, porter being two shillings a bottle. As is the case at home, the canteens had the worst description of articles, and charged for them the highest prices. It was very remarkable that Maltese and Greeks should be the keepers of them all, our own countrymen apparently not being allowed to do so. I often thought that it would have been better to be robbed by our own people than victimised by the Greeks, who hated us in their hearts, and were all of them Russian spies. It was entirely owing to the intelligence given by the camp-followers and canteen men that the attack of the 18th of June proved unsuccessful, the enemy having received due information hours before the attack began. The manner of communication practised by those spies, was in many cases quite original. One who kept a canteen up by the right attack, took a great fancy to shells, and every day about noon he sent some one to bring him any that had not exploded. He always sent in one direction, and to one certain spot, and, sure enough, there was always one of these missiles lying unexploded, seemingly as if it only wanted fetching. This curiosity in the canteen-keeper very soon caused others to have slight suspicions, and on examining carefully a shell that he had sent for, a nice scroll was found inside. The shell was a dummy, and his instructions were forwarded to him by this strange messenger; but how he communicated with Sebastopol never transpired, for he carried that secret away with him. He was hanged the following morning, on an eminence as close to the town as possible, so that his friends inside might see how it had fared at last with Giacomo. These fellows always died with their faces to the city, and, I believe, always what is called game.

Firewood we had served out to us, and in this and

many other respects, we were much better off than our allies, the French, whom I saw daily go out in fatigue parties to find it, having to dig up the roots of trees, &c.; and I have also often seen them come round to our tents, asking for any biscuits we had to spare, and (for we never refused them) receiving them gratefully. But it must not be imagined that we had always the pleasure of giving, and never received anything in return from our French comrades. They obliged us in numerous ways, and taught us many a dodge in campaigning of which hitherto we had no idea. And whenever we paid a visit to their camp, they treated us almost too well, I mean too well for their means; they were too generous, and any of us who, like myself, was in the habit of going among them, had to be extremely cautious in admiring anything they had, for if we happened only to praise a looking-glass, a fancy knife, or any of the nicknacks they had in their tents, it would be forced upon our acceptance, and they would have felt quite hurt had we steadily persisted in refusing. In respect of foraging, the French soldiers are far before our men, who are never taught to look after their food, or fuel to cook it with, expecting everything to be brought to them, a very bad habit to acquire, as all must allow, and one unfortunately that grows strongly upon English soldiers, many of whom would rather sit down, grumble and starve, than put themselves to the least trouble to look after food, or walk half a mile to get wood to cook it, and would sit down contentedly in the sunshine and neglect to erect a temporary bivouac to shelter them when it might change to rain. In this respect they somewhat resemble the nigger in whose hut a gentleman had taken refuge from a thunder shower, through the top of which the rain came pouring down. "I say, Cuffee, why don't you repair this roof?" says the gentleman. "Can't, Massa, rain too much now," replies Cuffee. "But why not do it in the fine weather?" remarks the gentleman; to which Cuffee, on the English soldier's principle, answers, "Ah, Massa, no use mending it in fine weather—then not want." I remember there was a great outcry about the green coffee beans that were sent instead of roasted; but I would guarantee that a French soldier would have been only too happy to get it in that state; he would very soon have found ways and means to roast it and grind it too. In the British army there is rather too much of that dissatisfied feeling with respect to rations that once possessed a soldier of Charles the Twelfth's. He had not received so fine a description of bread as he considered his due, and so taking it in his hand, he made his way with it to the king's presence. I forget the exact words used, but quoting from memory they were to the following effect:—*Soldier*—"Sire, do you consider this bread fit for a soldier to eat?" The *King*—"Let me taste it." The soldier giving it into the king's hand, to his astonishment and dismay saw him not only taste it, but actually eat it all, finishing with the remark, "It is not good, but it may be eaten." Soldiers should at least be taught the theoretical part of foraging, bivouacking, tent-pitching, and all the other numerous peaceful duties that he has to perform in war time; nor would there be much difficulty in doing this, for were only the men of each troop taken into a barrack-room one afternoon in a week, and the theories of the foregoing explained to them by some competent person first, and then each man questioned in turn about what he has heard explained, and how he would act under certain circumstances,—I say were this done, I feel positive that in six months most of the men would know how to cook, construct a bivouac, throw up a bank to shelter their horses in severe weather on outpost, to get clear water from muddy, to picket their horses, or to secure them in such a manner as would prevent them from straying, to make tents out of their blankets, &c., &c., of all which at present they have not the slightest idea.

CHAPTER TENTH.

The Crimea.

ON the morning of the 18th April, I was awoke out of a very sound and refreshing sleep by the adjutant calling to Sergeant-Major Rickards from the outside of the tent, directing him to go quietly round the troop, rouse the men, and tell them to turn out at once and without noise. Head-Quarters having arrived on the 17th, we were to take the field at once, and as I listened to the Adjutant's words, oh, thinks I, we are to have a slap at the enemy the very first morning,—and with great alacrity jumped up, but not a bit faster than the others, all vying one with the other in the attempt to be first saddled and turned out. When all were ready, we quietly filed off in succession down the hill towards Kadokoi, feeling our way in the dark cold morning as we went, then bearing to the left we took up position on the plain just beyond the watering-place, and dismounted. There we waited anxiously for daybreak, stamping round and round our horses, chafing at the delay, for we had been informed that an attack was then expected either from the enemy or from ourselves. We were also thinking a little about our rations, and whether we were to have anything to eat that morning, not feeling any desire to fight fasting; but we were relieved from that miserable idea by being ordered to undo our haversacks, when a supply of biscuits was passed round to each man. Having water in our choggles, (leather water-bottles,) here was meat and drink, and so with a desire to emulate Mark Tapley, we ate our biscuits, washing down each mouthful with a draft from the choggle, and made ourselves really jolly under adverse circumstances. Certainly it was a great deal better than none, and stayed our stomachs a little, half a loaf being better than no bread, a fact, by the by, which Jock Fairburn of "ours," when told so one day, emphatically denied, with a "No, I'll be hanged if it is;" but that was considered nothing out of the way for him, he having declared once to the colonel when a prisoner before him, that he would leave off drinking because it was " the *ruination of all evil.*" When the day began to break I found that we were upon the right of the Chasseurs d'Afrique, who, to my great surprise, had not only fires lit but coffee made, which they were drinking with much relish. After seeing this, I should not have been at all astonished had they produced chairs and little round tables, with cups and saucers to decorate them, out of their haversacks, which, like the bag of a wizard, appeared to contain nothing, yet produced everything that was required out of it. Being sent to the left flank by the adjutant with an order, and having delivered it, I was fortunate enough to be invited by a *sergeant-fourrier* of the Chasseurs to partake of a cup of coffee, and I need scarcely add, thankfully accepted the invitation; our trumpet then sounding

M

"Stand to your horses," I had to bid adieu to my friendly entertainer, and mounting galloped back to my place. This was the first time we had turned out, and we naturally expected to be at once engaged; a month or two later we knew better; but at this time our expectations became certainties, when the order was given for the squadron I belonged to to skirmsh, the adjutant cautioning us "not to fire until we got within fifty yards of a Cossack," and I really thought it was going to be something excessively like business. As soon as we had cleared the valley and passed beyond our advanced post, it sounded "Skirmishers out," and away we went to the right, while the Chasseurs extended in like manner to the left. The adjutant, who would always be wherever danger was, kept with the skirmishers, and observing a body of troops away on our right, despatched me to ascertain who and what they were. As I galloped towards them, I soon discovered that they were Turkish columns moving in line, and in the same direction as we were ourselves; but as that might not have been all the information that Percy Smith required, I went forward among them and saw their columns of the three arms, cavalry and artillery in front and flanks, and infantry in the centre, extending away continuously to the heights over the sea. Having informed the adjutant of what I had seen, I again took my place on the right of the advancing line; but we could not get within five hundred yards, far less within fifty, of a Cossack, for they would not allow us to get any way near to them. It was all one whether our pace was fast or slow, the Cossacks always conformed their retreat to our advance, trotting as we trotted, walking if we walked, and halting when we halted, keeping the same wide interval between us, so we had no opportunity of wasting powder or ball on them that morning. But the reconnaissance was successful so far as it had been a regular surprise, for we found their fires burning, and cooking utensils all in use, when we passed through the village of Kamari, having evidently disturbed them when about to breakfast. It was quite wonderful to see how extraordinarily snug a division of them had made themselves here, occupying all the cottages, and having dug out several scores of huts in the ground, which were covered on the top with brushwood, and so nicely concealed, that they were not discovered until some of our men, when riding over them, fell through, horse and all. The cottages, I suppose, were occupied by the nobs, while the huts were the residences of the privates. We, of course, could not leave these quarters just as we found them,—that would have been carrying politeness too far; so we set fire to the houses, and demolished the ground habitations. Here again was seen the forethought of the French Chasseurs; they seized upon the rafters, pieces of wood, and every other portable combustible that came to hand, while our men let everything burn, and yet, I have no doubt, that had they loaded their horses with firewood, some of the officers would have ordered them to throw it away. The enemy who, during our occupation and destruction of the village, had lessened their distance a little on our advance, immediately fell back to their original interval. On the top of a hill to our left, a party of Cossacks had taken up their position;

but the French rocket-troop, galloping to the front, sent two or three rockets amongst them, on which they dispersed so speedily, that one of them forgot to carry off his lance, which an officer afterwards secured, and carried back with him as a trophy.

Having extended the reconnaissance as far as was thought necessary, we commenced our retreat, the regiments retiring by alternate squadrons, until we reached the narrow part of the valley, when, forming close column, the skirmishers were called in, and we retired through the gorge by column of alternate regiments. We had nearly got through, when the trumpet suddenly sounded the "advance," followed by "gallop." The Chasseurs, who were then retiring, fronted at once, throwing down the firewood they were carrying, and came after us; but we were too late, the enemy got clear away, with a couple of prisoners. These were two navvies, who had followed the column in the morning anticipating plunder, and had remained loitering round, and in the village of Kamari, long after our skirmishers had left it, in fact, until the Cossacks were close on them, when they made after us, shouting as they ran, but they were too late, being pursued and overtaken. Our colonel, who was in command of all the cavalry, (the other generals being in England,) and consequently in rear, next to the enemy and watching his movements, saw this, and sounded the recall, but the enemy were too sharp for us, and the navvies instead of capturing were captured, and thus had an opportunity of visiting the interior of Russia free of expense. After this interlude, we quietly resumed our retreat, the

Chasseurs taking up the wood they had dropped, and all returning to our lines by ten o'clock, when we were quite ready for breakfast. Subsequently we managed always to have breakfast first, the cooks preparing for it over night, and while we dressed and saddled in the morning, they lit the fires and made the coffee or cocoa. This was preferable to going out empty, for I believe that every one, Scotchmen not excepted, will at all times fight better on a full stomach than on an empty one.

The position of our outpost in the valley I shall always consider to have been badly chosen. An outlying picket ought to be concealed entirely from observation, either by natural or artificial obstacles; and although our picket was posted remarkably close to the camp, no shelter of any kind was provided or constructed. The sentry's post likewise was equally ill chosen, on the slope of a hill which certainly commanded a view of the entrance to the valley, but it left the vedette entirely exposed. The Cossack, on the contrary, posted on Canrobert's Hill, could look right into our lines: being behind the crest, he need only peep over it, and so was not only concealed himself, but the whole of the picket were secure from observation. I shall long remember the first outlying picket that I mounted in the Crimea, which, as it will point out how careful men ought to be on outpost duty, I will relate. At dusk, it is customary to draw in the vedettes closer, and during the night to double them. During the last hour in the afternoon, just previous to the vedettes being doubled, an officer-like fellow rode up close to the vedette, a man of the name of Flynn, answering his challenge as "friend," and carelessly asking him which was the nearest road to the front, which he pretended not to be certain about. Then he changed the conversation, and by a few well-put questions, drew out of Flynn what was the strength of our regiment in men and horses, where we were encamped, and every particular; then, having got all the information he wanted, and doubtless seeing that he had a simple soul to deal with, turned suddenly upon his informant, and pulling out a pistol, told him that he was a Russian officer, and that as it would not suit him to go any further in our lines, he was going back to the Cossack picket, adding, "If you attempt to give any alarm until I get fifty yards away, I'll come back and shoot you." And this soldier actually, with a loaded carabine in his hand, not only allowed him to make this threat, but to ride away unmolested. While he stood there, nothing could have been more easy than to have shot him, without raising the piece or taking any aim, so long as the muzzle was towards him, for there would not be much variation in the flight of a bullet fired at so short a distance. But Flynn seemed to have been regularly bamboozled, and only too happy to get rid of his new acquaintance. He was one of those just-let-him-take-it-easy sort of men, who are content to do anything to which there is neither trouble nor thought attached. One who, even if informed from an authentic source that a comet would destroy the world twelve months hence, would be perfectly happy in the thought that there were three hundred and sixty-five days still left in which to eat and drink and sleep ere the end came. In the army, such a man is generally looked upon in the light of a good soldier, being what is termed steady, that is, in quarters; but on a campaign, from him and such like, "Good Lord, deliver us." They can use neither their heads nor their hands, and would be the very last to be selected if a post had to be surprised, an important despatch to be forwarded, or a village, where some of the enemy were hidden, to be stealthily examined. For anything of this kind, Flynn was physically and mentally unfitted, and he was still quite nervous when I relieved him. He then related the whole affair, and I acquainted Captain Bowles with the circumstances, who, in a very few words, but quite to the point, told Flynn what he thought of him. The utmost vigilance was now necessary, the position of the picket was changed, and patrols were sent out frequently all the night to the front and flanks, while the remainder stood to their horses' heads ready to mount. The night being remarkably dark the patrols had to be very cautious; and, in fact, the sergeant, four men, and I, had a narrow escape of being captured. We had gone too far and got close to the enemy's outpost, a proximity that we were not aware of until challenged; this explained the whole, we were at the bottom of Canrobert's Hill, and could hear the enemy mounting and scuffling about, just a few yards above us. Making no answer to the challenge, we retired cautiously in an opposite direction to where our own picket lay, and luckily none of our horses neighed as the enemy rushed down past us on to the plain, where we could hear them in extended order galloping about. Had we retired direct towards our picket we should inevitably have been captured; but waiting until the Cossacks had all swept past, we ascended the hill a short distance in the very direction they had come, and then circling round the reverse way, at last got safe on to the plain, when a few minutes' trot brought us all safe in. As we had been away nearly an hour the picket were all mounted, and having heard the noise made by the enemy when galloping after us, as they thought, made sure that we were captured. When we came off duty in the morning, Captain Bowles mentioned the matter in his report, and he and Sergeant Vallance had to go up to Lord Raglan's on the following day to give a full account of the whole affair.

It was about the 20th of May when General Canrobert resigned the command to General Pélissier,* and a marked change could be discerned in the tactics, which at once became more bold in their design, and were always carried out in the execution; and all this was attributed of course to the change of commanders. For instance, on the 3d of May, an expedition had sailed for Kertch, but was immediately recalled without any reason by General Canrobert. On the 23d, one of General Pélissier's first acts was to redespatch the force to Kertch; and on the 24th, the allied forces, disembarking a short distance from the town, commenced a bombardment which caused the garrison, after blowing up their magazines, setting fire to their stores, sinking their ships, and spiking a number of their guns, to move off (unmolested, though) towards the interior of the Crimea. Many considered at the time

* While penning these lines, I hear read by a comrade in the room the melancholy intelligence of his death.

that great want of judgment was shewn in selecting Kertch as the vulnerable point to attack; for had the allies first landed at Kaffa, where the peninsula narrows to about eight miles, and taken that town, and then Arabat, on the other side, the retreat of all the troops eastward would have been cut off, and the attack on Kertch could then have been made without a chance of its garrison escaping. However, as it was, an immense deal of damage was done to the enemy; the gunboats moving into the Sea of Azof, scoured it from one extremity to the other, destroying Arabat, and there capturing over two hundred vessels laden with grain; while Genitsch, at the other extremity, was destroyed, with nearly one hundred vessels, altogether causing a loss to the enemy of grain alone sufficient to have supported one hundred thousand men for four months. This is not taking into account the loss of guns, ammunition, and vessels elsewhere, including four steamers sunk by the Russians near Barianck; and so greatly did the presence of this force in the Sea of Azof intimidate the enemy, that instructions were forwarded to the garrisons of Soujak, Kali, and Anapa to abandon their posts, after levelling the fortifications and destroying the magazines. Six thousand Turks, afterwards reinforced by ten thousand more, one thousand French, and about the same number of English, remained to garrison Yenikale and St Paul's, the points commanding respectively the entrance to the straits; these places were strongly fortified against an attack by land, and the captured Russian guns armed the batteries.

On the day that Kertch was captured, (her Majesty's

birthday,) our cavalry were reviewed by Lord Raglan, on the plateau by the monastery of St George. I had then the pleasure of seeing General Pélissier for the first time, when it was the general remark among the men that he seemed "a determined-looking fellow," one who would give us some employment. Previously to this we had been rubbing along quietly enough, but not very satisfactorily, turning out day after day, going down into the valley and over the French Hill; we made many an advance as far as the Tchernaya and back again, but seldom got near enough to have a shot at the enemy. As time passed and troops arrived, especially cavalry, we began more and more to assume the offensive, and repeatedly drove the enemy beyond the Blackwater; but it was not until the 25th of May, when all the Sardinians had arrived, that it was determined to take up the old ground, lost by the Turks on the 25th October 1854. Mustering in force on the plain, the allies advanced, covered on the right by our squadron in skirmishing order as far as the Tchernaya, the enemy falling back as we pushed forward. After crossing the river, the Sardinians took up their position, which they at once began to entrench, while we still followed the enemy; but the country beyond the Tchernaya being densely wooded, the skirmishers were unable to advance in that order, they were therefore called in, and forming an advanced guard and support, kept on in pursuit. The path was very narrow, there being only room to march by sections of threes, with an extensive wooded cover on each side, where, had the enemy but placed a score of riflemen, very few of the advanced guard could have escaped; they might have been knocked over easily, without a chance of reprisal; but fortunately the enemy had not had the forethought to seize upon the opportunity, so we rode on unmolested. I was in charge of the advanced party of all, and seeing some Russians hurrying down a steep path with half-a-dozen horses, I felt exceedingly inclined to gallop across and seize them, but dared not do so on my own account; I therefore did the only thing which could be done in the circumstances—telling Pigott and Ovens, the two men who were with me, not to lose sight of the animals, I galloped back to the officer's party, and acquainting him with what I had seen, asked permission to follow after the horses and capture them. Lieutenant —— seemed to have no confidence in himself, and asked the opinion of Sergeant W——, who evidently did not know his duty either, for he replied, "Decidedly not, sir, we have no order to take horses." He might as well have said we had no special orders to capture a general, a gun, or baggage, or anything else that came in our way; as it was, I had to try to be contented, although it was enough to try the patience and temper of a saint to see those six fine horses, two grays, one chestnut, and three dark-coloured, all led comfortably away; and the two men grumbled as much as I did at "Green Forage's"* good nature, for horses being scarce, these six would have sold for a good sum. About a mile further on we came to a village where I thought the enemy had an idea of making a stand, for the rear guard

* A name that the men of the troop had given to this officer from his always inquiring, at Cairo, if the horses had had their green forage.

waited until we got within a hundred yards of the village, and I was just coming to the conclusion that it would be necessary to decide this small affair by a reference to our carbines, when they withdrew and continued their retreat through the village. On reaching it I sent Pigott and Ovens outside round the flanks and continued my progress, having first made a sign for the file of communication to halt until we saw that the enemy had got clear of the village. Riding slowly on at a walk, with my carbine cocked and at the "ready," I went through without seeing any one, until I had reached the far end, when I perceived a couple of Greeks in a house, and calling them out, endeavoured to gain some information from them relating to the enemy's movements, but I could make nothing of them, nor understand what they said, except two words, "Balaklava" and "Tchernaya." Thinking that some information might be gained from them if there was an interpreter present, I passed them on to the rear, and shortly afterwards we commenced our retreat, the Cossacks wheeling about, as is their custom, and following us in turn. We—that is, the two men and I—now formed the rear guard, but had not held that position long when I was relieved by Corporal Raynor; and on going towards the front, was told to take charge of the two Greeks I had made prisoners, and who were at present to be conveyed on. As the regiment was retiring very slowly, I and my party of prisoners were soon a long way ahead; and meeting General Parlby and his aide-de-camp, I was questioned as to who and what the prisoners were; and after informing him where I had met them, and my reasons for taking them, I could not help mentioning about missing the horses. I thought the General would have jumped off his horse with vexation. "The very thing we want, Townley," said he, turning to his aide-de-camp; "and —— was so foolish as to let them slip past." Then telling me that I had done perfectly right, and that I was to march back to the Sardinians, and there await his return, when he would see what should be done with the men, he went onwards. When I got back, I found that the Sardinians had taken up their position, which they were strengthening by placing guns to command the different approaches, and throwing up entrenchments. Behind them I dismounted, and sitting down on the ground with my two companions, pulled out of my haversack a supply of biscuits and cheese, and from my wallet a flask of rum, and this, with some water from the choggle, made a very good meal. Of course, the prisoners went shares with me in the repast, and from being dull and gloomy, became at once quite cheerful, I might almost say happy. They had the most of the chat to themselves, which was only natural, they being in a difficulty. I could partly make out that they were anxious to get home again, and that their wives would be fretting to know what had become of them. When General Parlby returned, they were had up and examined. I do not know what information was got from them, but it was all taken down; and about four P.M., when the covering parties were called in, I was ordered to go with them, and see them safe past the Sardinian outposts, which I did. They were still afraid of going by themselves, lest they should meet some French or Sardinian patrols, and asked me, as far as I could understand, to give them a paper shewing how they had been released. Having a pencil and pocket-book with me, I wrote a short note, stating that they had been brought away by the advanced guard, but were ordered to be released by General Parlby, and that I had seen them through the Sardinian lines, and on the straight road for home. Then shaking hands, I bade them good-by, and concluded that they were done with. But it afterwards appeared that they had not gone far when they were met by Lord Raglan and his staff, were again made prisoners, and turned over to the charge of Captain Macdonald, the provost-marshal; and the following morning, down came an order from Lord Raglan for the corporal who had taken these two men prisoners in the first instance, to go down to Balaklava, receive them over from the provost-marshal, and march them up to head-quarters. It was rather a surprise for me when I got notice to turn out instantly and go after them, as I had fancied they were by that time all snug and safe at home. On shewing my authority, I got the prisoners, who appeared quite delighted to see me, and came away most willingly, from which I inferred that the provosts had not been over kind to them. When about half way through Kadokoi, they suddenly halted, directing my attention to two women who were crouching at the corner of a hut, with an evident wish to keep out of sight; and the two prisoners, who were now quite agitated, made me understand by signs that these were their wives, and that they wished to be allowed to speak to them. I knew that they must have made their way secretly to where they now stood; that they had come from inside the enemy's lines into ours; that having done so made them amenable to military law; and that it would have been no more than my duty to call a provost and give them in charge. But I knew also that these two poor women had braved great dangers, having come for miles and miles in the dead of night through rivers, over hills, and across valleys, passing stealthily through the Russian and Sardinian outposts; in short, that they had risked their lives in many ways, just to know if their husbands were safe, or to be near them if they were in jeopardy; and although neither of them was young or beautiful, yet the faithfulness shewn by them towards their husbands in this trouble was worthy of all praise; and I should have been unworthy of the name of an English soldier could I have refused the simple request that they might be allowed to say a few words to each other. To tell the truth, I was rather pleased that it lay in my power to be able to do this little kindness: the women especially appeared to be most grateful; and when I endeavoured to make them understand that their husbands would receive no harm, they would have embraced my feet had I allowed them to do so. I took them up to the Adjutant-General's, Bucknal D. Estcourt,* to whom I explained the whole affair, which satisfied him perfectly, and he told me that they would be released as soon as they had seen Lord Raglan; so turning them over to the charge of the sergeant of the guard close by,

* He died within a month of this time, on the 25th of June, and was followed to his long home, on the 28th, by Lord Raglan.

I returned. It was about a week after this, when riding on duty through Balaklava, that I was agreeably surprised by again being brought in contact with my late prisoners. They were employed on the railway; but the moment they observed me, down they threw their pickaxes, and rushing across, commenced, in the demonstrative manner of the East, to shew their good feeling towards me; and afterwards they never failed when I passed to rush away from any work they might be at to shew their joy at seeing me, and to shake hands, a habit that I had some difficulty at first to get them into. They were perfectly comfortable, and received good wages, which I was very glad of, as had it gone otherwise with them, I should always have taken a little blame to myself for having in the first instance brought them from their homes. Not many months since, on looking over the Crimean despatches, I observed in the one giving an account of our operations and doings on that particular day, that it wound up with the intimation that "two prisoners were taken." Therefore it follows that some one must have taken them; and so, although not mentioned by name, yet by inference, I could say that my doings had been taken notice of in despatches; and this fact I sometimes joke about with my comrades, saying that I am the only one in the regiment who can lay claim to such an honour.

This bloodless expedition, although in a tactical sense one of great importance, did not half satisfy us, for we were not very well pleased at the present inaction, and were most eager that the initiative should be taken by our side, so that we might have an opportunity of paying off a trifle of the Balaklava score with accumulated interest. Ever since we landed we had been expecting the route for somewhere, hoping that one of the many current "shaves" flying about would prove correct, or that an engagement might take place, or an assault be made upon the town,—anything but doing nothing. For it was in this light that we had begun to look upon our customary turns-out in the morning, which only reversed King Pepin's famous manœuvre by "marching down the hill, and then marching up again," from and to our lines at Karrani, with but seldom a reconnaissance or a skirmish to diversify the sameness or to enliven the monotony. Not but that rumours were plentiful enough: their name was legion and their object nearly everything impracticable or unlikely. The most feasible were for us to form part of an expedition to be sent to Perekop, and so to cut off the principal supplies to Sebastopol, or to force the Mackenzie heights, and drive the Bear into his den, or to succour Kars or make a raid upon Odessa; but these and a hundred such like all ended in smoke, leaving us still discontented at what we considered the waste of time, and the inactivity of our generals. It was on the 16th of June that I made my first excursion to the front. Having borrowed a pony, I started immediately after dinner with the determination of getting down into the advanced trenches, and having a close view of the town we were besieging. First making for the flagstaff, I had a distant view of Sebastopol and the trenches surrounding it, with the continual steady fire kept up on and from the doomed fortress. On inquiry, I found that it would be a difficult matter to get into the trenches, there being a sappers' guard at the entrance of the ravine, who had orders to stop any one going in that direction unless on duty; but having come for the purpose of seeing the town closely, which could only be done from the third parallel, I went off towards the sappers' lines, where I might learn how best to attain my object. There I met with a countryman, and by a judicious application of sundry drams of grog, I at last got him to act as my conductor. Taking with me a bottle of whisky, also, to act as a mollifier for the guard, we made our way to the ravine, or "Valley of Death," as it had been named, from the number of shot and shell which had rolled into it at one time and another, literally paving its bottom. We walked together slowly, for my guide had by this time become rather obfuscated, walking irregularly and talking incoherently. On arriving at the mouth of the ravine the bottle proved an admirable "Open Sesame," and we were allowed to pass through without much further questioning. My new comrade informed me as well as he could, that it was now all plain sailing, and that I had only to keep on down the ravine, which would bring me in due course to the advanced trenches. As for himself, he had by this time sat down; he could go no farther. I found that it was of no use trying to get him up; he was past praying for, so I carried him to the side of the ravine, (I had left the pony in charge of the guard,) and placing him on the slope made him quite comfortable, putting a fifty-six pounder under his head for a pillow. To my inquiry whether he was "all right," he only answered, "Eh, man but that was rale gude stuff;" so leaving him I proceeded alone on my journey, knowing that I should find him all safe on my return, which, however, I was near enough not doing. Keeping straight on, I passed the first and second parallels, and when near to the third, instead of keeping on still round by the ravine, I must needs make a short cut across a slight elevation; I passed over its crest walking leisurely along, for I was looking at the town, which was now close to me, and wondering at the quietness, which, as the firing had ceased on both sides for a time, appeared to me most remarkable, and thus interested I scarcely understood the first shout from the men in the trenches for me to run; but the sharp pinging whistle of a rifle bullet that rang past my ear, had the effect of quickening my motions wonderfully, and I immediately darted off at full speed to gain the shelter of the sandbag revetments of the trenches in front, which I did not reach, however, before another leaden messenger whistled ominously past, with a proximity too close to be at all agreeable, and which seemed to say, "The next will be nearer." It was the 1st Foot who were in the trenches, "Pontius Pilate's bodyguards," as some one irreverently termed them; but their age had not caused them to deteriorate in the slightest degree; in fact, like old wine, they had improved by keeping, for a more jolly, comfortable, well-to-do lot I should never wish to meet with on a campaign, far less in the advanced trenches, where you may see a man for the first and last time, as none who went into them on duty over night knew whether they would come out again in the morning.

It has been said, and truly, I believe, that " Scotchmen, crows, and Newcastle grindstones are to be found everywhere;" and, believing this, I was not in the least astonished on being accosted again in my native tongue. The sapper I had left in the ravine had spoken Scotch at parting, and the first words I heard after the shout to run was, "Weel, my chappie, the whistle o' that bullet garred ye rin gey an' brisk; ye'll no likely come daunderin' doon again in a hurry to the third parallel, glouerin' frae ye."

It is almost needless to add that I was made to feel quite at home, while all the different points of the town were pointed out to me; but I was only allowed to peep cautiously round the corner of an embrasure with one eye. It was a Saturday evening, I remember, and what struck me most forcibly was the church bells, which kept ringing all over the town as sweetly, and beautifully, and calmly, as if war or bloodshed were unknown, and the roar of cannon, the noise of bursting shells, and the rattle of musketry were never heard near the spot. I had only to shut my eyes and hide from their view the soldiers with their muskets ready to handle, the pointed cannon and elevated mortars, the powder magazines and shot, and the sandbag defences, to fancy that I was far from strife,—and I had only to open them again to know that death held high carnival here nightly, and that by the day after to-morrow's setting sun, thousands of our men, of our allies, and of our enemies would have gone to their last account. The quietness I saw was only the precursor of the storm which was soon to burst forth. I remained where I was for about an hour, listening to tales of sorties and attacks, and how certain rifle-pits had been carried, and where Jack, and Tom, and Bill had specially distinguished themselves. Then I was shewn several sandbags, or rather what had once been such—for being riddled through and through with rifle bullets, they were now sievelike and consequently useless—still, to me they were objects of interest, telling of night attacks, and deadly engagements in the trenches; so I brought two away with me as souvenirs of my visit. Taking the low road on my return, I made my way along, picking up my guide and pony, who were both safe where I left them, on my way back again. It was generally known that the bombardment was to commence on the following day, and the attack on the day afterwards; and I had a chat with many who were for duty in the trenches on that and the next night. They all seemed joyous and hearty enough, and it was only at parting that any remark was made which referred to the coming struggle, and then only in such simple words as, "I'll see you again should all go right;" or, "Good-bye, Sebastopol will be taken when we next meet." But, alas! of the many with whom I parted that day, there were only two whom I ever met afterwards.

On returning that night, I met with a couple of sergeants and their wives, belonging to the 5th Dragoon Guards, who were going home in the same direction as myself. It was getting dusk, and on our way we met several of the French regiments marching down into the trenches, with their vivandières riding at their head on

ponies. I should say that Mrs A—— and Mrs P——
were riding on mules, sideways, of course, although they
had no side-saddles, and this style of equitation, or
muletation, amused the vivandières greatly, they riding
their steeds after quite a masculine fashion; and our two
ladies were equally amused at the French manner, so
both parties apparently derived entertainment from the
other's peculiarities. On our way home we called at the
" Iron Hut," Mrs Seacole's, where we had some refreshment, and a long chat with the old dame and her daughter
about the West Indies. Other excursions I made to the
front, and also to Kamiesch, which was far before
Kadukoi. At Kamiesch we could get something to eat
that was palatable, but at Kadukoi what was sold in the
so-called refreshment rooms had neither flavour nor
sweetness, nor would it satisfy our appetites, the feeling
after a repast there being just as if you had snapt at a
fly and missed it.

CHAPTER ELEVENTH.

Campaigning.

THE 18th of June was a mistake, the Russians being quite prepared for the attack; and after this a diversion on some other point was considered necessary; so we of the 10th were made very happy on the night of that day, by being informed that a wing of our regiment was to proceed the following morning upon a secret expedition with the Sardinians under General Marmora. This portion of the corps in great delight hailed the order with peculiar satisfaction, giving free scope to wild expectations of cavalry raids and foraging expeditions, which would bring about fresh adventures, and enable us to see new faces and fresh scenes in another part of the Czar's dominions. Leaving our *rowties*, (tents,) and taking only a change of linen with us, (for we expected to be away only three days, instead of seventeen, as it proved,) we marched from the camp near Karrani on the morning of the 19th of June. Being on the right of the leading squadron, I went on with the advanced guard, receiving orders to lead towards Kamara, and passing on the left of that village to cross the Tchernaya. Keeping straight across the Balaklava plain, we marched contentedly on, wondering where was our destination, and where our camping ground for that night would be, until we reached the river, which we crossed by a ford, and at once passed into a portion of country which we could not but regard with astonishment and admiration, wondering at the difference between this and the barren country we had come from, and admiring the high, finely wooded hills, fertile valleys, and murmuring streams which we now gazed upon. Riding through a beautiful valley, we came to the lovely but deserted village of Tchourgoum, where we pitched our tents beside the walls of an old castle, near to an enchanting stream, where stately poplars, rich grass, and beautiful flowers lined the banks. We had as yet seen nothing of the Sardinians; but the following morning, as we marched some miles farther into the interior, we passed them on the road carrying their *tentes d'abri*, and looking the most compact and serviceable little army in existence I should say. All the men were as neat as if they had just come out of the *tin boxes* which it was jocularly said at first the *Sardines* were to occupy only, being merely intended as ornamental and not useful, an idea which the battle of Tracter Bridge at once dispelled. Keeping to the left of a small river, which I was informed was the Chiliu, a tributary of the Balbec, and passing a village of the same name, said to have been once the abode of the celebrated traveller Pallas, we encamped a few miles farther on in a pleasant open glade, where many of the tents nestled under the large trees, which afforded a double shelter from the midday sun. The squadron I belonged to was placed on outpost duty this night under Captain Bowles, on a hill to the left of our camp. As it was a beautiful moonlight night, the time passed very pleasantly, at least as pleasantly as our horses would allow. Many of us endeavoured to snatch a few winks of sleep by lying down, but these were vain attempts alongside of our indefatigable steeds, who would not give us the least chance in life of enjoying a comfortable nap. Having a quiet horse, I tried, really hoping to succeed, but it was useless; he kept twisting and turning round one minute, and the next he was pawing at the horse next him, who was pawing and snorting in turn, each attempting to have a smell at the other; so I was forced to give up the attempt in despair, and getting on my legs again contented myself with building castles in the air until it was my turn to go on patrol. I may explain, for the benefit of the non-military reader, that the outposts are what are termed the eyes of an army, and when these are judiciously posted and do their duty properly an army is secure; while, on the other hand, when these are neglected no force can be considered safe. An army on the march in an enemy's country never attempts to break up its formation until the outposts are placed; when these are properly posted in advance of it they may be compared to a fan, the main body representing the handle, and the outposts the leaves which radiate from it. The proportion usually required for the duty of the outposts is one-third: for instance, an army of thirty thousand men would require, for security, ten thousand men as advanced or main guard and for the duty of outposts. The main guard for its preservation detaches one-third of its force, in three main pickets, each eleven hundred strong, one to be posted in front of the centre, the others on each of the flanks. These main pickets secure their safety by each detaching one-third of its strength to the front, forming three outlying pickets of about one hundred and ten men each, and posted in a precisely similar manner to the main pickets, that is, on the centre and flanks. And the outlying pickets have their safety looked to by a chain of sentinels termed vedettes. In this way it will be perceived that the main body is protected by the main guard, that this in turn is protected by the three main pickets, while these again are protected by the outlying pickets, who have the protection of their vedettes; but of course it entirely depends upon the nature of the country whether so many are wanted or not.

What I have mentioned is the proportionate force requisite for an open country; and the post of the pickets would be behind any elevations on the main roads, or behind any points where other roads branch off. In a close wooded country a smaller force would suffice, because where natural obstacles abound fewer men are required for defence. So we formed one of these outlying pickets, posted on the top of a hill covered with trees, which, while they sheltered us from the enemy's view, enabled us to have a good look at him. This was by daylight; at night it was another matter. Then, as you cannot distinguish what the enemy is doing, the want of this sense of sight must be made up by superior care, attention, and intelligence to the requisite duties which have to be performed, patrols being sent to the front and flanks at regular intervals, and so a constant watch is kept on the movements of the enemy. In the morning a troop was withdrawn, the other, to which I belonged, remaining for the day. The Sardinians had also an outpost here of Bersaglieri, who with their dark dresses, bandit-like hats and cock's feather plumes, could scarcely be distinguished from the greenwood in which they stood; and as I went and came past their posts, although I could hear the challenge, and answered "cavalier," still it took me a minute to discover where the sound came from. When posting the two vedettes, it was the corporal's duty, after placing his men, to patrol to a large flagstaff about a quarter of a mile farther on, and return. On most occasions it was my habit to go a considerable way past this to the crest of the hill, where, entirely concealed by the foliage, I could look at the Russian infantry vedette, who was walking about, as it were just at my feet; I could have pitched a stone upon him from where I stood. The Russian outpost was on the top of a hill just opposite, down the side of which a rude path had been cut, by which the sentries were relieved. At noon when I went to post our vedette, I had great difficulty in preventing one of the men, a hot young Irishman, from firing upon the enemy's vedette. I could not make him understand that it was against all rules of civilised warfare to fire upon vedettes; he kept grumbling to himself all the way back, and as I endeavoured to make it plain to him he could only answer, "Arrah, sure now, and wouldn't there have been one less!" We remained here a couple of days, and the next night we shifted our position, encamping in a narrow ravine that was in the side of the hill, on which our outpost was placed. This night we were ordered to strike our tents at midnight; and as the evening was fine and quite warm, most of us took them down at sunset, packing them up and making all ready for the march, for we had a pretty good idea there was something in the wind, and that we should meet the Russians in the morning. Lying down in the open air we slept comfortably until midnight, when the word was quietly passed to "get up," fires were soon set agoing, and camp kettles boiling to prepare our early breakfast, and by a little after two we were all mounted and waiting for the order to advance. Just as the day began to break we moved off cautiously; and when the sun rose higher we threw out skirmishers and pushed forward, but could not see any sign of the enemy, and by 4 A.M. were by this sudden march right into the enemy's lines. We were now near to Aitodar, on the right of which a gentle ascent led to the enemy's position, our skirmishers still pressing forward extended away to the left, while the Sardinians advancing in a regular crowd of tirailleurs attempted to force a passage up the ascent and carry the heights; but the enemy getting two or three guns in position, their fire completely swept the path, and the attempt had to be abandoned. In the meanwhile we had pushed forward and up a slight ascent, and the enemy's skirmishers coming to the edge of the precipice, knelt down and took deliberate aim at us, but they had evidently even worse fire-arms than our own, for the shots all went wide of the mark. It now sounded the recall, and I being on the right and having the shortest distance to go over, walked my horse leisurely in, the path being intersected with holes, feeling perfectly sure there was no danger; but "Green Forage," as we called him, hung on to me for not galloping in. General De la Marmora was close by the village, and there the squadron joined him, all watching the proceedings of the Sardinians in their attempt to carry the position. We heard afterwards from spies and deserters that these were only sick and invalids who had shewn front, and that had we persevered we must have succeeded in gaining a footing on the plateau, and there have turned the Russian position. As it was, after the Bersaglieri had retired, the enemy turned his guns on the general and his staff, four shells coming whistling over our heads. The old general viewed the first three quite complacently, not taking the slightest notice of them; but the fourth falling and bursting in a small garden immediately behind us, was taken at last as a hint to go, he quietly remarking, what I understood to be, "Ah, they are getting the range at last," and gave the order for the whole party to retire; so withdrawing as suddenly as we had appeared, we marched straight back to Kamara, where we encamped for the night. This was the 23d, and just after we had got our tents pitched and entrenched, a regular storm of thunder and rain came down upon us, filling all the water-courses, and swelling the river to overflowing; but closing our tents securely we in a manner defied the storm, which, however, in and about Kadukoi, I afterwards heard, not only destroyed property, but horses; and even men were drowned in it. Our horses had the worst of it, trying, poor things, to turn their croups to the drifting rain, and shaking themselves now and again to throw off some of the water that was incessantly pouring down. And all the while the thunder rolled and the lightning flashed; and as peal after peal shook everything around, we nestled closer and closer in our cloaks, thankful that the pitiless rain could not reach us, and sorrowing for the Sardinians, whose *tentes d'abri* we feared were not substantial enough to keep off the soaking shower. These four days' campaigning delighted all of us, being quite a relief to our late encampment near the wild and dreary plateau around Sebastopol; for we had been moving about through a splendid part of the country, in a valley that from Tchergoum gradually widened into beautiful meadows sprinkled with trees, tinted glowingly with wild flowers, and nourished by streams, upon whose peaceful bosom all this beauty was reflected.

On the 24th we were joined by another squadron, and, leaving the Sardinians, marched towards Baidar, there to be attached to Omar Pasha and his Turks. Crossing the Tracter Bridge and glancing to the left at the little inn, which gives the name to the bridge, we emerged upon the Woronzoff Road, *en route* to our destination. This road is truly a magnificent one, and a wonderful example of art overcoming nature. Cut for many miles entirely out of the solid rock, and with a descent on one side of several hundred feet, it passes among scenery not to be surpassed, I should imagine, by any in Europe. On our left hand the mountain range rose abruptly but beautifully in the foliage with which it was clothed to the summit; while, on the right, the descent is still more grand in its awfulness. When gazing over the narrow parapet on that side of the road, you look for hundreds of feet down into an abyss, the bottom of which is hidden in the dark green grass and flowers, which also flourished on its sides. On reaching the pretty little Tartar village of Vahnoukta, we filed into a field to its left, and in regular lines took up a position; then dismounting, we picketed our horses, and pitched our tents alongside of them. Everything was agreeable here, water convenient, and forage to be had for the cutting, in some instances for the fetching; and with the exception of one day, when the Tartar broached the rum, and getting drunk drove his araba into a hole, and so hindered our getting them, rations were plentiful and good; so the life here was all that a soldier could desire, had it only been healthy. And this camp life was made doubly pleasant by our daily reconnaissances and foraging parties, which, taking us away from this picturesque spot, led us onwards over beautiful hills and through wooded paths shaded by lofty trees, until emerging from the thick wood, we found ourselves surrounded by the magnificent scenery so characteristic of this portion of the Crimea, where lofty hills, flowering valleys, and sparkling streams, are all mixed harmoniously together as if by enchantment. So striking is the scene, that when it first bursts upon your view you feel as if it is almost too grand to be natural, and must have been called into existence suddenly by some magician's wand. While contemplating all this wonderful scenery, visions would spring up, causing one's thoughts involuntarily to wander back to the days of Genghis Khan the Terrible, when he and his hosts of armed and savage Tartars inhabited this beautiful valley, which, when they returned from any of their successful expeditions, flushed with pride and conquest, to the abode of peace, must have caused them to feel still prouder and still happier. It is impossible that any description of mine can give an idea of such loveliness, or even of the sensation of delight which it caused. Possibly our treeless barren camp near Karrani may have enhanced to us the effect of a view which to any eyes must have been eminently attractive. I shall never forget the first sight I had of the valley of Baidar. I was the advanced guard; and marching unthinkingly along a shady path, I came suddenly upon it, and was held enthralled for several minutes. Behind was the road we had traversed, scarcely discernible amid the dark foliage of the chestnut trees, and before us for miles was stretched out the most lovely landscape, with its flowery meadows like large nosegays, sprinkled with trees and groves of surpassing beauty, and encircled by wood-clad heights; on in front were the roads through it, which wound over silvery brooks that ran murmuring, slow and musical, and through small green fields with wicker frame-like fences, on to the two red-roofed villages, which, embowered in trees, formed a ruby centre to the cluster of nature's emeralds in which they were set. The deep silence, however, rather marred the beauty of the landscape, which wanted the busy hum of human life to gladden the ear, the blue smoke curling lazily upwards from the rural chimneys to charm the eye, and the gladsome greeting of some rustic inhabitant, with his

"Pleasant morning, sirs," to enliven our march; but there were no living things but ourselves, save the cheerful lark, the musical thrush, and the happy blackbird, to give spirit to the scene,—all, while beautiful as a vision, was nearly as silent as a cemetery.

At times extending these pleasant expeditions, we would ride to the farther side of the valley, and up to the pass of Pharos, through the fortified gateway away over the crest, from whence could be viewed a still grander scene in that realm of wild reality; for down, far far below, was the blue heaving sea, whose billows and breakers, as they appeared from the height, were only the smallest of specks; and again, turning from the giddy sight and looking upwards, a sight as grand met our gaze; on either side crag towering above precipice, precipice over crag, to the clear blue sky, all interlaced with verdure, vines, and wild flowers, in a beauteous confusion that charmed the eye. But this scene never appeared so exquisite as it did one morning when, on patrol, we ascended the path and reached its summit just as the "gates of morning" opened; the golden sun, rising from the sea, flooded its waters with splendour, illuminating the gray summits of the rocky pinnacles with delicate rosy tints and purple shadows, while from below the cloud wreaths coming up from the Euxine drew a semi-transparent veil over the scene beneath as they sailed upwards, splitting upon rocks, and forming themselves into ever-changing fantastic shapes, while through the rents in the curtain could be seen now and again glimpses of rock and wave, tree and stream, sea and shore, beneath all, adding the last touch to the fairy-like scene. With Omar Pasha we did not eat the bread of idleness, for every day we took part in some expedition or another, and had always the post of honour given to us of the 10th Hussars; which, however, was only our due: we could not have allowed the Turks to lead the way. The first day after our arrival, a reconnaissance in force was made to the left of Baidar, where our squadron, extending in skirmishing order, crossed the valley, over hedges, ditches, rivers, and ravines,—whatever came in the way. The fields were remarkably small, and fenced in with wicker-work hedges, which our little Arabs hopped over with the greatest ease. The trees being very closely planted round the fields, from the thickness of the foliage it became a matter of impossibility to keep the left hand man in view, far less to align oneself with him. I being on the right of all, found myself in a short time moving along quite alone; but knowing that the remainder must be to my left, I only inclined a little in that direction, still gaining ground to the front. Keeping on in this way for about a quarter of an hour, I at last began to be afraid that the skirmishers must have been called in, and that I was, for aught I knew, right inside the enemy's advanced posts, which surmise I afterwards discovered was really the case. I now turned direct to the inward hand, and, putting my horse to a faster pace, overtook Tom Nolan, who, like myself, was lost, and had seen nothing of the remaining skirmishers.

The country we were now in was even more densely wooded than the other portions of the valley we had passed through, and we, that is, Tom and I, having no desire to be made prisoners or to get shot by dropping into an outlying Russian picket, put our horses into a smart gallop, and so crushed through every thicket, splashed through every stream, and leaped every hedge that came in our way. I once thought that we were done for; when, having crossed a small field, and nearly reached the farther hedge, the branches of the trees hanging so low that we could not perceive what was on the other side, we could dimly discern something white glistening through the leaves, and taking it for granted to be a road, we together pushed our horses at the leap, holding down our heads to save our eyes from the branches. Our little steeds went at it with a rush which carried us crashing through and over, when, to my dismay, I saw that it was a clear descent of some fifteen feet, into a dry watercourse, which we were tumbling into. I had just time to think that the horses would break their necks and we our legs, when we fell; but our hardy little Arabs, with cat-like instinct, dropped on all their four legs at once; certainly they went down on their knees, but only for a moment, and the next they were on their feet again, and scrambling up the other side of the ravine as if nothing particular had occurred. We had not gone much farther when we met with a round-faced laughing little Tartar, who, unlike the generality of his countrymen, had a pair of pleasant twinkling eyes, and an honest look withal, that carried conviction and trust along with it. From what he tried to convey by gestures, we understood that we were but a short distance from a Russian outpost, which was situated in the wood, and consisted, as far as we could make out, of twelve men and an officer, our Tartar friend holding up first his ten fingers, then two, and afterwards his clenched fist. Our only regret was that we had not a few more of our comrades with us, as our guide seemed both ready and willing to lead us on to surprise the picket; two of us, of course, could do nothing. So making the Tartar understand that we wished to be taken towards the village of Baidar, he at once agreed to escort us, and in a short time we could plainly hear the trumpet sounding the recall. A few minutes brought us to our party, who had been formed up and waiting for us for half an hour, and had begun to give us up, coming to the conclusion that we were captured. Tom and I being the last to come in, orders were now given to move off; but I first took the liberty of acquainting Captain Clarke of the Russian outpost in the wood, which, with the Tartar's assistance, there would be but little trouble in taking. He gave, however, no credence to the story. I had but little difficulty in persuading our Tartar to accompany us on our return; and when we got to where the remainder of the troops were, we found them comfortably dismounted, and bivouacking by the banks of the river. We soon undid our mess-tins and had dinner also, giving a good share to our new chum, who was quite at home in a short time. Then all mounting but him, we moved back to Vahnoukta, Ned, as he was re-christened, still accompanying us; and I may add that he proved a most valuable auxiliary in getting supplies of provender while we remained at Baidar. Whatever *we* required, that is, *our* tent, to which he particularly attached himself, whether it was *braten*, (fish,) or *yarmoota*, (eggs,) or *sud*, (milk,) Ned could always procure it from the villages about, and it was the same with anything else that we wanted. We had only to make him understand what it was, and he would get it; but he was obliged to do a great deal of his trading after hours, in the night, for fear of the Cossacks. He made us understand that these fellows would enter a cottage or house at any hour, search it all over, take whatever they fancied, and if they found any English or French money in the possession of the inmates, they would be made prisoners, and probably their habitations levelled with the ground. But for cruelty and oppression, the Cossacks were lambs in comparison with the Turks, by whom nothing was respected, whatever might be its value or utility; and wherever they went, lawless desolation marked their track. All through the valley, wherever a house stood, the Turks visited it and carried off whatever was portable, and what could not be taken was thrown down and broken. There was one cottage there, in which resided a Russian lady, whose property and privacy had been respected by both English and French. She had lived there unmolested ever since our occupation, with a couple of servants and her only child, an infant of only some ten months old. When the Turks came, she was advised to remove to Backtsheserai, where she would be safe from them, but unfortunately she did not follow this advice, the previous kind consideration of her enemies having made her too confident; and one night, about ten o'clock, she was summoned by a party of Turks, who, on her coming into the hall where they were, with the infant in her arms, demanded from her money or valuables. Tremblingly she tried to explain that she had never been so treated; that she had no money to give them, nor articles of value, and requested as a favour that they would leave the house, as their appearance frightened her boy. This appeal to their mercy, made by a mother with her tender child, which would have been responded to at once, and an apology made for intruding, by the people of any other civilised nation, was totally unheeded by these wretches, who, perceiving the love she had for her infant, seized upon the child, and with fierce gestures made her understand that if she did not accede to their demands, her child would be sacrificed. It was of no use for her to solemnly declare she had nothing to give, equally useless were her tears and entreaties to spare her boy; they murdered him before her eyes, and tossing the mangled body bleeding on the floor, left her to mourn over it. An hour afterwards our patrol was passing, and hearing sounds of distress coming from the chateau, went in, and there saw the poor mother frantically weeping over the corpse of her darling. The patrol followed the murderers, and had they overtaken them, I am positive that the mere fact of their being our allies would never have been thought of, but a signal vengeance taken at once on the dastardly Turks. An account of this affair was sent to Omar Pasha in the morning, but he only replied that it was not Turks who had done it; it must have been Russians disguised in Turkish uniforms, and so these ruffians escaped the fate they so richly deserved, but only for a time, I hope; justice is sometimes lame, but often all the surer.

On the evening of the third day of our stay at Vahnoukta, we were agreeably surprised to see two carts arrive; and in the rear of our tents there soon sprang up a couple of green tents, one of which we discovered to be a canteen, with a supply of nearly everything that we were most in need of. The proprietor of this, a Greek, was a gentlemanly kind of fellow, and jovial with all of us, while at the same time he was quite a puzzle to every one, differing from most whom we had come in contact with, for he never appeared to look after the interests of his canteen as he ought to do, appearing as it were above his shop, and leaving all to his two assistants, who received the money and delivered the articles. Otherwise the master was very sociable, and we got to like him immensely. He would stand outside and joke and drink with us, paying his share, and often a great deal more. One thing we remarked in particular, and that was his great fondness for shooting. Every morning he might be seen, gun in hand, strolling leisurely away in the direction of Baidar. Often we cautioned him that his fondness for sport might terminate fatally, should he chance to stray beyond the bounds, and fall into the hands of the Cossacks. But all this he laughed at, saying that his dogs— he had a fine pair of setters—could scent a dirty Cossack a mile away, and would always give him timely notice of their approach; so we let him go on, as we thought, in his foolhardiness. But the end came one morning, when a French escort, composed of a corporal and file of men, marched into our camp, shewed their authority, and proceeding to the canteen, made the two servants prisoners, and then waited patiently for the arrival of the proprietor. About midday he came back carelessly, whistling, with his dogs at his heels; but the moment he caught sight of the French escort sitting inside his tent, his face turned ghastly white, and his attempt at a smile made one feel ill to see it. Although I now knew him to be a spy, one who probably, had he not been detected, might have given information that would have brought the whole Russian army upon us some night, yet now that near and certain death was staring him in the face,—the sand in his glass fast falling through,—I could not help feeling pity for him. I even admired him. When recovering from the first shock of surprise, he, like a brave man, seemed at once to resign himself calmly to his fate. He completely exonerated his two servants, declaring that they knew nothing of him or his designs, and were in no way his accomplices. He was going to leave his dogs behind to our care, and we held them back, but the poor things howled so dreadfully when he was marched away, that he stopped and asked us to let them come with him, adding, "I may as well have something faithful with me, for the last few hours of my existence." He evidently knew his doom—had staked all on the throw—his life against lucre, and having lost, made up his mind to his fate. He was marched off at once to the French head-quarters, and the following morning he was hung. The canteen and its contents by some, to us unaccountable, mode of reasoning, was given over to the Turks, who profess not to drink liquors nor to consume pork, and who had never spent a kopeck there, in preference to us, whom the poor spy, as he left, had desired should be his executors,—we who did profess to be partial to liquors, and had a liking for hams, to say nothing of what regular customers we had been, which alone should have given us a claim to the contents of the canteen. But all this was overruled, and the Bono Johnnies inherited everything, to our extreme dissatisfaction. Certainly in respect of plunder of any kind, we never had any opportunity, and this may perhaps partly account for the fact that Englishmen can never forage half so well as Frenchmen: they, being professed pillagers, can on a campaign live where we should starve. This state of things Mickey Free mourned in his day when he sang—

"Odds—think what a blunder, they wont let us plunder,
Though the convents invite us to rob them, 'tis clear;
And though each little village just cries, Come and pillage,
Yet we leave all the mutton behind for Mounseer."

Our sojourn among the Osmanlis was drawing to a close. The ground on which we were encamped was not only very damp and unhealthy, but being situated in the centre of the Turkish lines, where every description of filth and dirt is allowed to accumulate, disease, strong and deadly, broke out among us. One of the first victims was Captain Bowles, one of the best, if not the very best of our officers; who, after only a few hours' illness, expired at twenty minutes past eleven o'clock on the morning of the 25th of June, universally and justly regretted by every man in the regiment. He was the model of a cavalry officer, combining with the polite gallantry of a gentleman, all the zeal, activity, talent, and good sense so necessary to his profession. He was buried beneath two large wide-spreading chestnut trees on the right of our camp-ground, a pretty secluded spot, where a gentle rippling brook runs by the foot of his grave. As we performed the last solemn duties, and heard the beautiful service for the dead read over him, and fired the three farewell volleys over his remains, and took a last look at him as he lay uncoffined, Wolfe's beautiful lines on the death of Sir John Moore involuntarily recurred to me—

> " Little he'll reck if they let him sleep on
> In the grave where a Briton has laid him." *

On the 30th our veterinary surgeon, Siddell, died, and his remains were laid beside those of Captain Bowles, and by this time the cholera was carrying off our men by twenties; not a day passed but there were fatigue parties digging graves, and always several tenants waiting to occupy them. What rendered the sickness more appalling was its shortness, only a few hours generally elapsing after the seizure until death ensued: thus many cases proved fatal, when, if there had been time to send the men to Balaklava for a change of air, they might have recovered. This cholera seemed to be of a different kind to what I had seen in India: there were no cramps with this, but

* We had no sooner returned to Balaklava than the Turks disinterred the bodies of Captain Bowles and Mr Siddell. Intimation of the desecration of their graves reached us on the 8th of July, and Corporal Hauffe was despatched at once with some Turks in our service, to see if it was correct; and if so, to bury the bodies again. He discovered that it was indeed a sad reality: there were the bodies of our two officers ruthlessly torn from their graves, in the expectation of finding some jewellery. After carefully reinterring them the party returned.

a desponding helplessness seemed to overcome the victims, and make them a willing prey to its influence. I only saw one fight against the disease. He would not lie down, but kept walking about, and when getting too weak to do this, he made a couple of men drag him up and down the tent, and he recovered. Poor Davies, who had been talking two nights before with some of us, as to what had best be done when a person was taken with cholera, remarked, "I hope if ever I catch it that somebody will bring me a bottle of brandy : *that* will cure me if anything will." One present then said, "Well, Bill, I'll make this agreement with you,—should I be taken sick you will bring me a bottle, and should a similar misfortune befall you I'll do it for you." To this proposal Davies heartily agreed; and on the 29th June, when Alick heard that Sergeant-Major Davies had caught the cholera, and was then in the hospital tent, he got a bottle of the best Coguac which could be procured, and took it to him, but no persuasion could prevail on him to taste it. He would eat or drink nothing but what the doctor prescribed for him, and so was, as it were, anticipating the death which came a few hours afterwards. He also lies at Vahnoukta, poor fellow, in a picturesque spot near the village. Then there was Farrier Jones, who before going down to hospital went to his troop sergeant-major's tent, and requested him to draw all the money he had out of the Savings' Bank,—it was about £10,—and he desired that after his man was paid thirty shillings out of it, the remainder should be sent to his mother, for he said, "She wants it badly, and so will get it at once; if I left it till to-morrow, she would not get it for months;"* adding, that his mother was to have all that he died possessed of as well. I tried at the time to make him take a less gloomy view of the illness coming on him, but it was useless, and before he had been half an hour in hospital he was so ill that he could not sign the requisition which I had made out —being troop-clerk—to withdraw his money; in fact, Nolan, who took it down for signature, at Jones's request, signed "John Jones" at the bottom of the paper for him. He died that night, and his man whom he was so anxious to pay, never lived to receive the money. A curious and melancholy case was theirs. Jamie Lawler—that was his man's name—was beside Jones when he died, and asked in my hearing, "I wonder whose turn it will be next?" *It was his own;* before morning he was an inmate of the hospital, and when I and a fatigue party were digging a grave for the poor farrier, a message came to make it large enough for two, as Jamie Lawler was dead also. But this could not last long.

On the 3d of July our hospital returns shewed one hundred and sixty-one sick, out of our strength of six hundred and seventy-six, or one man in every five struck down by disease; so the authorities could not help perceiving that if we remained among the Turks, there would be but very few to ration in a month's time. But it must

---

* When a man dies in the army, an inventory of his kit is taken, and then it is sold. The paymaster takes the money and credits it first to the public. The secretary for war in a month or two gets to know the circumstances, and tells the deceased soldier's friends that there is so much money, which they can have by applying for it. Money drawn from the Savings' Bank goes at once to them.

not be imagined that the one hundred and sixty-one represented all the sick. There were as many more who would not succumb to the sickness, and kept crawling about outside, laughing and making light of the disease which they felt was daily weakening them. Colonel Wilkie was as bad as any one. I have seen him obliged to go off parade on more than one occasion; yet he remained at his post, never being a day on the sick list; and this noble example was if anything too well followed; many only going to hospital in the last extremity, which doubtless hindered their last chance of cure.

It was on the morning of the 5th of July that the route came for us to retire. The regiment was all out on a foraging expedition down to the right of the valley of Baidar, and we were passing through a long narrow defile between two hills, when the trumpet sounded " Threes about,"—" Trot." I remember that my first thought was that we had been cut off by the enemy; for I had just been remarking to the man on my left, how well the place was adapted for an ambuscade, that a few infantry on the heights, and a small party at the entrance of the gorge, could have slaughtered us all quite comfortably without our being able to prevent it in the least. So the trumpet sounding the retire, just appeared to confirm my anticipations, and I could not help reminding those around me, when we went about, to see that their sword knots were secure.*
We got safe through the defile, and were spanking home at a tremendous pace, all wondering what could be in the

---

* We only took swords with us on foraging expeditions,—no arms, the Turks being supposed to throw out covering parties for us.

wind; and when we got into camp, we found it was the route, and the men left behind were in a regular bustle, striking tents, saddling horses, and packing up. We, of course, added to the turmoil, most of our things being at sixes and sevens, having been thrown here, there, and everywhere by the others as they struck the tents. But an hour saw us all straight and mounted, with what stores we could bring away in a couple of *arabas*, and what we could not was destroyed. It was laughable to hear the regret expressed by nearly all on seeing a puncheon of ration rum stove in and spilt on the ground. Anthony, who was riding by my side, was inveighing against this sin and waste. I was explaining how much better it was to do this than to leave it to fall into the hands of the enemy, when he indignantly broke in with, " Ugh, to the devil wid yees; wouldn't it now be much asier and more economical to let us all fill our water-choggles, when not a drop would have been wasted; and now see to it!" On my reminding him that a few would never get into Balaklava if his suggestion were adopted, he rejoined, " Ah—and what if they didn't? Even that would not be so bad as throwing away the gifts of Providence in this manner. As it is, I shouldn't wonder but we are all dead of the cholera by the time we get home; and upon my word I hope that they who ordered the rum to be spilt will march into Karrani croakers, which would only be a fitting judgment for such extravagance." "Why, Pat," said one behind, "you are as bad as poor Dennis, who used to declare that 'some morning he would wake up and find himself a corpse.'" " Troth, and didn't the poor fellow do that same," he replied. This was too much for our risible faculties, and a burst of laughter from all around made him aware that he had made a fitting sequel to a story that had caused many a grin at Dennis's expense, although dead and gone, poor fellow. And in this way—laughing, chatting, and making fun of each other—we rode away from Vahnoukta, and reached our old lines at Karrani about five in the evening, without further hindrance or accident, barring to Nobby Pearce, whose thumb No. 3 of D troop took such a decided fancy to by the way that he actually bit it off. So ended our seventeen days' ramble with the Sardinians and Turks by the Balbec and in the Baidar valley.

CHAPTER TWELFTH.

Sebastopol and the Commissariat.

LOOKING back now at those days in the Crimea, six weeks appears a very short pace in the march of Time; and I could almost fancy our return to Karrani from Baidar valley, and the battle of the Tchernaya on the 24th of August, to be two events following one day after the other, instead of so many weeks apart. An attack was expected about this time, as bodies of troops had for days been observed massing themselves along the Mackenzie heights to our right; so, when at daybreak we heard the distant sound of musketry and the louder reports of cannon, and saw the smoke rising slowly over all, we paid very little attention, taking it as a matter of course. We had partly unsaddled and remained stationary, awaiting the order to turn out, which we knew would be sure to come at last, and then turned our attention steadily to the breakfast that was being got ready. As soon as this important affair was over, we began to stir ourselves; and seeing a bustle among the 1st Dragoon Guards and the Carabineers in the valley beyond Kadukoi, where horsemen were galloping in haste to and fro, and troops saddling quickly, we did not wait for the order to turn out, but got ready and mounted in anticipation. When the order came, we moved off at once down the hill, turning towards the left, crossing it past where the Army Works Corps was encamped, and came out into the Balaklava valley by the French watering-place. We had got about half a mile away, when Sergeant-Major Rickards, coming up to his man, remarked, "That blockhead Keep actually turned out without his carbine!" What more he was going to observe regarding Keep remains among the many things unsaid, for, looking at Riley,* he burst out, "I'll be hanged if you have got yours either!" Such was the case; his man Simon was no better than Johnny Keep. It would have been thought nothing extraordinary in him had he turned out without his saddle: the only way he could cause surprise was by turning out all right. This Keep was certainly the most curiously-formed dragoon ever seen: looking at him as a whole, he appeared as if he had been made up in dame Nature's workshop of all the odds and ends that had fallen under the bench. She had certainly been no ways grudging in respect of his head or feet: the latter it is impossible to describe, further than that they were large and without form: imagine a monster pair of wallets, well packed, and you will have a faint idea of his boots when his feet were cased in them. From these projected upwards a couple of supports, which, like everything else about him, were inverted, the thickest parts being at the bottom and tapering upwards, not gradually, but in

* Poor fellow, since I wrote these lines, he was found dead in his tent on the 27th of May.

P

sudden sinuosities; and while one leg was short, the other was shorter, differing in this respect from his arms, these being one long and the other longer, and the extremity of each adorned by a huge paw with tendril-like digits. His body might be compared to a sack of sawdust badly tied up, out of which emerged a short, thick neck: but short as this was, there was still an inequality, the right side being much shorter than the left; yet, as if to accommodate this peculiarity, the right shoulder rose sympathisingly to meet it; and when Johnny stood at ease, his head rested lovingly upon his shoulder. On the other hand, the left shoulder was as much down in the world as the other was up, and this gave him when walking a crab-like appearance of going sideways. His head, however, added more to his remarkable appearance than anything else, being, as I have said, a large one, and looking as if at some time or other it had been much larger, and was spoke-shaved roughly down without regard to shape, putting one in mind of a lot of holes and corners knocked together. His eyes certainly did not look crossways into each other, but they had a repugnance to turn in the same direction, so, while one cast downward carefully watched the left shoulder, the other stood sentinel on the right. His mouth was only a gap in his face, where food of every description instantly disappeared, closing with a snap after each mouthful, and leaving you to imagine that it shut with a spring, and would never open again. Add to all this a bushy pair of whiskers, which were so far ornamental that they partly covered the many ruts in his face, and therefore he had to be very thankful for them. Who enlisted Johnny in the first place, and what doctor passed him for the service, was never known; all we knew was, that he was transferred from the 11th Hussars to ours; and that as soon as he joined the depôt at Maidstone, he was sent out by the first draft to India. We certainly heard a rumour that Lord C—— had boasted that any man, who was twelve months in the 11th, however deformed, short of being a cripple, would be made smart and intelligent by his system of drill, and so Keep, having been caught in some wild part of the Yorkshire wolds, had been sent for his lordship to experiment upon. Rumour further said, that the first time his lordship saw him on parade he, the Colonel, fainted; and when, on coming round, he inquired what *it* was he had seen in the ranks, he was informed *it* was a private soldier, now belonging to his regiment, which caused him nearly to swoon away again, and he was only able to articulate, "Send for him." When Johnny was marched up left in front as usual, his lordship said to him with a deep sigh, "Well, Keep, how you got here, I do not know; but I do care, for one thing is certain, either you or I must leave the regiment; which is it to be?" "Well, my lord," Keep is said to have answered, "I have been in it the shortest time; I'll go to the 10th,"—and so *we* got him.

But I have wandered far away from the Crimea, and must return to Riley, who was sent back after Keep, also for his carbine. When we got on the plain, we pressed forward at an increased pace, hearing, as we passed across the valley, where once "rode the Six

Hundred," the increasing din of the battle then raging. To our left, on the crest of the rising ground, the white tents of the French shewed prettily out against the dark side of the hill, and farther on in front was the trim and tasteful camp of the Sardinians, made of branches and stems of trees neatly interwoven; but the occupants of both tents and huts of green boughs are yet further in front, fighting for life and victory. Still pressing on, we reach the brow of the eminence overlooking Kamara, and behind this dismount, eagerly wishing and waiting for the words to come, "Mount, and forward ;" while from both sides of the Tchernaya can be seen the puff, puffs from the rifles; and the ringing tone of the bullets comes clear, mixed with the shrieking sounds of rushing shells, as they cut through the air and alight a short distance in front of us. But the great struggle was over, and the numbers of dead and dying shewed where the fight had been severest and the loss heaviest. Beside the aqueduct, on both sides, they lay in heaps like "fallen grain,"—French, Sardinians, and Muscovs; and farther on in a narrow gorge between two dwarf hills, had evidently raged the hottest part of the fight; for the dead appeared as if they had fallen by ranks at regular intervals. The combat was virtually over, and the enemy, finding himself completely foiled and beaten back, was retiring, and there might now be a chance for the cavalry to avenge Balaklava. So evidently thought the Sardinian General, for the word was given for us and the 12th Lancers, to mount and move off to the front in pursuit. When the command was given, " Advance in columns of troops from the right of squadrons," all of us thought that the coveted opportunity had arrived at last. Blake, who was riding on the left front of me, evidently thought that some of us might not come back, for he turned deliberately round, as we were about to move off, and called out to me, I being on the right of the rear rank, " Willie, there's three sovereigns in my *bhonno*-coat pocket, which I left in the tent." Of course I understood at once that he thus made me his sole legatee, should anything happen to him ; but I replied, "Nonsense, Joe; we will first drive these chaps on, and then we'll spend some of your money tonight, when we return to Karrani." And my surmise proved the correct one, for the 12th, who were in front of us, had just moved off, when General Pelissier drove up in his little low phaeton, drawn by four greys, surrounded by his usual cavalry escort, and assuming the command, he countermanded our pursuit, and gave orders that the bridge should be retaken. Then followed the most sanguinary conflict of the day. The Zouaves, swarming down through the narrow gorge I spoke of, drove the Russians back again, and retook the bridge. Meanwhile, a battery of English artillery fired several shots after the retreating enemy, while, from both sides of the Tchernaya, small puffs of smoke could be seen issuing from behind every kind of cover, from bush and stone, shewing the position of our skirmishers and those of our enemy's. By noon the enemy, forming his battalions into close column, retired sulkily up the mountain to his fastnesses, there to ruminate on this his third and last unsuccessful attempt to drive the allies into the sea. I was greatly surprised at this time by the fortitude shewn by a Russian prisoner, who was brought in wounded in the arm by a musket ball. The limb hung helplessly at his side, and the doctors perceived at once that amputation must be performed. On being informed of this decision, he carelessly replied in Russ that they were to do as they liked, and stood perfectly unconcerned, smoking a short pipe, while his arm was cut off at the shoulder. A boy, of about fifteen years of age, and said to be his son, had remained on the field with his father, and so was taken prisoner with him, and the poor little fellow appeared to suffer most while the operation was performed. The dismembered limb was at once buried, while the two Russians, father and son, were placed in an ambulance, and sent to the rear. A day or two afterwards, a party was sent on fatigue to disinter the arm, to settle an argument which had arisen among the surgeons, as to whether it ought to have been amputated where it was—at the shoulder—or lower down. But I never heard what decision they came to; and after it was performed it seemed very little matter which way would have been the right one. The following day, having come across a Sardinian pony, which had followed our horses up from the French watering-place, I took charge of him, and picketing him at the back of my tent, found him afterwards of great service. He was as hard as nails, and could undergo an immense deal of fatigue, although not over eleven hands high. Eventually he got rather saucy and opinionated, and would only go up to the front by one particular road. This way he could be persuaded to gallop, but he would not even walk in any other direction. The same day (the 25th) that I found him, he carried my troop sergeant-major (Rickards) all over the Tchernaya battle-field, while I went up on the 26th. Far more able pens than mine have described that eventful day, so I will not trouble the reader with any account of what I then saw and felt. I may mention, however, that it was probably a fortunate matter for us after all, that General Pelissier had not allowed the cavalry to charge the day before, for I could now perceive that the enemy had his guns well placed to sweep the plain over which we must have advanced; and in the steep and wooded ascent of the other side of the Tchernaya, cavalry would not have been able to act effectually, whilst they must have suffered severely. On the other hand, it appeared that there was not much generalship displayed in his ordering the bridge to be retaken, for that being the only road for the enemy to retreat by, he could, as General Marmora did do, allow only as many to come across as he could easily destroy, this being one of the principles of war, and it was strange that he did not seize upon the opportunity. Days continued to follow days, weeks to follow weeks, and months months, and men began again to talk about another assault upon Sebastopol; but the day was not mentioned, we having gained experience from the mishap of the 18th of June; and so both the hour and the day were kept secret. The fire had increased perceptibly upon the 6th and 7th of September, and upon the 8th it was doubtless a *feu d'enfer*, as Menschikoff is said to have termed it, which gave us an idea that the hour and the day had come.

We remained all ready saddled to turn out, and about ten o'clock I was despatched with an order to Major Benson of the 17th Lancers for cavalry to patrol on all the roads to the front, and allow no one to pass to the front or rear, more especially camp followers. This precaution prevented any intimation of the intended attack being conveyed to the enemy. Precisely at 12 noon the cannonade ceased, and the attack was made; but, as is well known, it was not until the morning of the 9th that we were aware that victory had followed that attack. On that day a squadron of ours was sent up to the town as an escort, and then we had a good look at the Redan and Malakoff, from the summits of which the English and French flags were flying. But the pleasure of success was greatly modified by seeing scores upon scores of our fellow-creatures lying in heaps around these earthen mounds of death. And so close did they lie, that even at twenty yards from them it was an impossibility, as we followed one another in single file, to prevent our horses from treading upon the dead bodies. Looking at the price paid for the victory greatly diminishes its value. Gazing on the dead lying as they fell, every countenance inflamed by passion, the spirit leaving its impress on the clay, as it passed away in the deadly fight—looking, I say, upon this silent but terrible testimony, the thought would arise, perhaps war is but a poor thing after all—a little glory, a little triumph for the survivors; but this is poor gilding to the ghastly and touching sight before us. And while the news of victory caused illuminations, bonfires, and fetes in England, it also brought sorrow, and woe, and desolation to many a hearth and home. On the 10th I rode about by myself on my Sardinian pony, and by that time most of the dead had been removed and buried in large pits by thirties, but in the Redan a few Russian bodies still lay. By one of the embrasures a Russian in his long gray coat stood, apparently still alive and looking out; but my touch on the shoulder caused the body to fall backwards nearly into my arms.* This startled me so, that I involuntarily allowed it to fall; but the next moment I felt a twinge of remorse at not having caught it and let it down gently to the ground. His face was young, fair, and handsome, and death had evidently been instantaneous; his features, differing in this from all others I had observed, looked as calm as if he had been asleep. There were plenty of guns, bayonets, &c., strewed around, so that few of us went up there without bringing away some souvenir of the visit from the Redan or Malakoff. It was laughable to see how jealously and carefully Englishmen would carry off an old shako or pouch-belt, a bayonet or musket, not for its intrinsic value to himself, but for the store which he knew his friends at home would set by those articles, sent by a brother, or cousin, or uncle. The French now began to plunder the city, which they did in a style too complete for any but those celebrated campaigners to attempt. It was not only the large fish that came to their net which they seized upon, but they collared all the smaller fry that they saw drop into the nets of others. It was their peculiar privi-

* I noticed afterwards that it had been supported by the slope of the earthwork.

lege to sack the town, and no one else was allowed even to look on. How comical they looked, and how amusing it was to watch them as they came out with their different descriptions of booty!—some staggering under four-post bedsteads or large mirrors, which they had to lay down every fifty yards, and which nobody ever could be brought to purchase; while others, who confined themselves exclusively to the fine arts, took nothing but paintings, unless perhaps plate. Rough enough dealers were most of those whom I saw, but they were not hard to bargain with—a few francs would purchase anything they had. Round about Sebastopol three cordons of cavalry were drawn, and although any men of our army were allowed to pass, yet they had to give up whatever they had bought from the French, or secured by their own predatory inclinations. Therefore it was better to allow the Frenchmen to get past these three lines with their booty ere you attempted to become a purchaser, otherwise you might have the pleasure of getting your purchases taken from you, and of seeing the vendor walk deliberately up and repossess himself of the article.

Sergeant-major Laker being invalided home in the month of October, I was selected to fill his situation on the commissariat, which was to look after the rations and forage for the regiment; and for a few weeks it was a much easier appointment than the usual allotment of main-guards and outlying pickets. In owning this I am aware that I differ from many who, having staff appointments, are always crying and making a poor mouth about the hardships they have to endure, solemnly declaring to all they come in contact with that they are fagged to death, and, what with want of food and rest, they cannot and will not stand it much longer, assuring the listeners that they would greatly prefer to be at their duty. For my part I will own the truth: I always found a staff berth far easier than being at my own duty. On this occasion I discovered that being attached to the commissariat was not half a bad appointment, and so made much of it; the clerks were all a jolly set of fellows, and the few weeks I was on the duty passed very pleasantly. There was one great swell among them of the name of Turbot, who properly belonged to the artillery commissariat. Many can still remember his buckish style of dressing, and his always riding about in top-boots, with a hunting-whip in his hand. In conversation he could talk of nothing but the horse-racing and hunting he had had in Queen's County, or the beautiful women who at one time or other had been fascinated by him—most of us knowing, all the time he was relating these adventures, that the only hunting he had ever done was still-hunting, and the "foine craytures" he had bewitched could be only Biddy the housemaid, or Molly the cook—for Turbot had been one of the Irish constabulary. These traits of character were, however, very amusing, and were made use of by the other commissariat clerks, who liked no fun better than to trot out "Count Fathom," as we had christened him. I have already mentioned that there were some Greek girls who still remained at Karrani, and to one of these, named Theresa, Turbot was paying most devoted attention. She was certainly a very fine-looking girl, tall, and a good figure; and Turbot was never tired of singing her praises. One night Jack Blythe proposed that he and I should make a call upon Miss Theresa, and have a talk with her, so arranging as to be there when Turbot paid his customary evening visit. A few inquiries well put made us aware that he paid his visit about seven o'clock; so, dressed in mufti, we sauntered up in the direction of Karrani about six P.M. one fine afternoon. We reached the village all right, and very soon discovered the abode of Turbot's lady-love, when, knocking at the door and informing the fair Greek that we had brought plenty of rum with us, we were at once admitted. We soon made ourselves quite at home, there being an old lady and two young ones besides Theresa who resided in the domicile. Hot water, sugar, a bit of lemon, and the rum, were soon mixed and steaming on the table; and so, drinking and smoking—for the fair Greeks enjoyed a cigarette—and listening to a Greek song, which, although we understood not the words, sounded very musically, the time fled and the hour came when Turbot must arrive. We were just in the height of our enjoyment when a rap-tap at the door intimated that we were about to have an addition to our company. It was Turbot; and were I to live to the age of Methuselah, I should never forget the look of astonishment and horror with which he eyed us. We could see him perceptibly rising on the tips of the toes of his top-boots; and not recognising us in the dark, uncertain twilight, he demanded, with the air of a general officer, "Pray, what is your business here?" I simply replied, "Pleasure, my dear fellow, pleasure. Having heard inadvertently that you had some pretty birds caged here, we came up just to have a look through the wires, but the attraction proving too great for our sensitive natures, we passed through the portals to join them in their imprisonment, and were just hearing one sing when"—— I was about to add, "you spoilt our harmony;" but he burst in, not yet recognising us—" Are you fellows aware that you are speaking to a commissioned officer, to an assistant-commissary-general? Begone, both of you, this instant, or I will call in the provost-marshal,* and have you made prisoners!" At this outburst Blythe broke out into a hearty laugh, saying, "Bravo! Turbot, my boy!—stick to that, and only get Mr Cruikshank and Sir W. Codrington to believe it, and then possibly you may get others to forget that while at one time you may have made a very efficient and trustworthy *peeler*, you are now only one of the Q. H. B.'s, which, being interpreted, is Queen's Hard Bargains. However, my boy, you may depend upon it that everybody will know your ambitious ideas by to-morrow!" Finding that he was known, he endeavoured by a little coaxing to get rid of us; but we assured him that we were far too comfortable to think of going away yet from our fair friends, and advised that, as he was the only miserable person in the company, he had better go himself. At this proposition, Theresa, who was getting extremely good-natured with the rum and water, added her vote to the sentence of banishment by saying, "Go, go!" This was the unkindest cut of all, and poor Turbot un-

* Sergeant Elliot, of the 12th Lancers, assistant to the provost-marshal, lived a few doors from where we were.

doubtedly thought so, for, sitting down on a chair, he apostrophised the fair and false one, groaning out, " Oh, Theresa, Theresa! I've gave ye mate, I've gave ye drink —bought ye silks and satins, and jewellery for your hair —and now yees tell me to *go!* Och! I'll shoot myself! I will—I will!" As he appeared to take on so dreadfully, we, out of compassion, got up, and saying good-bye, left "Poll and her partner Joe" to make it up as best they could.

There was another celebrity who for a long time used to give the commissariat a call twice or thrice a week; this was the great O'F——, our interpreter. He was what is termed in the army "a nice man"—that is, one who, while keeping a particularly sharp look-out for Number One, is still most anxious to make every other believe, at the same time, that all he does is for the benefit of his fellow-creatures—one who seems to have a smile and a pleasant word for everybody, but who would not go an inch out of his way to do a kindness. O'F—— was, I heard, originally brought up as a Roman Catholic, but thinking that he could get on better in the world as a convert, turned Protestant. He then had to leave Ireland, and made tracks to Liverpool, where, putting on the appearance of a martyr, he very soon ingratiated himself with some of the religious folk in that town, who got him appointed as teacher in a school. There, however, he misconducted himself so grossly that it could not possibly be overlooked, and Mr O'F—— was obliged to fly. Enlisting, then, into the — Foot, he marched with his regiment for the East in 1854, and landed at Varna, when, by the help of his education, a particular aptitude for languages, and an immense amount of assurance, he brought himself into notice; and when we arrived in the Crimea he was appointed interpreter for our Turks, a number of whom were attached to the regiment.* O'F——, however, in his letters home, represented that he held the position of confidential interpreter to Lord Raglan. Of this there was no doubt, as some well-meaning friend published a letter in which it was stated. This, then, was he whom we styled the great O'F——, and who used to honour the commissariat clerks two or three nights a week, by calling incidentally, and having a glass and a game at cards with them. One night, while he was deeply engaged with Mannion and Naylin in a game at "twenty-fives," Jack Blythe slipped out of the tent, took the saddle and bridle off O'F——'s horse and hid them, and tied the horse up at the rear. When he thought it time to go home, we all turned out to bid him good-night, and then began the spree, O'F—— swearing that some one had stolen his horse, saddle, and bridle, while we all declared he must have walked down. By a good deal of persuasion we made him believe at last that he must really have walked down; and away he went up the hill; but the following morning he discovered that

* A true description of the O'F—— class is given by a writer in *Blackwood* for July, who says, "There are two classes of people not a little thought of and even caressed in society, and for whom I have ever felt a very humble estimate—the men who play all manner of games, and the men who speak several languages. I begin with the latter, and declare that, after a somewhat varied experience of life, I never met a linguist that was above a third-rate man; and I go further, and aver, that I never chanced upon a really able man who had the talent for languages."

the horse was gone, and again making his way down to the commissariat, offered a reward of a sovereign if it could be found for him. As he was one who was noted for looking at money a long time before he parted with it, and was always willing enough to do the consuming part of bottles of wine, which were purchased by clubbing round, but had never been known to pay his share, the money was taken from him without any compunction, and he was then shewn his horse, saddle, and bridle all safe. The money was spent as a matter of course, and he was invited to share in the purchase, but he was so nettled at having to pay for the first time in his life, that he refused to partake, and in high dudgeon rode off; and after this he also shied the Light Brigade. I have learned since, that when peace was proclaimed, he changed direction again, and took up his abode in Edinburgh, where he prevailed upon some good-natured people to keep him at college for two or three terms, until he was considered fit to preach, and then he was sent out as a missionary, to propagate the gospel among the Turks. Not many converts will the great O'F—— make, I fear.

Although fighting was daily going on, we had amusement as well. At times a friendly match at cricket was knocked up between the two Elevens of different regiments, and an exciting game was sure to ensue, the bowling and batting being as carefully watched and criticised as if the game was being played at Lord's, and as if there were not another and a greater game going on, where other balls than cricket, thrown by 36 and 64-pounders, were bowled down between the trenches and Sebastopol. There were also horse-races at Karrani, and theatrical entertainments up at the Naval Brigade and elsewhere. As may be expected, the stage and dresses and scenery were of the most primitive description, while tall grenadiers and stalwart dragoons were the Desdemonas and Ophelias of the dramas. But this was nothing new to us Indians, who for years had been accustomed to see the female parts taken by smooth-faced or close-shaven specimens of the opposite sex. I may say likewise that it has been my lot to witness, both before and since, many female performers who sustained their parts in different pieces much worse than those *gentlemen* I saw as *ladies* on the boards of our little Drury in Kirkee. There are many now, doubtless, who lay in Poonah in the years 1852-4 who will endorse my opinion, if they recall to their memories the finished acting of Private O'Niel of the 3d Bombay Fusiliers, on whom a shawl, gown, and crinoline seemed to fit not unbecomingly, and who, in features and action, thoroughly personated a woman. But I must own, at the same time, that their appearance behind the scenes sent to the winds all one's ideas of their fine acting and the affecting tale they had told so well but a few minutes previously; for there was to be seen the gentle Fanny sitting comfortably with a short black pipe in her cheek, or the neglected and wayworn Maid of the Mill imbibing a pot of porter with gusto. So time did not fly with leaden wings: our days were so regular, and our dinners also, that we cared very little about peace. What we were most anxious for was a regular pitched battle, and used often to wonder how it was that we had allowed the Russians thrice to attack us in force, each attempt being so well planned and well timed that it would have been successful but for the dogged courage and determination of our men, and yet we had never once returned the compliment by attempting to force their position. Surely, thought we—ignorantly perhaps—there must be one vulnerable point in the enemy's defensive armour, one link not sufficiently tempered, which a vigorous stroke would break. But no! with parks of artillery, thousands of cavalry, and hundreds of thousands of infantry, the allies steadily remained in front of Sebastopol, keeping up certainly a destructive fire upon the place, but in no other way assuming the offensive or annoying the enemy, except by sending off one expedition to Kertch, which was successful, and one to Eupatoria, which was for no purpose whatever, we supposed, but to get rid of Omar Pasha. There is one thing to be remarked, however,—the enemy had his advanced posts pushed much farther out than ours were; had we adopted similar precautions, a surprise, as at Inkermann, would never have occurred. It is requisite for security that an army should at all times have its advanced posts placed as far as possible to the front, when any attack in force could be met by a superior one, as soon as it was discovered on what point the real force of the attack was to be made. Where a good position has been taken up, and the enemy is in front and ready to attack, there may not be the same opportunity to place the outposts at a distance: but even then it becomes all the more imperative to have the outlying pickets pushed as far towards the enemy as possible, with supports proportionate to the strength and vicinity of the enemy. Had this been carried out, the attack on the 5th of November would have proved a miserable failure. And another lesson is given us by what happened the other day in Virginia, at Spotsylvania Court-house, when a division of the Federals, creeping cautiously forward at four A.M. on the morning of the third day's battle, never fired a shot until they were close upon the batteries, and then, with a shout and a rush, were in among the Confederates, and captured 4000 prisoners, several pieces of cannon, and two generals almost while at their breakfast. In India, during the mutiny, another example was given us by Major-General Windham, who, by neglecting the usual precaution of placing his pickets, allowed Tantia Topee (I think it was) to catch him and his force comfortably napping, the first intimation they received being the enemy's cannon-balls hopping through and over their tents, and they barely managed to escape with their lives, losing guns, tents, and equipage. The greater portion of these, however, were retaken shortly afterwards by Sir Colin Campbell, a more energetic and practical general. But at these things we could only guess and wonder. So little is really known of what is going on out of one's own regiment, that we learned more about the doings of the allied army from home papers than from what we either heard or saw, unless we were really ourselves engaged in the enterprise.

CHAPTER THIRTEENTH.

The First Anniversary of Balaklava.

"IT is an ill wind that blows nobody good," and had it not been for the Balaklava charge, the 10th Hussars would have remained in India, for simultaneously with the news of that mismanaged affair came the order for us to proceed immediately overland to the seat of war.

The first and unsuccessful assault, the affair of Tchourgoum, the battle of the Tchernaya, and the last assault and fall of Sebastopol, had followed rapidly in succession; and almost, as it were, before we were aware of it, the 25th of October was drawing near, the first anniversary of that disastrous charge,—disastrous only in its immediate results, for it added fresh glory to that name which the British cavalry have always retained for daring and determined courage. On the morning of the 25th, as I looked from the entrance of my tent, I could not prevent my thoughts from reverting to that eventful day twelve months back; for before me lay the Valley of Death. Imagination completed the outline by one of the most prominent of her laws, that "a likeness in part tends to become a likeness of the whole;" therefore as I gazed and gazed on, my imagination repeopled the valley with the actors in the tragic strife.

The cavalry standing at their pickets, in front were the four redoubts occupied by the Turks on a range of low hills, crossing the plain from beneath the heights of the plateau to the opposite ridge near the village of Kamara. The Turks are lying lazily smoking around the guns, all so quiet—too quiet—it was only the lull before the storm, which speedily burst. Dark masses can be seen debouching suddenly from my right, but far in front are the Russian guns on the eminences, and in the valley commences a cannonade on the outposts held by the Turks. The garrisons of these, after a feeble and short defence, desert their guns and fly for their lives, save the solitary English artillerymen in each of the redoubts; these preferring death to shame remain, spike the guns, and are slain.

But onward still come the Russians with an overwhelming force of all arms—artillery, cavalry, and infantry. To oppose these odds, Maude's troop of Artillery, with the Scots Greys in support, gallop out and take up position on the slopes between the outposts; and although only armed with six pounders, they stem the torrent until the ammunition is exhausted. The troop then retires, leaving behind many horses and men, and the captain, who was severely wounded by a shell which burst on his horse.

The fire of the enemy's artillery is loud and fierce, the roll of his musketry draws nearer and becomes more dangerous; his guns darting out from the columns and dotting the plain at intervals, fire shells up at the heights; and then from among them dash forward two large columns of cavalry, at speed able apparently to annihilate all that may come before them. At this moment three heavy guns—two Turkish and one French—in position on the heights, open fire on the right column of the Russian cavalry, and with such effect, that it wavers, halts, turns, and gallops back. The left column still, however, holds on its course, passing over and down the opposite slopes on to the plain, where they are met by the Greys and Enniskillings, (they charged together last at Waterloo,) covered by the 5th Green Horse and 1st Royals. They meet, and ours are swept back for about a hundred paces by the avalanche of Russian horsemen, fighting as they go, red coats, fur caps, and gray horses being conspicuous amid the dark masses of the enemy, and the fate of our dragoons seems uncertain for a few minutes; but the English cheer is heard above all, whilst they fight on. Hodge with the 4th Dragoon Guards advance like a wall and bury themselves in the flanks of the Russians; simultaneously, the 5th Dragoon Guards charge in support of the Greys and Enniskillings. For a moment sword cuts and lance thrusts are exchanged, then the Russians turn and fly over the slopes. The combat has been short but decisive, the enemy retires, beaten back behind their guns.

While this is going on, the infantry have not been idle, for a party of about four hundred horse had detached themselves from the enemy's column, and, charging up the slope, make a rush for the entrance of the valley. But the 93d are there in line waiting, not a move in their ranks, not an attempt made to form square.* Calm, cool, and determined they stand, and when the advancing foe came within range, fire in a destructive volley which shakes the squadrons to their centre. But they still advance; and as nearer they come, all feel anxiety for the brave Sir Colin and his men; again, when but thirty yards apart, the glittering barrels are seen to drop to the present, and a stream of withering fire is poured in from right to left of that little band. The work is done, backward they go, yet again try to turn the tide, and wheeling, attempt to turn the right flank; but are forestalled by Captain Ross, who, wheeling back his grenadiers, gives them a volley which drives them back in confusion, and they fly to the rear with the remainder of the column, pursued by the fire of Barker's battery.

To lookers-on there was something almost theatrical in the grandeur of this portion of the spectacle; the French posted on the heights, and the English passing along the slopes, appeared like spectators from the benches of an amphitheatre, watching the two bodies of cavalry "meeting in mortal shock on the level grassy plain, which, enclosed on every side by lofty mountains, would have been a fit arena for a tournament of giants."

The enemy then, beaten at every point of his attack, is preparing to return. Now is the time for a charge of the Light Brigade, who have not as yet been engaged, and in

* Sir Colin Campbell, on being remonstrated with for giving such an opportunity, replied in the memorable words, " I would not even form four deep."

the confusion, there will be an opportunity of retaking the guns lost by the Turks. This is all observed by a staff-officer,* who points it out to the generals, but they cannot see the advantage; time, valuable time is now lost in riding from one to another, and considering the matter; they delay and hesitate for minutes—which seem hours, and the decisive moment has passed never to return. At last, the word "forward" is given, and the staff-officer already spoken of, in desperation places himself in front of the advanced line, waving his sword and encouraging the men on. A puff of smoke shews that the enemy's guns had got into position, but before the report, a scream is heard, and the staff-officer's horse, still carrying his master's dead body, gallops past the advancing troops to the rear. He had been struck by a shell in the breast, and death must have been instantaneous. The advancing line is galloping on to the attack, but the favourable opportunity is gone—the enemy's confusion is over, his formation is recovered, and as the Light Brigade sweeps along, it can be seen that they are rushing to destruction. Never did cavalry shew more daring to less purpose. Received in front and flank by a fire, which strewed the ground for half a mile with men and horses—they waver not—halt not; the cry is still "forward!" and driving through the battery they cut the gunners down at their guns. But behind are the enemy's supports of cavalry and infantry. What chance have the surviving few, against numbers, with fresh horses and men? None! these bold hearts can do no more to retrieve the day; but what are left can

* Captain Nolan.

rally and fight their way through again. This they do, and back they come, "but not the six hundred."

My dream was nearly over; still I could see the valley covered with the slain—the rider in his armour, and the steed in his harness just as they fell. And where lay the fault?—in delay. No misconception of an order, as has been said, only delay. In these affairs all depends upon decision and promptitude; and even when it could be plainly seen that the move was a bad one, why was it not supported by all the available force present? For any movement threatening the Russian flank would have diverted part of the concentrated fire that was poured upon the doomed troops.

My reverie was brought to a close by hearing a hearty shout of my name. On turning round, I found it was Jack Blythe of the Light Brigade commissariat. He was quite blown by his walk up hill, but, on recovering his wind, he informed me that a few of the survivors of the eventful charge were going to give a supper to the remainder, and a few particular friends besides, that evening; and he had brought me an invitation, I having the honour to be one of the latter.

Returning thanks, of course, for the compliment in being one of the chosen few, I still could not help saying to him, "But what, in the name of all that is great and wonderful, had you to do with the charge of Balaklava!" adding, "You were all that time, and are now, only an issuer of the good things of this life, and not one of those whose calling made them dealers around of death and destruction."

"Softly, softly," was his rejoinder; "you forget where the cavalry were picketed at that time, and so I must remind you that it was in the valley—in the very centre of the stramash; and the commissariat was just alongside; not the most enviable situation that day; for the shot and shell pitched among us, and over and through our casks and stores, in a manner that is pleasanter to talk about, now that it is over, than it was then. Affairs got so warm at last, that we were obliged to levant with scarcely half the stores, considering discretion the better part of valour, and that it was more advisable to move off with half, than stay and lose all—perhaps the number of our mess as well. Deuced glad I was to get clear with a whole skin; and between you, me, and the gate-post, I am more entitled to my Balaklava clasp than many who wear it for being at Scutari at the time; or some of the staff-sergeants who get medals 'for distinguished conduct in the field,' and never saw a shot fired in anger, or drew a sword in action."

"Well, well," I replied, "I've no doubt you went through all you state, and probably a deal more, if your extreme modesty would only allow you to relate it; but I should feel rather diffident in sitting down with so many warriors,—I who, as the Indians would say, have not as yet taken a scalp. Might I not run the chance of a roasting for my presumption?"

"Never you fash your thumb; there will be none there who would take such a liberty with a friend of the givers of the feast. We ask no one's permission. We invite whom we will. Are you satisfied?"

"Perfectly, and as I am more than anxious to come, weaker reasons would have been sufficient. But you have not mentioned the time you heroes meet."

"At seven o'clock to-night, precisely; but I can stay here no longer; for although you are not the first I have called on this morning, still there are a score or more to invite yet. Do not be late, for if all come who are invited, there will not be much room to spare. Good morning."

Before going further I will explain how soldiers became commissariat clerks. When the commissariat was organised afresh and sent to the seat of war, a staff of clerks was appointed by Government at a salary of ten shillings and sixpence per diem, to do the extra writing and correspondence required in that department. Those men were principally taken from the constabulary of the three kingdoms, the greater portion being from the sister isle. These had evidently been selected without reference as to their capabilities or fitness for the situations to which they were to be appointed. All was done, I believe, through interest, and what was the consequence? It was this, that when the army landed at Varna, and afterwards proceeded to Devna and Unah-Barad, it was then, and only then, discovered that not one in six (and I am speaking within bounds) were fit for their appointments. Doubtless they could all read and write, but a great deal more was requisite.

Clerks were wanted who, acquainted with the routine of public office business, were able to write as well as answer letters, make out returns both of and for supplies, &c.;

and these men—clever constables enough, I dare say—were now found to be utterly incapable of doing what they were intended for.

In this strait the authorities naturally fell back on the ranks of the army, and there easily found the material they required. Sergeants, corporals, and privates were now engaged, and paid two shillings extra daily, to do the duty of the ten shillings and sixpence a day men. All that the latter did was to go from the stores to Varna or Balaklava, and give in the requisitions for what might be required. All the writing and correspondence was done by the former. To this class pertained Jack Blythe, Tom Oliver, (dead, alas! poor fellow,) and M'Pherson, and they all belonged to different regiments. These joined the commissariat at Varna, and did duty in it until the peace, when they rejoined their regiments. It is not with any intention of casting reflection on these commissariat clerks that I make this explanation. I only wish the neglect of Government to be brought to notice for not seeing that qualified persons were selected. With respect to the men themselves, they were as jolly a set of fellows as any one would·wish to meet.

To return to my tale; in continuation, I may mention that there was very little necessity for the last reminder of Blythe's; as the company I should meet there would be inducement enough of itself, without taking into consideration the opportunity of having a good supper—an affair about as scarce in the Crimea, as swallows at Christmas, or a flake of snow in the dogdays, and which was safe of itself " to draw a good house;" likewise bearing in mind where this was to be held—the commissariat, the headquarters of all things eatable and drinkable—the place where plenty reigns supreme. When one thought of all this, it must have been the gout in its worst form, a broken leg, or a certainty of meeting the man who had ran away with your wife, that would have kept any one away.

As none of these accidents, luckily, had befallen me, I got there at the time appointed, and was then introduced to about forty of all ranks and regiments, from the private to the sergeant-major—from the 1st Royals to the 17th Lancers. All had here met on an equality; military distinctions were for the time laid aside; the greeting between Tom and Jack, and from Harry to Bill—all had come not only with the purpose of being themselves happy, but with the intention of doing all in their power to make others so.

A hut, from which the stores had been cleared out for the occasion, was ready for our reception, and as far as time and circumstances would allow, had undergone a raw kind of furnishing. Tables and forms had been erected on a rough principle certainly; but then consider we were on a campaign, when empty barrels are thought to be excellent substitutes for table-legs, and deal beams for tops were reckoned first-rate. For a table-cloth, some large bran-sacks had been ripped open, washed, and stitched together lengthways, making a cover not to be despised. The forms were made in the same primitive manner, having candle-boxes for legs instead of barrels. The lighting part was got up in a superior style—in fact, the place was quite illuminated. From every beam was suspended ten or a dozen candles, fixed in large round wooden sockets, grand to see; but the chandelier *par excellence* was in the centre; it had formed part of the plunder of Sebastopol, having been purchased of a rollicking Zouave, who, not finding a purchaser nearer, had brought it from the town nearly to Kadukoi, when Jack Blythe, with an eye to what was coming off, bought it and a teapot, for ten francs and a drop of grog.

By very little after seven, all were assembled; and first having a jorum of grog each, as a stomach settler and a tonic, we sat down, between forty and fifty in number, to supper, all of whom, with the exception of myself and three others, had formed part of "the six hundred." And I was informed, that what with those who were invalided, and others who had fallen victims to the severe winter, this small band comprised nearly all the survivors in the Crimea.

Yet all here had distinguished themselves in one way or other, and in a manner which, although not probably known to the powers that be, or mentioned in official despatches, was well known—patent, if I may use the word, to all those here assembled; for, like the truly brave, they were the last to speak of what they themselves had done. What I did learn was always from the mouths of others, who, when relating what had happened, would jealously keep their own light from shining, for never did they mention themselves. And thus numbers have been passed over in silence,—the principal fault lying with captains of troops and commanding officers,—for the spirit of the men themselves would not allow them to supplicate for what they considered ought to have been given as a matter of right.

But I must return to the supper—and what a supper it was that we sat down to! Roast beef and roast mutton, ducks and geese, pork and giblet pies, and tarts, and fruit from Kadukoi! No expense was spared; and it was such a feast that my mouth waters even now at the bare recollection of it; therefore it may easily be conjectured how much more so then. What a relief it was to our daily fare of beef or pork, biscuits or bread, as the case might be, and no superfluity of either. Then there were the drinkables—rum of course galore, a strong sprinkling of the mountain-dew, bottled ale and porter in dozens, wine, and even champagne, in cases. What a contrast this plenty must have been to those who, recalling the last 25th of October to their memory,—the scarcity of everything that day, shot and shell excepted,—now saw the abundance here laid out. But if any had such thoughts, they kept them secret.

Troop Sergeant-Major Josephs of the 11th Hussars took the chair, faced by our worthy friend M'Pherson of the Commissariat Department. Everything being ready, it needed but little persuasion to fall to, and this was followed up with a zest and will that campaigning alone can impart. Beef, pork, mutton, giblet pies, &c., all visibly and rapidly disappeared under the united efforts of that forty and odd good men and true there assembled. But all this did not prevent the jovial laugh and joke from going round, or the kindly inquiries after those who were, either from duty or sickness, unavoidably absent from the gathering.

Supper over, and all things cleared away, "the materials" were placed on the table for the preparation of a large bowl of whisky-punch. A looker-on at this moment might have observed a humorous, well-pleased twinkle of the eye pass round the table, followed by a shifting in their seats, to place themselves more comfortably, and a squaring of the elbows to get as much available room as possible; in short, a desire seemed to possess all of making themselves as "cosy" as lay in their power. Honest old M'Pherson, being deemed to have most experience, was requested to brew the first bowl of his native drink; and from the silence observed during the proceeding, one might have imagined that all the company were "frae the land o' cakes," where, while the toddy is brewing, not a word is spoken, in case it might distract the mixer's attention from the *great* object in front of him. When all was finished, the lemon was sliced into it, and the whole set fire to for a few seconds, just by way of proving its strength—then a glass or two were ladled out, and the opinions of a few asked as to its quality, &c. All declared it excellent, although Jack Oliver added, "That a thocht mair whisky wadna hurt it." This, however, was overruled; and when the glass passed round, it drew forth commendations from all present—Celt and Saxon being alike loud in the praise of the bowl.

The first toast proposed, as a matter of course, was "Our Queen." Then followed the other members of the Royal Family, including the Duke of Cambridge; then the Navy, and our allies the French; all of which followed each other in succession.

The chairman then rose, and after reminding the company to fill their glasses, and calling their attention to the day, proceeded to say "that there was but little necessity for his so doing, as we had one and all met to commemorate the conflict at Balaklava." He continued, "I will not attempt to recapitulate the proceedings of that day, which to those present is unnecessary; but will simply recall to their minds that, out of so many who advanced, but few returned. Each of us lost there, not only one or two comrades whom we prized and loved, but I may say twenty, and some of us more; for what is a regiment but a large family? And it is while thinking of those—while bearing in remembrance all their honesty and sterling worth—it is, I repeat, while thinking of all this, I am confident that every one present feels at the recollection, as I do myself—'too much for words.' Comrades, I will conclude by proposing, The memory of those who fell that day." This was drunk standing, and in solemn silence.

After a pause of some duration the chairman rose again, saying, "With the remembrance of Balaklava, I beg to give the healths of our leaders. I am aware that more than one has stated that Lord Cardigan never charged with us at all; others, that he returned after only going part of the way. As regards the first statement, any here of the 17th Lancers can contradict it; for they know that his lordship, accompanied by his aide-de-camp, led the first line, and so I'll say no more on that head. With reference to what else is said, we soldiers know

R

that any tremor (I'll not say fear, for it is nothing akin to that—it is more of an over-anxiety or nervousness that we feel) is always before an advance; it is never at or after it—then our whole thoughts are occupied with the enemy in front, and how to get to them. So it is as unlikely as improbable for any one to return at such a moment, far less a general; and those who say they saw him must have been differently situated from us, whose attention was taken up solely with what was in advance, not with what was behind, in which latter direction *their* eyes may have been. I'll say no more on this unlikely topic, but proceed at once to propose the health of Lord Lucan, coupled with the names of Lord Cardigan and Sir James Yorke Scarlett."

Their healths were drunk with all the honours. Several songs followed after the toasts, our worthy vice-chairman being the first called upon, to which he responded nobly, giving us "The muckle big Priest o' Kilbogie" in the real Scotch Doric. Sergeant Reardon of the 1st Royals then gave us "The Price of my Pig" in capital style. Others followed, among which was one by Bob Scott, who, after a slight demur and a little coaxing, gave us

BONNIE JEAN.

"And is it you, my bonny Jean,
    Just come to meet me a' your lane?
Oh, blessing on your hazel e'en,
    They smile to see me back again!

"Wi' weary fit and heart o' dole
    I've wander'd India's sunny plain;
But cft it cheer'd my very soul,
    To think ye wish'd me back again.

> "Welcome, my bonny Hieland hills,
>   Ye mind me o' the days o' yore;
> I flee frae care and a' its ills—
>   Your peaceful scenes to leave no more.
>
> "But come what may, my only dear,
>   Together we 'll be blythe and fain;
> Though wanting much o' this world's gear,
>   I 've brought a leal heart back again."

Bob sang this with much taste and feeling; but to me its greatest attraction was its being sung in my own country's language. Next came M'Pherson's, and never before did any song seem so beautiful and affecting as on this evening, when in a hostile and foreign land, and as one might say, in the very "shadow of death," I heard a song that breathed of the joys of love and of "my native land;" and there are few, if any, who would grudge the soldier—perhaps on the eve of battle—the solace of those sweet sounds to which his ear may soon be deaf for ever. And why should he not snatch whilst he can—from amid the days of danger and nights of peril—the few pleasant hours—these oases in his life's desert, which, when they do come, from their very scarcity occasion a joyousness surpassing belief? I had not previously heard, nor ever can forget this beautiful song—

MY NATIVE LAND.

> "My native land! my native land!
>   Now near thy coast-crags, high and hoar;
> I see the surf that strikes the strand—
>   I hear its hoarse and restless roar.
> Before the breeze we gaily scud,
>   With straining stay and swollen sail;
> And while we stir the foaming flood,
>   All hail! my native land, all hail!

"Through Afric's sands the gold ore gleams,
    On Asia's shores the diamond shines;
But there, beneath their sun's bright beams
    The black, a bondsman, pants and pines.
Proud parents of the *fair* and *free*,
    O'er roaring surf, and rolling swell,
With happy heart I look on thee,
    All hail! my native land, all hail!

"What Briton's breast but deeply draws
    The breath that sighs thy shores adieu!—
But throbs as oft a thought he throws
    From far, on days of youth and you?
You! whom my heart hath sigh'd to see,
    When hope was faint and health was frail;
How gladly now I gaze on thee.
    All hail! my native land, all hail!

"Bound on, bold barque! with powerful prow,
    Through whitening waves, that round thee roar,
From port the pilot hails us—now—
    Hark! hark! I hear the plunging oar.
The anchor drags the clanking chain,
    The seamen furl the flapping sail,
Thick throbs my heart—and yet again—
    All hail! my native land, all hail!"

After this song, which was well received, the conversation "changed round" again to what was done that day twelve-month. One of the first that spoke was a corporal of the Royals, of upwards of twenty-five years' service. When the regiment was ordered out, he would not stay with the depôt, but insisted on going with his comrades. When informed that he was to be left behind, I was told that he said, "What have I done that I should be served in this way—and the only opportunity during all my soldiering that I've had of getting a medal? I'll go; and chance whether I come back or not." He certainly was, and is—

for he still remains in the regiment—the finest stamp of an old soldier it ever was my lot to see. Some one had asked him how he came by the medal for "Distinguished conduct in the field," inquiring, at the same time, "if he had taken a Russian general prisoner, or anything of that sort."

"Nothing of the kind," was old Bob Swash's reply. "I think they wanted some excuse to give it me, for, bless you, I did nothing deserving of it. You see I had my horse killed under me, and then managed to get another that was running about: this I mounted, and an unlucky shot killed him also; and the colonel seeing this as well, ordered me off home. There was a good saddle on the last one, so I took it off, and, putting it on my head, came away. They made a bit of work about it; so I got the medal. That's just the truth of it; and I don't wish any one to imagine I did more."

"I only wish," struck in a sergeant of the 4th Light, "that all those who wear them, Bob, had earned them as well; but when we see them principally decorating the breasts of staff and hospital sergeants, it causes us chaps to lay but little store by 'distinguished conduct' medals. I say, 8th," he continued, turning to one of the 8th Hussars, "how was that affair of your sergeant-major's brother settled?"

"Oh! all hushed up," was the reply.

"What was that, Watson?" asked several at once.

"Why, I thought nearly everybody knew about it; but as it appears not, I'll tell you what I know of the matter. After the 8th had formed up on the plain that morning, the major, I believe, placed Sergeant —— under arrest for some trifling affair or other, and, as a consequence, his belts and arms were taken from him. Instead of being sent to the rear—the place for a prisoner—he was still kept in the ranks; and when we advanced on the guns, he went along with us unarmed. Like many more that day, he never returned; but whether he fell by the sword or bullet of the enemy, none knew; if by the sword, he was an easy victim, being unable to defend himself. There was a deal of bother about the matter at first, and I fully expected that his brother would have reported the matter; but I suppose he thought better of it—it could not bring the dead to life again, and would doubtless have injured his prospects; so second thoughts were probably best, as he was an old soldier with a family."

"Yes," remarked one of the Royals, "it is of very little use reporting any of those over us to a still higher authority; because the report itself must go through what is termed the proper channel, which is probably through the very man's hands you are making a complaint against. He takes care, then, first to give his version, after which he will mention about your complaint, styling it as both 'frivolous and vexatious;' and should he not be able to refute your statement, he will either represent it as being altogether a malicious affair, or he will cast reflections on your character, which will cause your communication to be, if not actually disbelieved, at least listened to with inattention and regarded with suspicion."

"Ah!" says another, drily, "it's very little use going to law with the devil when the court's in hell."

"True for you, my boy," chimes in one of the 17th, "but it's not exactly law that we want in the service—there is too much of that—but what we require badly is a little justice, of which latter commodity there has at all times been a great scarcity. For instance, here is Jack Farrel, who, with another sergeant and under a heavy fire, went back and carried a wounded officer off the field. This was done at the risk of their lives, for, while doing so, a round shot carried Jack's shako off his head. And what has he got for doing this? one would naturally inquire. Why, nothing—absolutely nothing;* unless having been passed over for promotion twice be considered any recompense. And this is not the only hard case: there was Corporal ———, for instance, who charged along with his squadron, passed the batteries, and, being a cool fellow, seeing that nothing more could be accomplished, while waiting would only be certain destruction, he rallied fifteen men together of all regiments, and briefly explaining the case, ordered them to follow him, which they all did, and, cutting their way through again, got all back except three. Now, neither of these have been recommended for either the French medal or for the one for 'distinguished conduct in the field.'"

"There is but little fair play in the service," said one

---

* Six years afterwards, justice was done him at last, he being gazetted for the Victoria Cross in the latter part of 1860, while he was in India; and I believe this would not have been done even then except for this paper having appeared in the *United Service Magazine*, November 1859.

of the Green Horse—5th Dragoon Guards. "I could tell of something equally glaring, but it does no good; only, had it been an officer who performed these deeds, what a hero he would have become! The only thing like justice that I have seen done was for our friend Quinn of the 47th, who from a corporal has been promoted to a commission. But what was it, after all, pray? Why, only an ensigncy in the Land Transport Corps ;—just putting a brave lad like that out of the way—buried in a manner, and where he would not have another chance of distinguishing himself."

"Or more probably getting extinguished," quietly remarked one of the 4th Royal Irish.

"Well, for my part," said one of the bonnie Greys, but whose accent betrayed him to be from the other side of the bridge, "I cannot imagine what yees all have to complain and grumble about. By yer talk yees ought to have this medal and the other medal. The devil tie ye up with medals, say I. Why, here sits Phil Hannigan, who kilt and druv afore him more Roosians that day than all on ye put together, and niver a word have ye heard him spake about rewards of merit and crasses of the lagion of honour."

"Was you, then, in the Balaklava charge, Phil?" inquired one of the 13th; "I had no idea of *you* being there."

"Troth, then, I did not suppose you had," was the indignant answer, followed by "it's aisy seen you didn't belong to the hivy brigade, or you wouldn't had the laste occasion in life to ax that question."

"There are several of us similarly placed," said one of the 4th Light; "and if you have no objection, we should much like to hear the particulars."

"Objiction! Not a bit of it; but with the greatest pleasure in loife, my boy, though faith, not loiking to blow my own trumpet—I should have preferred it to have been towld by some one else.

"I daresays most on yees remimbers the first charge of the hivies, and thir wor the Greys and Inniskillings in front. Scotland and Ireland for iver, my boys! But sure it's dirty work this talking, my tongue is jist loike a rasp; so jist fill the tumbler with a drop of nate potheen—*nate*, mind yees—for wather nivir did agree with me; and sartain shure am I that it's not a bit of improvement to good whisky at all, at all. Oh," smacking his lips, "that's something loike! Well, as I wor telling yees, the shamrock and thistle wint hand-in-hand slap into the center of the Roosians. Iviry one fowt well, but I loike a divil; my blood was up, and at them I wint. It was Donnybrook that oncet I thowt wor a foine place for a scrimage; but, ifecks, it was nothing. The plain beyant bate it intirely, bedads. I began to think they'd never ha' done. They kept springing up faster than I could cut them down, jist for all the world loike that baste who, if one head was cut off, two come in its place,—what was his name?"

"Janus," said some one.

"The divil Janus ye! Is it yerself ye mane, ye two-faces-under-a-hat looking rascal. Shure it wor that baste who took apartments near Lake Lerna, and stopt there in spite of ivery one, until Mr Hercules came, with a knife in one hand and a glowing torch in the other, and murdered the brute—bad luck to the name, I can't rimimber it; but there, I warrant yees all know who I mane. Well there I stood out and fowt—one down another come on, until troth I finished them. It wor jist at the time I saw ye light bobs about to charge—and I was thinking of jining yees, only rather puzzled how I was to lape my horse over the Roosians that lay round about—when I heard my name shouted by some one behind, and on looking round who should it be but Lord Cardigan."

"Oh, Phil, Phil! you told it quite different the last time. You said it was Lord Lucan then," shouts one of his comrades.

"Did I? Faith then bedads it was—avecoorse it was. *Wipe and return your sword, Sergeant Hannigan,*' says Lord Lucan to me; *'you've done enough for the day; and had ivery man done half as much, not a Roosian would have left the field alive.'* And it was well for *thim* that he spoke, as the light brigade had not made their charge then, and thir wor time enough to have saved yees, but his lordship would not let me stir a fut towards ye. But a dacent boy he was for all that, as he not only dismounted and give me a hand to make a lane through the Roosians, but, what wor better, gave me a dhrop out of his flask, and rale good stuff I can tell ye his lordship carried too, d'ye mind; and"——

Here a burst of laughter from all present stopped the worthy sergeant at this point of his story. He tried to look serious for a time, but could not, so joined in the laugh against himself at last, saying, "Ah, ye might laugh; but iviry word I have towld ye is truth, although ye are so unaccustomed to it, that nivir a one will belave it whin ye hear it spoken."

"Well," says old M'Pherson, "I've heerd mony a ane, but that bates a', certainly." Turning to me, he continued—" I'd strongly adveese Paul Mannion o' yours to look to his laurels, for by my faith Sargent Hannigan will grup them awa frae him."

I replied, "Paul, I am sorry to say, is at present in hospital, and now, I fear, would not be able to cope with our friend. But in good health, and other things in his favour—like Hannigan has to-night—' the hoith of company,' and plenty of the best of liquors, he would prove a dangerous rival."

"By the by," said an Inniskillinger, "was it Paul who was orderly sergeant on church parade, when the officer inquired if all were present, and replied, as he saluted, 'All prisint, sir, barring the Catholics, and thim I got in my cap.'"

"No, no, my dear fellow, that was not one of ours at all," I replied. "That was Paddy Rooke, at Maidstone; he that used to remark, after parading his squad, 'Bedads, my boys, yees are all clane: the divil himself could not find fault wid one of ye; but, shure, *I must report somebody!*'"

"Faith, I shall always remember Paddy Rooke. When I joined," said one of the 12th Lancers, "he was drilling me, and I thought I was getting on first-rate before this;

but from the moment I got under his charge, there was nothing I could do right; and one day—I shall never forget it—when, after having exhausted all his powers of abuse, as I thought, he walked up, and, having placed me in position, exclaimed, 'Now there ye are, wid yeer three hot meals a day, and ye scarcely know how to walk about. But I'll take them good clothes off your back, and turn ye out of the barrack-gate; and thin, what would yees do?'"

"But Paul," I said, "does in no way or form resemble him, and as he appears to be a stranger to most of you, I will give you a slight sketch, so that if ever you should drop across the individual, you will know him. Just imagine to yourselves a fine smart fellow, standing six feet in his stocking soles, as straight as an arrow, and shoulders as square as a church; with blue eyes, ruddy complexion, and hair of the same hue as Father Malichi's coadjutor's was. To all these qualifications you may add that he can run or wrestle any man of his inches, and leap over anything his own height. However, it is for none of these last that he is most remarkable, but for being the greatest liar in the regiment,—an hour ago I would have said in the division; but the tale I have heard since has made me cautious as to making that assertion."

"I shall always think of the yarn Paul told me when I first went to India," added one of my own regiment. "I may first remark that Paul pretends to hold in great contempt us Fox Maulers (twelve year act men) especially if they are not particularly tall. You may all perceive that I am not much over five foot six on a brick now, and at the time I speak of I was not that. The first night I went to stables, Paul was in charge of the squad, strutting up and down the centre of the lines with his shoulders back, arms bent, elbows outwards, and his head up; his eyes being far above any object of my stature. By some accident or other, however, he looked down, and twigged me eyeing him from between the horse's fore legs. Walking majestically towards me, he called me to him, and looking down at me, as Gulliver must have looked when he saw the first inhabitant of Lilliput, he condescendingly asked my name. On being told, his next inquiry was 'who enlisted me?' I told him Sergeant Jones. 'It's very little credit you are to him,' was his reply, continuing with a knowing wink and nod, 'and it's a good job for him that he wasn't recruiting for the 4th Royal Irish, for if he had it would have been something like two years' imprisonment he would have got for the same mistake. Bedads Colonel Chatterton would take no excuse.' Sinking his voice to a confidential whisper, he went on: 'When I joined the 4th, I stood five feet ten inches and a half under the standard, and the sergeant that gave me the shilling was immediately called in, tried by court-martial and reduced for enlisting *me*, so you may form some idea what his fate would have been had he sent a sample like you: but, as I said afore, I don't blame *you* a bit. I blame the man that gave you the shilling. Now just look across the lines at that man the second from the top—you see what a strong fellow he is, with an arm on him like a scaffold pole—but you see he is but barely five feet ten,—now he is a volunteer from the

Fourth. Whisht, I know what you are going to say,—how did he get into the regiment? Well, I'll tell you upon conditions that you promise never to breathe a word of it to a living soul—because the chap don't like to hear it spoken of now-a-days.' (I of course gave the required promise.) 'Well now—whisper—he was druv in along with thirty-five other young colts into Cahir barrack-yard —and by some mistake he was included, for forage was drawn for thirty-six; and shure I would not tell it to every one, but I think I dare trust you—he lived on oats for more than three weeks—and took his water out of a bucket—devil a haporth else; and when the colonel came to hear of it, the affair took his fancy so much that he had him enlisted, but he was never mounted at a general's inspection, being always put on stable guard or sent into hospital for a day or two just out o' the way like. Now wouldn't you think that odd?'"

After the laugh had subsided which this tale caused, I ventured to remark that they were doubtless now well satisfied as to Paul's abilities, which (as regards telling a good lie with a circumstance) were far above mediocrity; but if they wished for further testimony I was prepared to oblige them.

"For my part," said old Watson of the 4th Light, "although perfectly convinced that the 10th ought to have the belt for telling anecdotes, I must own at the same time that I like to hear a good one told, and so for one am agreeable to hear a little more of Paul."

The others all being in the same mind, I commenced. "After the 86th Royal County Downs arrived at Poonah,

Paul remembered that an old comrade was then adjutant of that regiment, and he and I took a trip over, he to see his old chum, I to have a look at the regiment. We arrived all safe, and spent a very pleasant morning, Paul having gone to see his friend. At midday he had not returned; so I with a few of the 86th went over to the canteen to pass the time until dinner. I suppose I had been in the canteen about half an hour, when I found that my companions had all strayed to the other end of the place, where a large and listening circle were assembled round some person or persons unknown. Being always a social sort of animal, I did not relish my lonely position, so sauntered down and joined the others. To my great surprise and gratification, I found that Paul was the centre of attraction, and was delighting the ears of his audience with an account of a tremendous brute of a horse, in the 4th Heavies, which had killed several, and thrown everybody that had ever ventured to throw a leg across it, until Paul took him in hand and conquered the brute. And from that day forward he was known in the regiment by no other name than 'Mannion's horse.' When I joined the party he was explaining that although *he* could manage him, still there was no one else could. But I had better try and give it in his own words :—' Ah my boys, in spite of all his tricks I was as fond of him as if he had been my child, for when he did choose to go quiet —very seldom, though—it was a rale pleasure to ride him. He would step so springy and elastic that after a long day's march you would jist feel as fresh as when you started. And oh! to feel him under you at a gallop, there's no words can describe the pleasure—so light in hand, and yet his speed so great, and withal so easy—you would scarcely be conscious of going along at all; then at a lape I can compare the feeling to nothing else than the hop of a bird; but shure I could spake in his praise alone until night. Thim rough riders and such like had many a try, but faith no sooner were they on than aff they came, and he became such a terror that not a man dare mount him. The colonel took advantage of this too, for it was quite a common occurrence—if any good soldier got into serious trouble and the colonel did not wish to try him—for him to say, " Let the prisoner have fourteen days on Mannion's horse ; " but the invariable answer was, " I 'd sooner have a court-martial, colonel." And small blame to them for making such a choice : it shewed their sense, as they could get over a court-martial, but they wouldn't get over a broken neck so aisy. And it was not long before an order was given that no one was to cross the horse but me; and I remember an old sergeant being placed on the shelf and very nearly reduced for ordering a man to ride him one day I was upon guard. I was just marching the relief round, past the riding school, when I sees poor old Flinn leading him up. By grate luck for Flinn, the riding-master was standing outside, and as soon as he sat eyes on the pair, he shouted out, " Where's Mannion ? " " Halting the relief," I answered, "here upon guard, sir." He then sent for the orderly sergeant, and towld Flinn " to take the brute back," adding, when he had gone, " I wonder if they want that man killed too." And when the orderly sergeant came he placed him under arrest, and the colonel was as near trying him as not.'

"Some one here said, 'But, Mannion, did you never come off him?'

"'Well, I did, and at the same time I didn't. Ye might think that odd, but it is true; and troth it was the nastiest trick that ever he sarved me. It was after we got to Edinboro', in 1844, that I formed one of the escort for Lord Belhaven, the Queen's Commissioner. On turning out that morning, I thought that I never knew him in a sweeter temper. On mounting, he walked off as quiet as a lamb, and scarcely whisked his tail until we got into Princes Street, then he made up for all. Seizing the bit in his teeth, and throwing his head between his legs, he gave himself a shake, that nearly shook me out of the saddle; then setting his back up, for all the world like a camel, he gave about a dozen bucks in the air, and such a height that I thowt he would never come down again. Once, upon my soul, I counted about thirty afore he come to the ground. He and I was both pretty well puffed: he with trying to throw, I with trying to bate him out. He went along pretty quiet for about a hundred yards, and I began to think that, finding it was impossible to shift me, he had gave in; but nothing of the kind; he was only collecting himself for another rally, and by an entire change of performance. His first manœuvre was by a side rush against a carriage that was passing, for the purpose of jamming my leg against it; but a vigorous application of my right spur defeated that movement. He then rushed sideways in the opposite direction, kicking and bucking all the time. I sat very quietly, thinking to myself, "It's all right, my boy, you'll get tired first of this game," when I found myself sitting quietly in the saddle in the middle of the street; and I was confounded to see him capering along in front. He had kicked himself clane out of the saddle!'

"Flesh and blood could stand this no longer; I was obliged to speak; so I said, 'What! clean through crupper, breastplate, and girth? Paul! why man, it's impossible!'

"'Not a bit of it, my boy,' was his unabashed reply; 'sure, didn't all thim things break long before?'"

"Well, upon my word," said Watson, "that's nearly as good as Hannigan's battle of Balaklava."

"There was only ae thing that he was deficit about," observes old M'Pherson, "which was the name of the beast. Now I'll tell him that. It was Heedra, ye ken, Hannigan."

"And who moight you mane by He-edràa?" said Hannigan, mimicking him, at which there was a laugh all round.

"Weel, like the Scotch, I'll answer ye ae question by axin anither. D'ye mind o' a Major Gordon bein' in the Greys? No. I thocht ye didn't, for ye micht hae rekalektit hoo he, an' a countryman o' your ain, had an argument aboot the pronunciashun o' a word, and the Major didnae hae the warst o' it."

"Bedads," shouts Hannigan, slapping the table, and jumping up, "I'll forfate half-a-dozen of wine, if you can prove that ever an Irishman had the worst of an argument with any Scotchman that hailed from 'Maidenkirk or Johnny Groat's.'"

"I accept the half-dozen, wi' mony thanks, Hannigan, for I think, when I've tell't my story, that ye'll gie in yersel'. Weel, it's mony year sin' this happened, when clergymen were no so plentifu' as they are noo in the army, and at some stations the commanding officer used to read the services himsel' in the riding skule. The Greys were layin' at Ipswich in 18—, and Major Gordon, wha was frae the north o' the Tweed, like mysel', used, when reading the Church services, to pronoonce an orra word here and there rayther broad. Ae Sabbath, when reading the Creed, the Major pronounced, in rayther a queer way, 'Suffered under Pontious Pilate.' A countryman o' yours, Barney Blake, exclaimed, 'Who is Ponshoos Peelate, I wonder?' The Major paused at this, and layin' doon the Prayer-book, said, 'Ah, Barney, is that you at your jokes again? just come oot here, my man.' Your countryman stept to the front; three taps on the drum, and a court-martial assembled; he was tried and found guilty, the triangles rigged out, and Barney received a hundred lashes, without having said another word. When the floggin' was done, the Major resumed the Prayer-book, and went on with the service as if nothing had happened. I think ye'll own noo, Hannigan, that your countrymen had the warst o' that argument."

"Ugh! that was no argument—a fellow taking the mean advantage of his position only."

"Faith, Phil, I think it was a pretty forcible argument, and I for one give it against you," I said.

A whole chorus of voices here decided the affair in Mac's favour.

Sergeant Reardon, of the Royals, gave us now, in splendid style, Tennyson's "Charge of the Six Hundred," and it being the first time any of us had heard it, it was vociferously encored.

The mirth now grew fast and furious; song came after song, story after story, joke followed joke, until we had encroached well into the "wee short hour ayont the twal," and our worthy vice gave us a hint to go, by saying that he "thocht it was nearly time we were breaking up." But it was hours after, when we got Mac in the centre, and sang, "For he's a jolly good fellow,"—hurrahing until we were hoarse. Then it was, "We are nae fou," and "We won't go home till morning;" then winding up with "Auld lang syne," which was sang three times over, we broke up, all happy at parting, and happy in having met. It is but eight short years since, and where are they all now? I spent the last anniversary with the 11th Hussars, and they only mustered some nine men who were present at Balaklava.

CHAPTER FOURTEEN.

To Winter Quarters and Home.

THE weather having set in cold, and there being some prospect of peace, it was determined to send the cavalry into winter quarters. Our destination was Ismid in Turkey, where were sent also the 8th Hussars and 17th Lancers; the brigade being under the command of Brigadier-General Shewell. The remainder of the cavalry were sent to Scutari. On the 13th of November the regiment embarked on board the *Himalaya*, the *Assistance*, and the *Kangaroo*. I was in the latter, and in a very short time we were under weigh, passing Cossack Point, and taking, as it turned out, a farewell look at Leander Creek, the monastery of St George, and the old castle with the hospital below; all of us anxiously looking back to each well-remembered spot as it gradually faded from our view amid the dark waters and mist-covered hills. Away back again across the Euxine, and in two days we were again floating calmly amid the caiques on the blue dancing waves of the Bosphorus, past the Golden Horn and into the Sea of Marmora, when, changing our course, we steered up the Gulf of Ismid, and the following afternoon dropped anchor alongside of the town. Ismid, the ancient Nicomede, is built upon the side of a steep hill, the streets being in terraces, that run parallel with its base. There are the usual mosques and minarets, the bathhouses and numerous fountains common to most Eastern towns, not forgetting the never-failing abundance of dogs and vultures—the scavengers of the country—and the accompanying dirt and vermin. However, one good thing was, that water abounded—marble fountains were in every street, and down the centre of the roads which led up from terrace to terrace, a stream of water continually flowed to the sea. I must allow that the interiors of the houses were kept very clean, but the Turk's idea of cleanliness does not go beyond his own door; outside is deposited all the filth and refuse from the interior; but luckily the heavy rains and hill streams carry away a good portion of this. It was our lot to disperse the remainder, and in a few days after our arrival the streets were cleaned, and a degree of order instituted that would have delighted even a sanitary commissioner. But all this was done under protest as it were, the inhabitants viewing the cleansing operations with horror and surprise; they could not understand nor appreciate such innovating ways. We were soon able to go about without getting over the ankles in mud, &c. But outside of the town was beyond our jurisdiction; and there Turkish habits and customs allowed dead cattle to remain rotting in the sun, until the dogs had devoured the flesh; and if the authorities had not been stirred up, and caused the carcases to be removed, we would in no time have had cholera or fever breaking out amongst us. In one respect the Turks are remarkable above all other nations we had come in contact with, and that is for unswerving honesty. Thoroughly conscientious in this respect, they imagine that every other person is similarly disposed. On our arrival in Ismid we were quite surprised to see tables, chairs, handsome narghillies, and glasses, lying carelessly out of doors; as for locks they were never used; but I am sorry to add that some of the *mauvis saujets* of the brigade, who did or would not understand the difference between *meum* and *tuum*, soon caused the Turks to be more careful and less trusting than they had been. All tribute, however, to the Osmanli for this virtue, which, like unto charity, covereth many sins. Our customs and habits were so different to theirs, staid old Turks could not for their lives understand how it was that we congregated together in cafés, and sang songs with uninterruptible choruses, and drank, not coffee but porter, and ate—oh! horror to their ideas—oysters, beds of which were as plentiful in Ismid, as "leaves in Valambrosa," but which to them, up to this period, had been entirely useless. With them true enjoyment consisted in sitting cross-legged on cushions, smoking narghillies and sipping coffee from small cups, talking in monosyllables, and making up a conversation with gestures of nods and shrugs. But whatever surprise they might feel at our ways, it was never expressed or shewn: apathy seems to be a virtue with them; I verily believe that had one of us gone in among twenty of them and committed suicide, not one of the party would have appeared in the slightest degree interested or shocked at the occurrence. Our creature-comforts were well looked after

—canteens sprang up in every quarter, and a large singing saloon was erected by M. Missouri, of Constantinople, at the quay, which, as a matter of course, did a roaring trade, and consequently had, in a short time, several rivals. In these met, every night, parties from the three regiments, when the best singers delighted their comrades with their harmonious performances. Our bandsmen occasionally brought down their instruments to these reunions and gave us a treat; and in this way we managed to pass the long nights in winter.

The 8th Hussars occupied the lower portion of the town, the 17th Lancers the centre, and we of the 10th the higher part; our only disadvantage being the distance we were from the stables, which were by the sea shore; they being some empty storehouses converted to their present purpose. The houses being all built of wood, it was wonderful, from the careless way in which the Turks used fire, that a conflagration had not broken out before and destroyed the town. While we were there a fire did break out in a small granary, but fortunately it was near no other building, and the evening was calm. Being only a short distance from our quarters, at the first alarm there were soon plenty of men on the spot, and they quickly had it extinguished. The Turk who owned it sat complacently looking on, smoking, while we worked, he repeating now and then "God is great." After the fire had been smothered, down came the town fire-engine, about the size of a small handbarrow, which two men had carried easily; and as there were apparently neither hose nor buckets belonging to it, it may be guessed how soon .

the Turks would have extinguished the fire. The first thing we did was to make a drain across the road, and there plenty of water soon collected, and a few buckets and willing hands did the rest.

The General having appointed Sergeant Temple of the 17th Lancers deputy provost-marshal, and given an order that he was to be assisted by a regimental provost from each corps, I was fortunate enough to be selected by my colonel to fill that appointment in the regiment. As two shillings per diem extra was attached to it, the appointment had the advantage of being lucrative as well as arduous. We were kept employed all day and a good portion of the night—in the daytime exercising the prisoners, and at night patrolling the town; but beyond the walking and late hours there was nothing fatiguing or irksome. The principal duty of the provosts was to prevent the sale of liquors before midday, and the dodges of the canteen people and our men to evade us were numerous and amusing. In my opinion the very fact of not being allowed to drink causes soldiers often, when the opportunity offers, to take a great deal more than they otherwise would, simply because the liquor is prohibited; and sutlers being aware of this, sold rum in coffee, tea, and milk. A Greek named Constantine, who had a shop close to our main-guard, had always a couple of sentries posted watching for my arrival at the time he was selling liquor inside, out of hours. Lounging carelessly against a post or corner of the street, I could observe them signal my approach; and the consequence was, that when I walked into his shop he would be selling everything but liquors. Not a quart-pot or glass could be seen anywhere, while I could read in the customers' faces that some had nearly choked themselves in bolting the rum or beer, and from the twinkle of Constantine's eye that he considered himself particularly clever in deceiving me. The old rogue would just be saying when I entered, "Not a drop, until twelve o'clock, me sell to my fader;" and then, turning to me, he'd continue, "Tell this man, sir, that I can't serve him now," &c. The clever Constantine forgot that I could get to his canteen by another way, and while covering his front by two vedettes he neglected to take similar precautions to his rear. So, one morning, making a detour of about a mile, I gradually circled round and took my friend Constantine in reverse; and there I found him in full swing, drawing and pouring out as hard as he could, never perceiving me until I asked the question, "Holloa! is this twelve o'clock?" It was only nine, and, taking him red-handed as it were, he could make neither excuse nor defence. I gave him a fright by closing up his shop, and bringing him before the brigade-major, who, as it was Constantine's first offence, gave him a caution, which rendered him more careful for the future. Another morning I was going round after reveillée had sounded, and having my suspicions about a small coffee-shop that had just opened, I dropped in quite promiscuously, and called for a cup of coffee. The proprietor did not know me, and, in answer to his question whether I took it with milk or without, I, smelling a rat, replied, "With milk, if you please." As I had suspected, I was served with a cup of *rum and water*, hot, strong, and sweet. His surprise may be imagined when I introduced myself to his notice as assistant to the provost-marshal, requesting him to close up his shop and attend the general's quarters at noon that day. Another gentleman pretending to sell cooked fish kept a thumping large bottle of sauce for them. From the taste many of the men suddenly shewed for fish, I came to the conclusion that the sauce was neither Lazenby's nor Harvey's. The fellow who kept the shop was, like Major B——, "sly, sir, devilish sly," and he foiled me for nearly a good week. The bottle containing the *sauce* I could hear of, but never could see; there was only the pan full of fish simmering over the fire, and a few customers waiting until the fish were cooked. But I caught him at last. One day, having made my usual call, I left, apparently satisfied that all was right, and, going round the corner, made a halt, waited a few minutes, and returned sharp on the fishman. There was a bit of a bustle, and an attempt to get between me and the fireplace; but it was too late, all was discovered. A large tin jar, in which he pretended to keep olive oil to fry the fish, was so constructed that, while oil came out of the neck, a hole under the handle let out rum, there being a division in the centre. I had often looked at this jar, but had no suspicion about it before. The fishman now had to pay the penalty of his ingenuity by appearing before the general for orders to leave the town. At Scutari, some months afterwards, I was also nearly out-generalled by a quiet, plausible fellow who sold handkerchiefs and other cotton goods by the roadside; but anything to drink—"Oh no! he knew better than that, for wouldn't he get flogged and turned out of camp? Why should he run such risk?" This and such like was his talk, while I could see that he was laughing at me, and taking considerable credit to himself for the style in which he threw dust in my eyes. He had chosen a good position, having a most excellent view of the front, while his rear was protected by a small wood, where I had every reason to believe his stock of grog was kept, though I never could find it. I was the more annoyed because of his confounded civility, as I could not pass without his wishing me "Good morning" or something of the sort, to which salutation I always took care cordially to respond. It almost appeared as if I should never catch him, although I daily met men coming from the direction in which he was, in a state which among civilians is termed "fresh," and in the army comes under the head of "drunk." Ismail, from having his scouts well posted, was not to be easily had; so I was obliged to bring craft against craft. Pretending that my suspicions were disarmed, I passed his stall for three days without taking the slightest notice, and then sent a comrade of the name of Avery to him for a bottle of rum. In the meantime I made a circuit, and placing myself in the plantation behind, remained an unseen spectator of the transaction. When Avery arrived he asked for a bottle of rum, for which the other demanded, as I found afterwards, three shillings—three shillings for what cost the vendor sixpence! On receiving the money Ismail called his assistant, and sent him and Avery to the plantation, and I immediately fell back, concealing myself behind a tree. Avery was taken by his companion towards another tree, about twenty yards from where I stood, and at the foot of this raised a turf-covered lid, disclosing a large wicker basket full of bottles, which had been neatly let into the ground, and so nearly defied detection. The fellow's consternation, when I looked over his shoulder and passed a compliment on the neatness of the whole concern, was rich to see. I only wish I could depict it as I saw it! Ismail and his man were taken to Scutari, where they had the pleasure of seeing General Storks next morning, who in a few words decided the whole case, and the Greek was, of course, turned out of camp. These kind of fellows who followed our men in the Crimea and Turkey sold the very worst description of liquor, for which they charged the most exorbitant prices. Most of them were Greeks, whose sympathies were all on the side of the Russians, and who, of course, considered robbing us and selling bad liquors highly commendable actions.

When over at Scutari about Ismail, I was greatly astonished to see among the provost prisoners, a private of the name of R———, whom I had known years before in the 1st Royal Dragoons. Upon inquiry, I found that he had been convicted of breaking into and robbing a store, and received six months' imprisonment. It was one of those general stores where everything was sold; and R———, having discovered a loose board at the end, he used to break into the store after hours, and bring away cases of liquor, which he disposed of at so much a bottle to his comrades, who thought that he was an agent for some one. It appears that he carried on this plan for several weeks, until the robbery became so perceptible that the owner set a watch for the thief, and R—— was taken in the act. Yet this man had been educated and brought up as a gentleman. His uncle was a physician in extensive practice; he had received over £500 left him since he was a soldier, and "all the good it had done him," as Paddy would observe, "was harm," for he had spent and fooled it all away in less than twelve months, and while doing so, had several courts-martial, and at last sank so low as to commit this robbery;—a sad ending for one whose fate might have been far different, and who had brothers, officers in the army.

But to return from this digression to Ismid, and its streets. Dangerous obstacles, such as deep holes, water courses, and great stones, lay all up the centre of the roadways, rendering it quite an Alpine feat to ascend or descend them after nightfall, and there, in my provost duty, I often found some unfortunate wight, who, heavy laden with liquor, had sunk in the slough, to rise no more by his own exertions. Any one who served there must remember the steep paths, which, full of these snares and pitfalls, made travelling even by day a difficulty; and I often felt surprised how the natives, with their slipshod shoes, ever made headway up the town at all. Bad roads and impassable streets, however, are common to all Eastern countries, and when there we can easily perceive the reason that Mohammed was so particular in not allowing his followers to partake of strong waters, being unquestionably convinced that no drunken Mohammedan could ever safely make head against the perils which beset his path, but would inevitably break his neck before he reached his destination. Even the provost-marshal made a grand mistake one dark night. There was a by-road which led from the brigade lane to his quarters, and in the very centre of this was an old dry well, without any paling or parapet round it. Going home one night, about the " witching hour, when churchyards yawn," he forgot this well, and dropped down to the bottom. Coming past a few minutes afterwards, I was astonished to hear sounds resembling groans, coming apparently out of the ground. I was giving the well a wide berth, but hearing this noise, went towards it, and to my surprise discovered that it was poor Temple, who was in this sore strait. I ran home, got a rope, and dragged him out, he, however, making me promise that I should not speak about it. And I would not have done so now, but that all reason for secrecy is over, for he, poor fellow, lies in the churchyard at Kirkee, where he died, troop sergeant-major in the 17th Lancers.

On the 2d of December, a man of the name of Cox committed suicide by shooting himself in a stable, simply because he could not find his kit, and had been told by the commanding officer, that if he did not find it he would be liable to get punished. So he went home, loaded his carbine, and destroyed himself. It appeared strange to me afterwards that he should have been so particular as to go and have lunch at a canteen before he committed the act. He called in, asked for some bread and cheese and a pint of ale; said he might as well have a glass of rum, finished it, and sauntered quietly away. In five minutes more there was the report of a carbine, a rush of some soldiers, and there they saw the disfigured corpse of their comrade, and a discharged weapon by its side.

At Ismid, I luckily found some of the commissariat clerks I had known in the Crimea, who had a house of their own, and lived there like princes. Mrs Sheridan, who belonged to the 8th Hussars, messed them and did their washing. She was really a very saving, hard-working woman, but had for a husband one of the most rackety customers in the corps. Anthony, for such was the name given him by his godfathers and godmothers in his baptism, was one of the most thirsty souls I ever saw, and many were the shifts and contrivances he tried to get money out of his better half, and many were the out-of-the-way places in which his frugal helpmate used to hide her money from him. One day he was on the spree—no unusual thing with Anthony—and being, in military language, completely stumped,* had been on a private exploring expedition through the house, endeavouring to find one of his wife's secret hoards. He had just, as he afterwards informed us, made a last appeal to one of the many saints in the calendar, to direct him how to seek and find, when he declared he saw the edge of something shining, sticking out from under the table leg—(a candle-box, by the by.) Dropping on his knees in ecstacy, for the purpose of seizing what he found to be a sovereign, and ejaculating a thanksgiving to St Bridget, for directing him right, off he ran, and, with some comrades, was speedily converting the pure gold into pure spirits. Poor Mrs Sheridan was wondering how it was that Anthony came

* " Cleaned out, or hard up."

to dinner, and went away again, without ever even asking for the price of a pint; but when he came home drunk after stables, and had money in his pockets, the suspicion that she had been robbed burst upon her. An immediate search made the surmise that her sovereign was gone a certainty, and then ensued a mingling of questions and reproaches at the helpless Anthony, who neither knew nor cared what she said. At breakfast-time the following morning, we were all highly amused by her reproaches and Anthony's excuses and denials, especially when she broke out with, "Oh, Anthony, Anthony, if the devil was only to pop in now, and be looking for a liar, wherever *should* I hide you?"

Christmas was now drawing nigh, and although away from home, the occasion was not to be allowed by any of us to pass over without its celebration to the best of our ability. We had neither tables, chairs, nor forms; but what of that? we were equal to far greater emergencies. We procured wood, a saw, a hammer, and a few nails did the remainder. Each room or mess acted independently; some, like the one I belonged to, preferring the substantial to the artificial, were content with plenty of green leaves for decorations; while others would have painting and curious devices. There were eleven of us in our small room, where, when all were present, there was bare space to sleep; so as no one was absent from the Christmas gathering, there was but very little room for guests; yet we managed to have three. Blake and I being on the provost, looked after the preserves, fruit, and drinkables; the others saw to the roast beef, goose, and plum-pudding.

At 2 P.M. on Christmas-day fourteen of us sat down to enjoy ourselves at our own expense, at a most substantial meal; and we did it honour with real relish, keeping up our festivities through the night as if we had been in a Christian land. There were no candlesticks, certainly, but wine bottles were excellent substitutes; and although not so imposing were quite as useful. Plates to serve the different courses on were certainly wanting, and tumblers and glasses were at a discount; but there was no lack of that true comrade-like feeling—of all being anxious to please and wishful to make the evening pass agreeably, that content with which a dinner of herbs is far more acceptable than when a stalled ox graces the board where strife abounds. All were happy and comfortable, and this state of things even the slight excess in drink did not interrupt. Being on provost, I had to leave the company early; in consequence of which I witnessed a curious sight. The two trumpeters, Daly of the 8th Hussars and Johnny Brown of the 17th Lancers, each represented the band of their respective regiments. Both were short and stumpy, and both in a marvellous degree were partial to a "dhrop" of anything—no matter what, hard or soft, mixed or "nate," it was all one to them. They were the most inseparable of chums, so inseparable that we named them the Siamese Twins. If you wanted Brown, look for Daly, and you could not miss him also; should Daly's presence be needed, find Brown and you secured the other too; so they were fitly named. And what connived at this Damon and Pythias feeling was this peculiarity, that Daly, when drunk, was able to walk, but could not sound a note upon his trumpet; while Brown, on the contrary, could do anything in the sounding line, but was unable to walk a step. So this was how they managed it: Daly carried Brown on his back round the quarters both of the 8th and 17th, at each corner Brown winding out the "First and last posts." It was their particular fortune, that however drunk they might be, they could not be confined, as there was no one to relieve them; so they got drunk when they liked, and kept up the carrying game, and it was this I had a laugh at on leaving our Christmas party that night upon provost duty.

It was almost a necessary consequence of the great seclusion of the place, that we should have a desire to make ourselves as jolly as possible. This feeling extended likewise to the officers, some of whom may remember a small sentry-box-looking affair, which was perched at the end of the pier; and how upon a certain night about twelve o'clock, some of them rallying down in that direction upset everything they came across, and among other things hoisted the sentry-box over into the water. But doubtless they are not aware that in this box at the very time was a man lying recumbent, snugly curled up asleep, who was awoke by finding himself and the house in which he was snoring shoved over and floating away among the waves. Fortunately he was a good swimmer, and the drink having partly got out of his head, Blake had little difficulty in making his way to the shore, where he landed dripping wet just in time to hear one of his unconscious friends remark, "What a lark it would have been, if any one had been inside!" "Faith," said Joe, (he was a man of few words,) "it was a dale nearer a murder than a lark yeez were committing." The box was carried out to sea and never more heard of, and the sight of the pierhead was as good as an emetic to Blake ever afterwards. Warner Cook of ours met with his death poor fellow, about the same time. He went to bathe from the end of one of the numerous piers, and being taken with cramp sank to rise no more, and his body was never recovered.

I only saw one Turkish funeral, and as a description of it may be useful to some of the parochial authorities at home, who, from their economical propensities ought to be thankful for, and willing to act upon the hint, I will relate the occurrence.

One afternoon about four o'clock I was passing down the lower end of the town, when I observed a Turk lying down beside a wall smoking, and his wan and tired appearance caused me to regard him more attentively than I should otherwise have done. When I came back about ten minutes afterwards, he had put the pipe down and turned his face to the wall. Wishing to see whether he was asleep or not, I looked at him closely now, and discovered that he was dead, having passed away from among the living, uncared for, untended, unknown by the numbers of his fellow-creatures who kept "passing him by on the other side." Even when I called the attention of the passers to the corpse, they would only look at it for a second quite uninterested, and then with a muttered "God is great," would wend on their way. Those who lived close by knew nothing of him: he had been a stranger among strangers, and had wandered to Ismid to die. I went up to the Turkish Governor and told him of the case, and that he had better give orders for his interment. He, a little, fat, gray man, came down with me, looked at the body, and—there are no coroner's inquests in Turkey—gave an order for it to be buried. To my astonishment a coffin was brought in a few minutes, into which the poor fellow's body was placed, and being put on a porter's back, was carried away to the burial ground, and I alone followed to see the last of him. Going into the first graveyard, the porter deposited his burden on the ground, while he dug the grave, a deep narrow hole. When ready he dragged the coffin to the hole, and placing it in a slanting position, opened a lid at the bottom which I had not before observed, and the body slid out into the grave. Throwing in a piece of cake, and twisting the face round towards Mecca, he shovelled the earth in upon him, then shouldered the coffin and carried it away, to be ready when it was wanted for somebody else. Our burial ground was in a small corner of the Greek graveyard, which we had neatly walled off and planted with shrubs. A gravestone which we erected tells who are buried there, and the Greeks promised that it should remain undisturbed; but whether they have kept their promise is doubtful.

I have said that the Turks are notoriously honest; and I can also state that the Greeks are as notoriously the reverse, and not only so, but they delight in deception. I firmly believe they would sooner earn ten pounds by fraud, than a hundred in an honest or honourable way.

Of course, I only speak of those I personally came in contact with; but so far as that experience went, I had never occasion to alter my opinion. Our Government suffered accordingly. The Greek contractors, in conjunction with some of our officials, robbed it wholesale, not by paltry driblets of a few pounds at a time, but by hundreds, or I may say thousands. If things had been carefully looked into after the war, it would have been found that Turks once in our employ, were still returned as effective, and pay drawn for them, months after their death. Numbers sent out by Government to look after its interests, and well paid to do so, lived not only far above their income, but yearly remitted home sums which were treble and quadruple the amount of their salaries. "Fine doings," some will say; while others declare "it is all fudge, and could not be done;" but those who lived and profited and saved money on it, could tell, if they dared, how the hundreds were got, how receipts were given for oats that were never received, vouchers given for stores that were never drawn, and accounts cooked up and signed as correct, that were thousands of pounds deficient. A case that occurred in Ismid will shew how a part of the rascality was managed, and how reckless every one had become, because no supervision was kept upon them and their actions. A Greek on the opposite side of the gulf of Ismid contracted to supply wood for the use of our army in the Crimea, and a commissariat clerk was sent to see the wood weighed and put on board of the vessels that were to convey it, and he had to give a certificate as to the quantity placed in each. The contractor and he were not long before they came to an understanding with each other, and ship-load after shipload was forwarded to the Crimea and Constantinople, which contained a half, and still oftener only a third, of the quantity represented in the vouchers. Whether any of the other clerks turned informer, or whether after peace was proclaimed the officials at Stamboul commenced looking into things more closely, I never learnt, but whichever way it was, when transport No. 196 was unloaded, the wood was weighed, and a deficiency found of many thousand okes—a Turkish weight of about two pounds English. An official letter was then written by the authorities, inquiring into the discrepancy; and unfortunately this gave the confederates time. The commissariat clerk whose duty it was to see every oke weighed and put on board, and who had certified to having done so, made it his business to go off at once to his Greek co-adjutor the contractor, and they at once set to work to make up each a check-book that would agree with the amount of wood that ought to have been sent: in two different ways they made these books tally to a single oke. I myself saw afterwards the commissariat clerk's book, and each day's work was plainly set forth by dates and marks in this fashion 𝍬, with a supplementary total at the end of all, shewing the total each day shipped, and the grand total sent. So things were all cut and dried when the assistant commissary-general arrived from Constantinople to investigate the matter. All that could be done he did, but the time wasted in correspondence gave them the start; there were the two books to look at, and the contractor and clerk ready to swear that what was there set down had been put on board ; so all the investigator could report was that there was no proof *but plenty of suspicion.* Had the authorities not written in the first place, but come down sharp upon them, nothing in the world could have saved the guilty parties ; but redtapeism must have its course, and the result was their escape. Many such, and even more glaring instances than this happened, which, if they were related, would scarcely be credited, but which would shew that peculation of the very worst description was not confined to Turkish officials or to the officers of the Czar. At Scutari it was a notorious fact, that the men there could see no accounts nor have any settlement, and more than I are aware, that the paymasters' accounts of many a regiment, up to the present time, have never been balanced for the period when the war was going on. How much easier still could false charges be made for stores that were never delivered, or in fact never sent to the Crimea, by fraudulent contractors in collusion with conniving officials, who did not deem it robbery because it was John Bull who had to pay for all. Here can be seen the rottenness of a system that we take so much credit for. News of the armistice, and the peace which followed, reached us in course of time at Ismid, when a number of our horses were sold by auction to the natives; and, taking over some others from the 8th Hussars and 17th Lancers, who embarked from there for England, we prepared to march by land to Scutari, there to await our turn to go home likewise.

It was on the 23d of April that, packing all our valuables on our horses, we bade adieu to our winter quarters, being followed by a crowd of Bono Johnnies who really seemed sorry at our departure. Whether our sojourn had enlightened them, or only caused them to be less contented with their lot, I must leave wiser people to determine. During our stay we had certainly given an impetus to trade, and a stimulus to exertion, having both by example and precept caused them to be more cleanly in their streets and by-ways, and also more careful with respect to dead carcases lying rotting in the roads; so if they continue to act up to these, their general health no doubt benefits. We marched to Scutari in three days, going through a very pretty, though rather mountainous, portion of the country, where roads were rough and bad; but the sight on the second day of a small French factory, with a score or two of pretty girls looking at us from the windows, added a charm to the small town which the longest and worst road in existence would not have obliterated. Our horses always rendered it imperative that we should be encamped apart from the remainder of the cavalry; so instead of our occupying the pleasant zinc barracks, or the commodious quarters at Ismail Pasha, where, by the by, the 13th Light Dragoons were burned out, we were put by the seaside some three miles away, where everything was quiet and nothing to disturb us, save the tortoises which were crawling all about over the ground. The remainder of our horses were here transferred to the Turkish Government for a consideration of, I believe, £20 a piece. I expect, however, that it was on the I.O.U. principle, and only swelled the already too large debt of the Porte to this country, a debt which I fear is like those of a certain nobleman, that will not be settled until the day of judgment. I have already related how the Turks treated our steeds to music, and how I parted from my faithful old four-footed companion, Donald. The piece of his mane lies before me now; and as I look it causes vividly to spring up in my mind's eye his whole form, his flashing eyes, his flowing mane, his proud and noble bearing, and, best of all, the remembrance of his courage and docility, the latter being a virtue greatly to be prized from its scarcity. As in days of yore, I can in fancy see him looking towards me, expecting the piece of bread which I always brought him in my stable bag; and still I can see on his left flank the singular mark of a lady with a parasol in her hand, which was caused by the hair on that part being of a darker shade than that which surrounded it. It doubtless was the particular brand with which his first master had marked him when a colt running wild among the mountains of Herat. Poor Donald! As I look at the plait of black hair, I think I would willingly go on a pilgrimage to see you, and find it difficult, even after the lapse of eight years, to check the thoughts which will return to you, and turn my mind to the conclusion that we shall never meet again. Our first squadron sailed for England on the 22d of May; and I followed with the second, on the 5th June, on board the steamer *Brenda*. We steamed away from Constantinople that evening, bidding adieu to the famous city, into the Sea of Marmora, crossing that through the Dardanelles; as we cast our eyes over which, came thoughts of Leander's nightly path across its waters to Hero, his lady love, of

"Mr Aikenhead and the most famous victory," and also the sad reflection that the Greeks of old and Lord Byron's fancy are quite different in all respects from those of the present day. Still on we sailed, passed the sunny Grecian isles, and up the Mediterranean Sea, staying at Malta for coal, but for only a few hours, just long enough to get a glimpse of the town and the Cathedral of St John, its massive marble floor, and the silver railings that the cunning monk painted so that the French never suspected that they were not iron. On again on our voyage, passing between the two forts—St Elmo and Ricasoli—which defend the harbour; getting just a glimpse of the African coast, said to be Tunis; and in a few days more to the pillars of Hercules, easily discerning the hill of Gibel Tariff, 1200 feet above the sea level, hours before we reached it. When looking up at it, however, one would never suppose it had the immense strength it really possesses, and it is only on the side next to Spain that the rock appears in any way impregnable. To all appearance Edinburgh Castle is equally invincible. On the side facing the bay the slope is slight and gradual to the summit; but here is the weakest part naturally, which has been rendered by art the strongest. Above the town is the fortress, where are numerous galleries, tier over tier, cut out of the solid rock, from which point guns that command all the approaches. The east and south sides of the rock are much steeper than this, however, and they also are strongly fortified. The bay, which is seven miles wide and about eight miles long, is also well sheltered. The batteries are all well concealed, and few looking at it from the sea would ever dream that it is half so formidable as it is, or that a thousand cannon were ready to speak with iron tongues to any enemy who dared to attack the key of the Mediterranean. Here could be procured tobacco at 8d. a pound, and cigars at 1s. 6d. a box, an opportunity most smokers availed themselves of. We remained but a few hours at Gibraltar, and were away again on our road home. Passing Europa Point, we could see the fortress of Cueta opposite on the African shore, while on the European side we could feast our eyes upon the Andalusian mountains, whose tops sought the clouds. The Queen of Spain's seat was pointed out to me, where she had vowed to remain until the Spanish flag topped the highest pinnacle of the fortress; but that event has not happened yet, and in all likelihood never will. We were now breasting the wide waters of the Atlantic, keeping close into the Spanish shore, which at this part of the coast is rocky, the land rising abruptly from out of the sea. Pretty little cottages peered at us over the cliffs, while further inland could be seen spires, which told of churches and monasteries. Passing through Trafalgar Bay none could help thinking of Nelson—his last victory, his glorious death, and all that he had done for his country. All that we were now wishing and praying for was soon to be accomplished. The word "Home" was spoken to us by every breath of wind that fanned our cheeks, and by every swelling wave that tossed our vessel towards it. We looked at ships that met us, for they had come from some English port; and at those steering in the same direction as ourselves, for they were bound for the same haven; and so enjoying our quiet thoughts, we gazed across the sparkling waves, and counted the hours and the minutes that must elapse ere we saw the white cliffs of Albion. While thus reflecting on board ship, a kind of misanthropical feeling comes over one, a wish to separate one's self from one's fellows, and to lounge over the vessel's side, communing only with the deep waters that run rushing past, as if their passive sympathy were most congenial to one's mind. Crossing the Bay of Biscay, that for a wonder was perfectly calm, we sighted Star Point, and then the Lizard, and sailing steadily on up the English Channel, we passed between the Needles, through Southampton water, and at 9 A.M., on the 20th of June 1856, were safely anchored in Portsmouth Harbour, within a few yards of the old "Victory." Our marches, our fighting, our voyages were done, and we were gazing once more upon the green shores of Old England—"Home, sweet home!"

That afternoon we disembarked, and were marched at once to the railway station *en route* for Birmingham. Everything wore roseate hues, flags were flying, bands were playing, and crowds welcomed the soldier's return from the wars. When in the railway carriage I did nothing but sit looking at the hills and dales of home, and although years had passed since I last set foot on English ground, it only appeared like yesterday when I made a couple of jumps on the strand at Gravesend, before stepping into the boat which was to convey me on board the ship *Brahmin*, that for four months was to be my home, and the next shore I leaped on that of Asia. I had since then gazed on many a fair and beautiful scene, but as I looked across the smiling fields, and saw the happy homesteads, I felt that I had never seen anything to compare to them, and could not resist pointing rapturously to each rural spire, each pleasant village, each verdant lawn, each snug farmhouse, everything as I travelled on appearing to get more and more homely, and, for that reason, to me more and more lovely. We arrived in Birmingham at midnight, but even at that time crowds were waiting to receive us, and give us a hearty welcome to the hardware village. We slept in barracks that night, and the following day re-commenced soldiering at home.

CHAPTER FIFTEENTH.

Three Days at Woolmer.

THERE is an old adage, "To be at peace a nation must always be prepared for war;" and for the saying to hold good, she must keep her soldiers well practised in campaigning, and no better practice could be given than that which is practised at the "Flying Camps."

In the summer of 1859 Government made arrangements to have Woolmer Forest as a kind of supplementary camp to Aldershot, where the brigade could be marched in turn, and thus give all a practical insight to camp life as it would be were they on service. This, I believe, was the intention at first, but the plan was afterwards in a degree modified.

In accordance with division orders a brigade composed of the three arms, under the command of Colonel Ellis, of H.M. 24th Foot, proceeded from Aldershott to Woolmer Forest, on Saturday the 9th July 1859. The brigade consisted of the right wing of the 10th Hussars, a battery of Artillery, a detachment of the Military Train, H.M. 24th Foot, and the Wiltshire Militia. The reveillé sounded at 2 A.M. for us of the 10th Hussars, and by 3 A.M. we were saddled and ready for breakfast, which had been ordered to be prepared for us at that hour; but blessed are those who expect nothing, for they will never be disappointed. As for us, we were doomed to be so,—at least with respect to our bread and meat. Coffee there certainly was, and hot, if not strong; still that by itself makes but a poor breakfast for soldiers going on the march. However, it was no use grumbling, hoping, like Jacob Faithful, "to have better luck next time;" and as consolation may be derived in a slight degree from the misfortunes of others, we could solace ourselves with the reflection that even then we were not so badly off as the first brigade which went to Woolmer, for on arrival there it found, to the dismay and sorrow of all concerned, that there were no rations at all, as the authorities at Aldershott had arranged that it should be rationed at Woolmer, while those at Woolmer had arrived at the conclusion that the rations had been brought with them; so they were obliged to starve for that day, and as best they could to grin and bear it.

Starting about four o'clock, we passed through Farnham, with swords drawn, drums beating, and banners waving, long before the good people of the town had even dreamt of rising. It was a lovely morning, with not the semblance of a cloud to darken the bright summer sky; the sweet pure air invigorated us, and we felt so fresh and lively that none envied the Farnhamites their rest. Being the vanguard, and as our horses walked fast, we were obliged to halt and dismount several times, to allow the others to come up, which delayed our arrival until about ten o'clock.

At first the appearance of Woolmer Forest was by no means pleasing, as it resembled too much the sterile place we had left; but as we proceeded through, it lost in a great measure its wilderness-like look, and the cheering idea dawned upon us that we would find this a far pleasanter spot than we had at first anticipated.

The position was taken up by the Infantry and Artillery; the 24th being on the right of the camp, the Wiltshire on the left, and the Artillery in the centre. The Military Train were placed on the left of the line, in front and at right angles to it, while we were posted about three hundred yards to the front of the line, and parallel with it. A small plantation protected each flank; and on the far sides of the woods, pickets were placed to look to the security of the flanks.

On arriving at the camping-ground, we were delayed a considerable time waiting for the waggons, there being one for each troop to carry the tents, cooking-kettles, horse-blankets, picket-posts, ropes, &c., &c.; and a longer time elapsed in getting these out, and measuring the lines, as the space was termed, which we were to occupy. At last we made a start, and linking our horses together, left them in charge of eight men, the remainder being told off for different duties,—some to draw forage and fuel, others to put down the picket-posts and ropes, heel-pegs and head-ropes. When this was all done, and the horses picketed, two hours had elapsed—two hours in doing what we could have done formerly in fifteen minutes; ay, in less, for in 1854, when inspected by Lord Frederick Fitzclarence in India, the regiment halted, took up a position on the drill ground, filed into the lines marked out on the spot, dismounted, picketed their horses, took off their accoutrements and baggage, all in eight and a half minutes; and put on all these things again, unpicketed their horses, mounted, and formed up in even less time; but at that time there was no delay waiting for a military train, no time lost in driving picket-posts in the ground, with sledge-hammers, and hauling the picket-ropes tight. I am speaking of India; and when we marched from there by the overland route to the Crimea, every man then carried head and heel-ropes, and head and heel-pegs, on his horse, the head-rope being fastened round the horse's neck, and the heel-rope, rolled up and doubled in a circle, was attached by a strap to a ring on the near side of the saddle, and hung over the shoe-case. The head and heel-pegs were carried strapped on the top of the valise.

Picketing our horses then came like A, B, C, to us, for when the lines were marked out, the men filed in at one end mounted, as they came off the march, the rear rank being on one side, the front rank on the other. On arriving at the further end, the leading files turned inwards, the remainder turning in succession, taking up their position and distance as it came to their turn, and dressing towards the hand they formed to. When this was done, the order was given to dismount, when every man was in his place; then head and heel-pegs were driven in, head-ropes fixed, and heel-ropes put down; the shackles now fastened on, and the horses were secure.

But what a great difference there was between the Indian shackle and those that were served out to us for use at Woolmer; the former being light, strong, and useful, while the latter were quite the reverse, being heavy, cumbersome, and useless. There were certainly plenty of buckles, straps, and rings, (neither of which form any part of the Indian shackle, which is completely made of leather,) and yet with all these additions they were easily broken, the least plunge of a horse being usually sufficient to do so, for either the strap gave way, or the leather which joined the ring to the shackle broke; and thus what was apparently strong enough to have held an elephant securely, was scarcely serviceable with these quiet horses, and would have been utterly useless to fasten the little Arabs that we had once upon a time.

I observed that the principal fault in the construction of this ponderous affair was through there being a thin piece of leather used to connect the ring with the shackle, and as the heel-rope is fastened to the ring, all the strain is upon this piece of leather. The Indian shackle is very simple in its construction, and of great strength. It is made of a strap of leather about four inches wide and twenty-four long; the sides are folded in, the edges meeting in the centre; a button is now formed at one end, by doubling the end back and rolling about a couple of inches up tightly, and this is made secure by cutting a hole close to it, and just large enough to pass the roll through, when it is pulled tight, and which forming a button, that end is finished. The other end is next doubled in, so as to form a loop large enough, and no more, than will hold the button, which is sewn together with a leather thong; a loop is now made for the rope to be attached to, by again doubling up the button-hole end; this is likewise fastened by sewing, and a leather thong is afterwards tied tight round all, and making it, as it ought to be, the strongest part, for on it and the button lie all the strain. The shackle should be greased about twice a month; if this is done, it will last a long time, and a horse fastened by it might break the rope but never the shackle.

Another failure at Woolmer were the iron heel-pegs, or pins, for even, long as they were made, the least exertion (which any person may prove by trying) draws them out of the ground; while another most serious fault is their weight, for one of them, ring and all, would weigh more than half a dozen wooden pegs. A wooden peg has not only the advantage of being light, but if lost or broken it can easily be replaced; also when in the ground it swells from the damp, and thereby offers a great resistance when any attempt is made to pull it up.

Some will doubtless consider that the dragoon's horse has now too much to carry—an opinion with which I quite agree; but at the same time would be very loath to recommend that whatever secures the horse, ought to be carried, with the tents and other baggage, by the Military Train. A nice affair it would be certainly, after getting to the camping-ground, to be obliged to wait until their arrival, before any attempt could be made to picket the horses. As regards the extra weight which the horse would have to carry, it would not altogether exceed ten pounds, which might easily enough be taken away from the weight the horse has at present to carry, without proving in the least detrimental, but, on the contrary, beneficial to the service.* It ought also to be remembered, that it is not the largest horse which will either carry or endure most; as, for instance, those which we brought with us from India to the Crimea were much less than the English trooper, rarely measuring over fourteen hands, yet they carried, and carried with ease, in addition to what is now borne by the cavalry horse at home, two blankets,—one under the saddle, the other on top of the cloak,—head and heel-ropes, pegs, a water-deck, forage-nets, &c.; and yet with all this additional weight to carry, twenty or thirty miles a day was apparently easy work for them to do, as after having a roll on the ground and being watered, they would be as fresh as when they started.

It will be urged that as they were stallions there is no comparison between them and the horses at home; but the late lamented Captain Nolan, in his work on "Cavalry Tactics," gives the preference to geldings for lasting powers on the march. He relates, when the 15th Hussars were in India, an account of two squadrons being ordered to march from Bangalore to the Deccanee Hyderabad, a distance of some five hundred miles. This opportunity was

* In a paper that appeared in *The United Service Magazine* for November last, entitled, "The Dragoon, his Horse, and their Training," I have pointed out where and how the extra weight could be taken off.

embraced for the purpose of testing the lasting qualities of the stallion and gelding, a squadron of each forming the wing—when the latter, in this long march, proved themselves superior, in enduring fatigue, and keeping in better condition while doing so, than the former. With respect to the superiority of the breed, it is the duty of Government to get the best animals procurable for the work, and the duties of the cavalry service. I'll allow that I prefer a small horse for cavalry, as it will be found not only more compact and of better proportions at about fourteen hands than at sixteen, but hardier, more enduring, and faster in its paces. Of course this is meant generally speaking, for there are exceptions to every rule.

I may mention that Colonel M'Dougall, in his "Theory of War," preferring the larger animal, states that "The effective force of cavalry is in direct proportion to the momentum of its charge; or in other words, the weight of a body in motion is multiplied by its velocity. Hence velocity and weight being considered as elements in the effect of a charge, the greater momentum will be obtained by light men on powerful horses." I however humbly and respectfully beg to differ from this assertion of Colonel M'Dougall's, and I think that most cavalry men will agree with me, when I state that the smallest horses are usually the swiftest. This will be seen at any field day, when with the same weight to carry as the larger animal, in a charge the others will invariably be found in front. Large horses look grand and imposing, but they lose in speed, and if the country was rough or rocky, the small horse would cross it like a cat, and with a facility which the other would be incapable of. I would put light men on light active horses; and will further suggest that cavalry horses should have no stabling in the summer months, but be made to rough it in the open air, and in winter have them kept in open sheds that would only afford shelter from the weather. They would not look so well, I 'll allow, their coats would not look so glossy, nor might they appear so fat, but they would be far more fit for service, should they be required, whether it were to meet an enemy in a foreign land or to repel an invader from our native shore. However, in the event of either coming to pass, I hope that we will not be encumbered by picket-posts, &c., and delayed waiting for their arrival; besides, on service, a cavalry regiment of eight troops would require no less than twenty mules to carry those articles.

However, to return to the subject, Woolmer;—after the horses were picketed and fed, to look after ourselves became the next consideration, so tent-pitching was the order of the day. Each troop had four tents—one to every twelve men. The tents were placed in double rows at the top of the horse lines, the tent doors opening in that direction. The officers' tents were pitched in rear of all. It being the first time for many of ours to be under canvas, as the greater portion were young soldiers, more time was occupied at this than there should have been, but taking all into consideration it was not done amiss. We then had dinner, when we tested the commissariat rations of bread and meat, both of which were first-rate in quality, especially the bread, it being the best I had eaten in England, and was quite a relief and a pleasant change from the sour, stale stuff supplied from the commissariat at Aldershott.

The ovens and shambles here were quite in the primitive style, the first being formed of clay, or nearly so; the shambles was a kind of scaffold fixed upon some loose planks, on which the cattle, as they were disposed of in an off-hand manner, are hung up and dressed. The whole, of course, was in the open air. After dinner we finished our houses, and then the intrenching of the tents was the next thing to be looked to. At this we all worked well and with a will, the pickaxe and shovel plying merrily, and, in "the twinkling of a bed-post," we had secured ourselves against any amount of rain that might choose to drop or pour down upon us.

After looking to his horse—at all times the first consideration with a dragoon—intrenching his tent ought to be the next thing he does, and when the appearance of the weather is unfavourable, this is frequently done immediately the tent is pitched. In this instance, however, as the weather was remarkably fine, we deferred it until after stables. A case in point will perhaps shew how requisite it is to do this first, and what may happen if it is neglected. About three weeks previous to our going to Woolmer, the 12th Foot marched into Aldershott, taking up their quarters on Cove Common, close by the 5th Dragoon Guards. When their tents were pitched, they did not intrench round them, in consequence of an order having been issued—to the effect that " the ground was on no account to be cut up;" an order that simply meant that it was not to be done so unnecessarily; at least, I would read it so. The regimental authorities, however, took it in the literal sense, and would not allow the men to put a pickaxe or shovel in the ground. That night—it was a Saturday—one of the heaviest and severest thunder-storms, accompanied by rain, came on, that had been experienced for years; nothing I ever witnessed could be at all compared to it, except the opening of the south-west monsoon in India. The lightning flashed, each flash followed by the sound of thunder, which, low at first, increased as it rolled nearer, until it would burst overhead in a deafening peal, that shook all around; while during the intervals the rain was heard pouring, plashing down in torrents; and in all this was the unfortunate 12th lying, or, as I should say, standing in their tents, through and under which the water ran in floods. I saw them next day, and it was truly pitiful to mark the drenched appearance they had, with everything on and about them wet through. When the storm was over, they were then allowed to dig and trench round their tents, and no rain fell for weeks afterwards. So the old adage held good of "locking the stable door after the horse was stolen."

Having been a-foot from two o'clock in the morning, there were none of us required rocking to sleep that night and upon a little straw with our cloak and a blanket to cover us, slept a sounder sleep than many that night may have done upon a bed of down. In truth, an old soldier could no more sleep comfortably on a feather bed, than a civilian, accustomed to such a luxury all his life, could have a refreshing slumber upon hard boards. Speaking from experience, I remember when on furlough, that my poor mother, God bless her, would put me in the best bed, thinking it must be such a treat; but I could no more sleep among that sea of feathers than if it had been stuffed with broken bottles instead,—of the two I fancy that the latter would have been preferable;—and even now, years afterwards, the troubles of that night and its nightmares are as vivid in my mind as they were then. I tossed and tumbled, and changed position, all round and round that bed—threw the clothes off and pulled them on again, till at last exhausted nature could bear it no longer, and I was obliged to beat a retreat with a portion of the bed-clothes on my arm, taking refuge on a sofa in the next room, where I found the rest and pleasant dreams that were denied me in the feathered four-poster, for no sooner was this diversion executed than it was followed by a degree of success I scarcely calculated upon: sleep, heavy, sound, and refreshing, now stole over me, burying for the time in sweet oblivion all my former cares, troubles, and annoyances. I need scarcely add that I insisted upon retaining possession of that couch for the remainder of my stay.

But I have again wandered far away from Woolmer, to which let us return. The next day being Sunday, we expected to have but little to do, there being only "church parade" in orders, and that over, we looked forward to some ease and comfort for the remainder of the day; but our anticipations were far from being realised, as after dinner a message came, intimating that Her Majesty would in all probability pass through the camp in the evening. And now the hurly-burly began: tents were turned inside out and back again, then put square; blankets laid over the straw for a carpet; places that had been already swept were swept again, and everything in and about the tents put as ship-shape as possible. Then all the saddles had to be placed on end, and in line, when there was such pulling up and pushing back of these unfortunate saddles—propping up those that, from the unevenness of the ground, would not keep in their dressing. Then it was tried if the horses could not be brought up and kept in a straight line also, but after getting them as near the mark as made no matter, the obstinate brutes would not remain so, unless every man stood to his horse's head and kept him in the right position; and that could not be managed, for we were wanted elsewhere—as a crusade had been ordered against some poor inoffensive bushes, not because they were in our way, our horses' way, or any one else's way, but simply because in obeying nature, they had grown beyond *their* original *line* of dressing—*the ground.*

So, with one thing and another, we had but little peace until the time drew near when Her Majesty was expected; then we were told to remain inside our tents, unless the royal cortége passed, in which event happening, we were to fall in *in line* outside. Lucky dogs were we, that our position lay in advance of the others, for the remainder of the brigade, who were encamped near the road, were all on parade in full fig., awaiting Her Majesty's coming full two hours before the time. Her Majesty arrived between five and six o'clock, passing slowly along the line formed to receive her, bands playing, and people cheering, as only the loyal hearts of Old England can cheer.

On Her Majesty arriving on the extreme flank, some of the soldiers' rations, tea and bread, was presented to her, which she condescended very kindly to partake of, and, I understood, spoke very favourably of it. I guess, however, that it was as good of the kind as a soldier ever gets. I have had, and lately too, stuff served out said to be tea —there is certainly no Act of Parliament against it being called so—which I should find it very difficulty to describe. The best idea I can convey of what the mixture is like, will be in the words of Lieut. Gavin, who, being orderly officer one day in India, the tea was reported as being unfit to drink. Walking into the room, Lieut. Gavin took up a mess-tin full of the concoction, and having tasted it, turned to the orderly, inquiring of him in an undertone, "What is this, sergeant, tea or coffee?" "Tea, sir," was the whispered reply. This was sufficient and satisfactory seemingly, as the officer turned to the complainants and —according to formulæ laid down for the regulation of complaints in the service—said, "*It's very good; indeed, I never tasted better in my life.*" If this was the case, Lieut. Gavin's experience must have been very limited.

In fact, a soldier's rations are seldom or ever even of an average quality. In towns the gentry get the best of the meat, so the contractor sends the worst to the barracks. In large camps, however, like Aldershott, the soldier ought to be fairly rationed, to have a little good along with the bad; but I am sorry to say that the meat there was something like the nigger's wife, "all worser." I remember one day when the rations were extraordinarily bad, the meat especially, when it was cast by a board of officers. That was of no use; and then a board of medical officers was ordered to examine it, and they arrived at the same decision as the first board, when it was sent back to the commissariat, and the proceedings of both boards forwarded to the authorities. We all imagined now that the meat was cast at last, and waited anxiously for another lot to come; but one, two, three, and four o'clock passed slowly and anxiously, but without the sign of a dinner, or the makings of one; at last, about five o'clock, the old same lot came back to us again, like a bad shilling. A board of field-officers had been ordered to assemble at the request of the Commissary-General, and as they had not got to eat it, brought in a verdict against us, by saying that the meat was of a fair average quality; probably, had it been for their own consumption, a different decision would have been given. From this we were satisfied that it was useless to complain of our rations in future, and although frequently afterwards we had both bad beef and sour bread issued, we made no more complaints, but took them thankfully, consoling ourselves with the thought, that it was a deuced deal better than none. There is certainly this advantage in commissary beef, we know that it walked to the slaughter-house, and now-a-days it is a consolation to know that it was alive shortly before being skinned; but as regards the quality, that's another pair of shoes, and I fear will never be altered while the contractors and commissariat clerks pull so nicely in the same boat together. Not six months since, a *gentleman* on horseback was pointed out to me, who, two years before had been a sergeant in the commissariat—he had been a butcher, and his duty at that time was to pass in the cattle to the commissary stores, and send any back which were not up to the mark. He, while in this capacity, and within a couple of years, saved enough to purchase his discharge, and rent and stock a farm "over a thousand pounds," my friend added.

Her Majesty made no further inspection than passing in front of those that were formed up to receive her, and immediately returned to Aldershott. I fancy that Woolmer would have pleased her Majesty more had the parading of the troops been dispensed with, for at Aldershott there were at all times plenty of men under arms to be seen; and after a drive of so many miles, our Queen should have seen her troops in a rough state, with jackets off and shirt sleeves tucked up, going about their occupations if they had anything to do, and if they had not, lounging about smoking and chatting with their comrades, having a careless look, as if they knew they were far, far off from barracks or barrack regulations. It is this that makes camp life so agreeable, there being a cheerfulness and freedom from restraint when so situated, that cannot be felt in a place that is walled round—a feeling something similar to what is felt when the stock and belts come off after a long guard on a sultry day. When rambling about through the forest, or sitting comfortably round the bivouac fire, one can partly imagine that strong love the Arab has for the desert, and the gipsy for his tent; and soldiers from their style of life have something akin to this in them. Year after year is spent going from town to town, from country to country, from one quarter of the globe to another, all of which tends to give them a liking for change—a dislike to be settled or to stay very long in one place, and from this a sort of vagabondism springs up, which, gaining strength daily, becomes inherent in their nature. Just watch a soldier when he gets leave, whether it is for a day or a month. As soon as he clears the barrack-gate he feels a new man, his spirits are at the highest, and, like a boy just freed from school, he goes bounding forward, trying to forget all that lies behind. And it is something of this that is felt under canvas, where there is not that formality, that martinetism, which can only be satisfied by a species of humbugging—wrongly termed by some " order and discipline," but which is only the remains of the sad soldiering times of some seventy years back, those *good old times* when flogging, cocked hats, queues, tights and gaiters, were what made a soldier well conducted in quarters and brave in the field. There is still a strong leaven of that obsolete period amongst us, and those infected can be easily known by the pertinacity with which they cling to their duties—their Brahma and Vishnu, their leather stocks and pipe-clay. Paying but little heed to what is of importance, and directing their whole attention to small matters; such a thing as the fit of a buckle or a button not in line, being considered by the would-be martinet, as an opportunity not to be missed for finding fault, or to accuse the victim of culpable negligence, and apparently that is *their* mission; to be great in small things they consider an equivalent for whatever else of importance they (and others) know themselves deficient in.

On Monday morning we turned out at nine o'clock, and had a most splendid ride among the woods, round the woods and through the woods, then across a wild-looking part of the country, where not even a house could be seen for ever so far, until we were among the trees again, the lark singing sweetly overhead, and the mavis answering it with musical notes from amid the branches; the plover starting and soaring upwards from under our feet, or perhaps a nest of young ones, startled by us from their nest, and even when trying to get clear away they would get bewildered, double back, and run among the horses' legs, while the old ones were flying round and round, screaming their wild cry, as if beseeching us to be careful of those that could not as yet take care of themselves. And so we kept riding on until we found that we had wandered into one of those beautiful narrow grassy green lanes, with trees on either side, whose branches, overhanging and entwining one in another, made a perfect shade from the noonday sun; such beautiful spots as are only to be met with in our own land.

And what a healthy place that Woolmer must be! I declare I did not see one graveyard about the place, and a person might really imagine, from the robust, ruddy look of all the people, that they never die, but, like the folk of that village in Kentucky, "are obliged to go somewhere else" to "shuffle off this mortal coil." Certain am I that an undertaker does not earn his salt at or about Woolmer. The young people have a rosy glow upon their cheeks that would make any Londoner quite envious; and as to the old folk, how strong and hearty they are, and how fast and firm they walk about! I can see even now in my mind one old man who attracted my attention when there. It would have puzzled any one to guess his age: it might be a hundred, or it might be a hundred and fifty; he seemed so old, so very old, yet so young, for he was a green old age. He was still active, straight as an arrow, and had a cheerful mellow voice, that was as good as a song to listen to.

A hearty laughing country lass, in answer to our " Good morning," wished that we were always to remain, and mine, I am sure, was not the only response to it—" I wish we were." By this time we had got close to the village of Liphook, but did not enter it, which I was sorry for, but time would not allow us; so filing about, we retraced our steps to camp, feeling sorry to drag ourselves away from so much that was lovely.

We left for Aldershott at an early hour on Tuesday morning, when all the bother which had been previously gone through was again enacted; all the water-decks, picket-posts and ropes, head ropes and heel ditto, pegs, nose-bags, tarpaulins, &c., &c., with a great waste of time and trouble, were collected and counted. And the same mistake about the breakfast happened: there was the coffee, but no bread. We had to get that at Aldershott, so off we marched, hungry as before. How much more like common sense it would have been had we drawn our rations from Aldershott the day we marched out, and from Woolmer the day we marched in; it would have made little difference, as we would have still had the same number of rations at Woolmer.

We arrived at that splendid specimen of the skill of our Royal Engineers—the Cavalry Barracks, (where water was not only scarce, but muddy,) at about half-past eight A.M., all safe and sound, and I daresay all weighing two or three pounds heavier than when we left, our only regret being that our stay had not been for three weeks instead of three days, yet grateful that we had had even that short enjoyment.

THE END.

www.ingramcontent.com/pod-product-compliance
Lightning Source LLC
Chambersburg PA
CBHW021208230426
43667CB00006B/610